A NOTE TO READERS..............................5

ROBOT LAND...7

IVAN THE FOOL.......................................63

A DAY TO REMEMBER...........................111

GHOST MANUFACTURING MACHINE...127

OSAMU TEZUKA...213

Table of Contents

by
Osamu Tezuka

translation
Frederik L. Schodt

lettering and retouch
Digital Chameleon

Dark Horse Comics®

publisher
Mike Richardson

editor
Chris Warner

consulting editor
Toren Smith for **Studio Proteus**

collection designers
David Nestelle and **Lani Schreibstein**

English-language version produced by **Dark Horse Comics** and **Studio Proteus**

Astro Boy® Volume 4

The artwork of this volume has been produced as a mirror-image of the
original Japanese edition to conform to English-language standards.

Published by
Dark Horse Comics, Inc.
10956 SE Main Street
Milwaukie, OR 97222

www.darkhorse.com

To find a comics shop in your area, call the Comic Shop Locator Service toll-free
at 1-888-266-4226.

First edition: June 2002
ISBN: 1-56971-679-X

10 9 8 7 6 5 4 3 2 1
Printed in Canada

A NOTE TO READERS

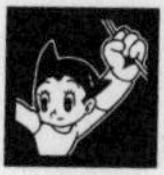

Many non-Japanese, including people from Africa and Southeast Asia, appear in Osamu Tezuka's works. Sometimes these people are depicted very differently from the way they actually are today, in a manner that exaggerates a time long past, or shows them to be from extremely undeveloped lands. Some feel that such images contribute to racial discrimination, especially against people of African descent. This was never Osamu Tezuka's intent, but we believe that as long as there are people who feel insulted or demeaned by these depictions, we must not ignore their feelings.

We are against discrimination, in all its forms, and intend to continue to work for its elimination. Nonetheless, we do not believe it would be proper to revise these works. Tezuka is no longer with us, and we cannot erase what he has done, and to alter his work would only violate his rights as a creator. More importantly, stopping publication or changing the content of his work would do little to solve the problems of discrimination that exist in the world.

We are presenting Osamu Tezuka's work as it was originally created, without changes. We do this because we believe it is also important to promote the underlying themes in his work, such as love for mankind and the sanctity of life. We hope that when you, the reader, encounter this work, you will keep in mind the differences in attitudes, then and now, toward discrimination, and that this will contribute to an even greater awareness of such problems.

— Tezuka Productions and Dark Horse Comics

ROBOT LAND

First serialized between May and September 1962 in *Shonen* magazine.

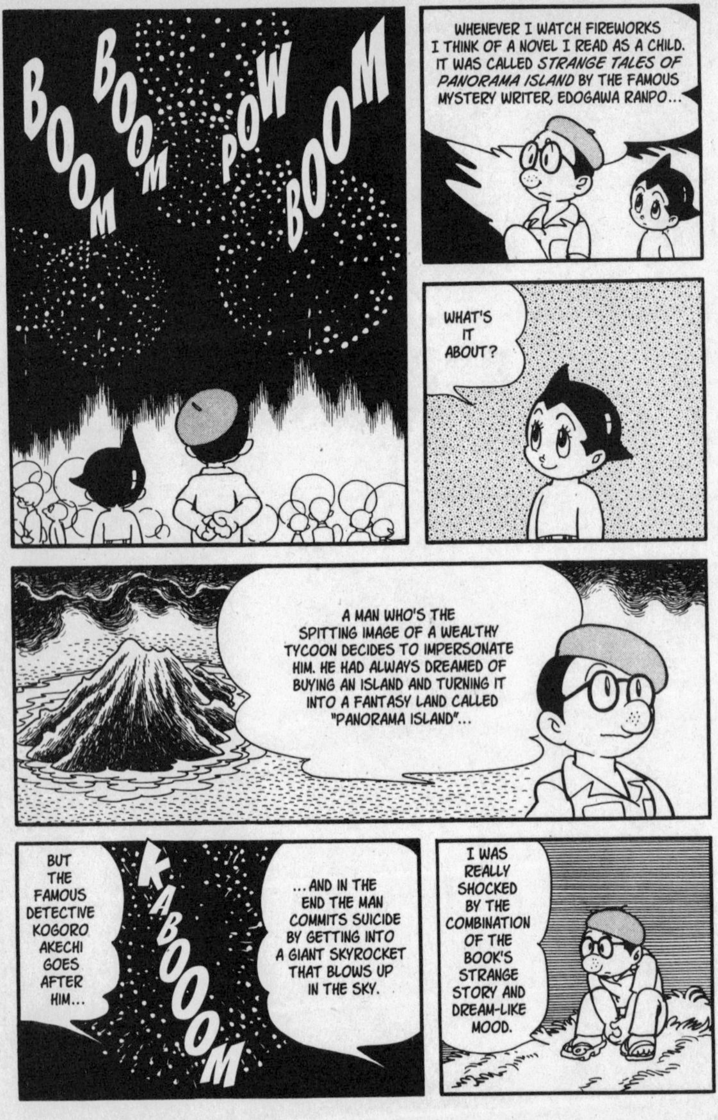
BOOM BOOM POW BOOM
WHENEVER I WATCH FIREWORKS I THINK OF A NOVEL I READ AS A CHILD. IT WAS CALLED *STRANGE TALES OF PANORAMA ISLAND* BY THE FAMOUS MYSTERY WRITER, EDOGAWA RANPO...
WHAT'S IT ABOUT?
A MAN WHO'S THE SPITTING IMAGE OF A WEALTHY TYCOON DECIDES TO IMPERSONATE HIM. HE HAD ALWAYS DREAMED OF BUYING AN ISLAND AND TURNING IT INTO A FANTASY LAND CALLED "PANORAMA ISLAND"...
BUT THE FAMOUS DETECTIVE KOGORO AKECHI GOES AFTER HIM...
KABOOOM
...AND IN THE END THE MAN COMMITS SUICIDE BY GETTING INTO A GIANT SKYROCKET THAT BLOWS UP IN THE SKY.
I WAS REALLY SHOCKED BY THE COMBINATION OF THE BOOK'S STRANGE STORY AND DREAM-LIKE MOOD.

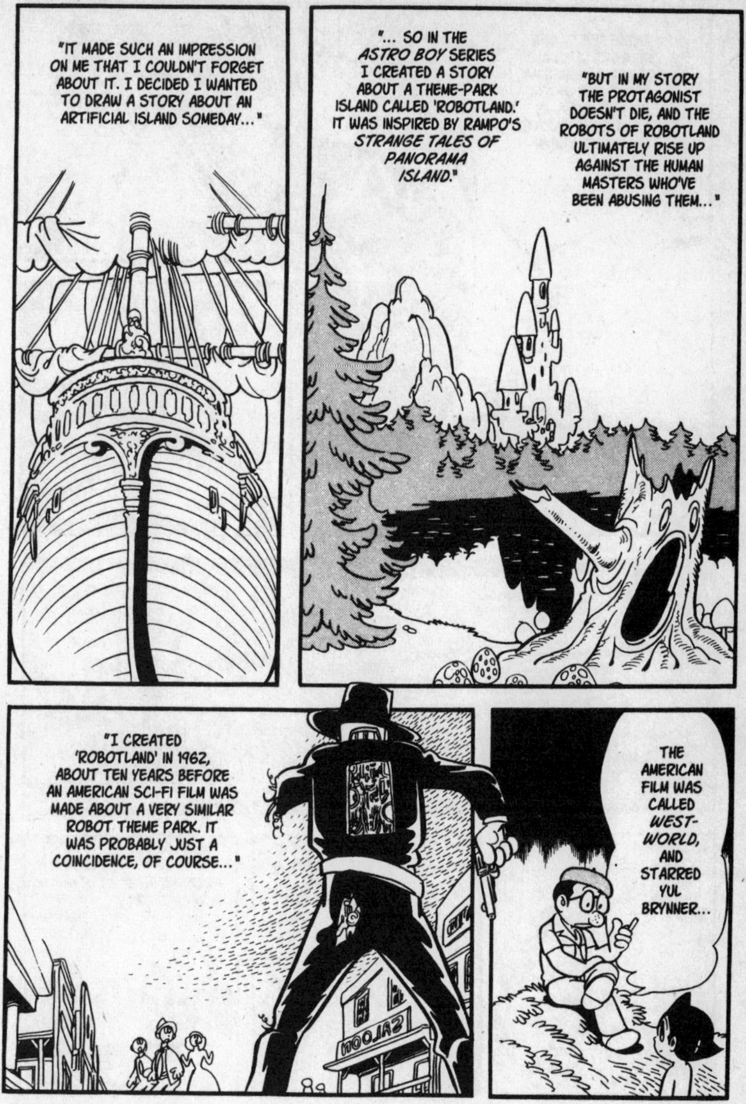
"IT MADE SUCH AN IMPRESSION ON ME THAT I COULDN'T FORGET ABOUT IT. I DECIDED I WANTED TO DRAW A STORY ABOUT AN ARTIFICIAL ISLAND SOMEDAY..."
"... SO IN THE *ASTRO BOY* SERIES I CREATED A STORY ABOUT A THEME-PARK ISLAND CALLED 'ROBOTLAND.' IT WAS INSPIRED BY RAMPO'S *STRANGE TALES OF PANORAMA ISLAND*."
"BUT IN MY STORY THE PROTAGONIST DOESN'T DIE, AND THE ROBOTS OF ROBOTLAND ULTIMATELY RISE UP AGAINST THE HUMAN MASTERS WHO'VE BEEN ABUSING THEM..."
"I CREATED 'ROBOTLAND' IN 1962, ABOUT TEN YEARS BEFORE AN AMERICAN SCI-FI FILM WAS MADE ABOUT A VERY SIMILAR ROBOT THEME PARK. IT WAS PROBABLY JUST A COINCIDENCE, OF COURSE..."
SALOON
THE AMERICAN FILM WAS CALLED *WEST-WORLD*, AND STARRED YUL BRYNNER...

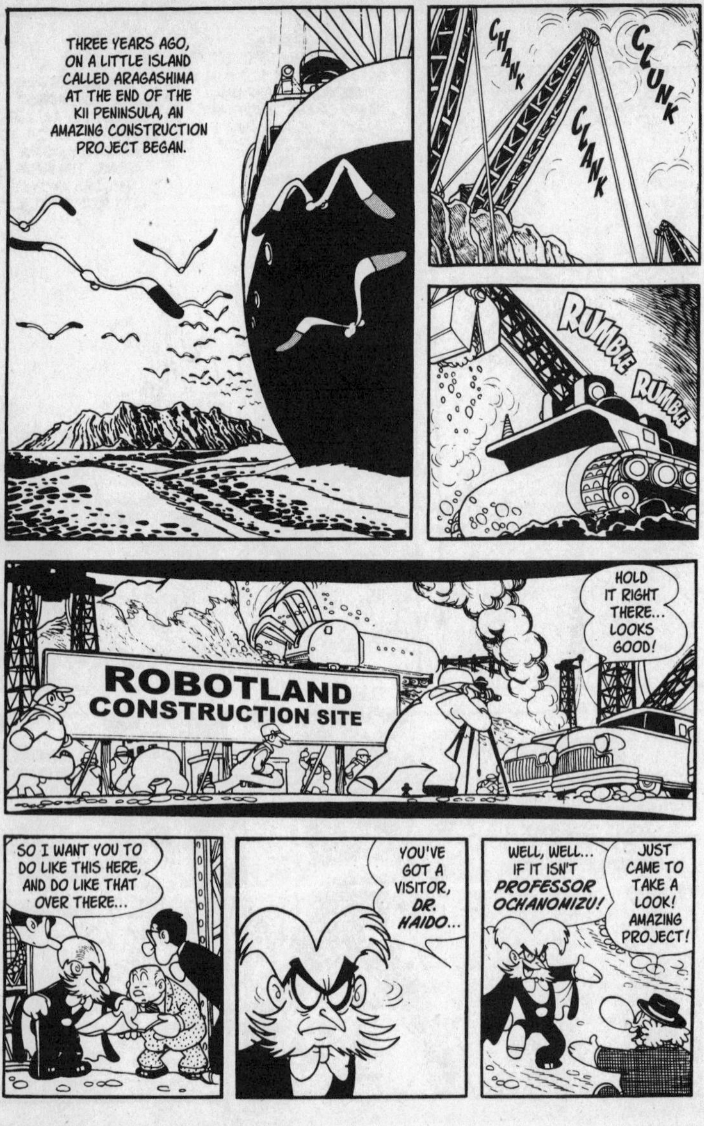
THREE YEARS AGO, ON A LITTLE ISLAND CALLED ARAGASHIMA AT THE END OF THE KII PENINSULA, AN AMAZING CONSTRUCTION PROJECT BEGAN.
CHANK
CLUNK
CLANK
RUMBLE RUMBLE
ROBOTLAND CONSTRUCTION SITE
HOLD IT RIGHT THERE... LOOKS GOOD!
SO I WANT YOU TO DO LIKE THIS HERE, AND DO LIKE THAT OVER THERE...
YOU'VE GOT A VISITOR, DR. HAIDO...
WELL, WELL... IF IT ISN'T PROFESSOR OCHANOMIZU!
JUST CAME TO TAKE A LOOK! AMAZING PROJECT!

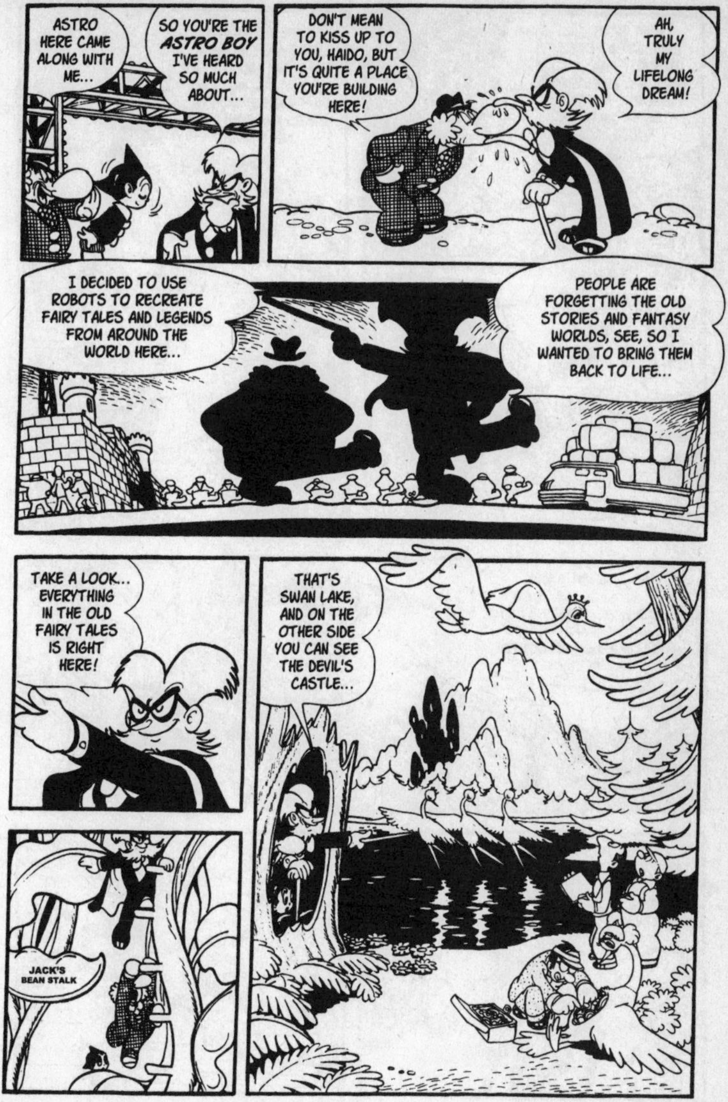
ASTRO HERE CAME ALONG WITH ME...
SO YOU'RE THE ASTRO BOY I'VE HEARD SO MUCH ABOUT...
DON'T MEAN TO KISS UP TO YOU, HAIDO, BUT IT'S QUITE A PLACE YOU'RE BUILDING HERE!
AH, TRULY MY LIFELONG DREAM!
I DECIDED TO USE ROBOTS TO RECREATE FAIRY TALES AND LEGENDS FROM AROUND THE WORLD HERE...
PEOPLE ARE FORGETTING THE OLD STORIES AND FANTASY WORLDS, SEE, SO I WANTED TO BRING THEM BACK TO LIFE...
TAKE A LOOK... EVERYTHING IN THE OLD FAIRY TALES IS RIGHT HERE!
JACK'S BEAN STALK
THAT'S SWAN LAKE, AND ON THE OTHER SIDE YOU CAN SEE THE DEVIL'S CASTLE...

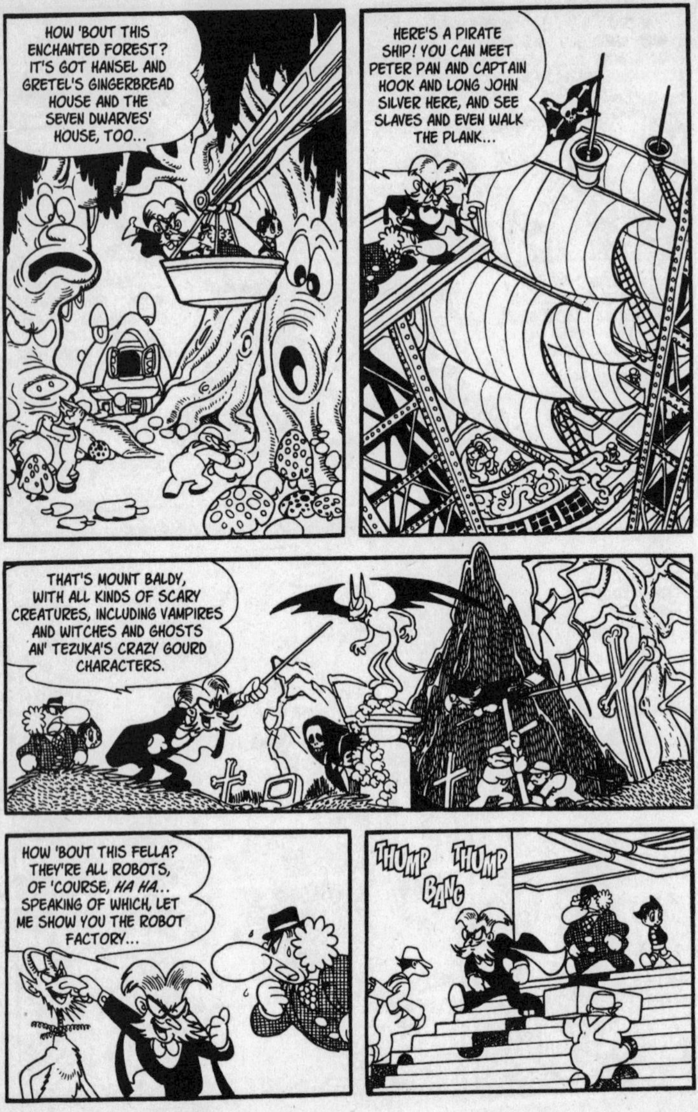
HOW 'BOUT THIS ENCHANTED FOREST? IT'S GOT HANSEL AND GRETEL'S GINGERBREAD HOUSE AND THE SEVEN DWARVES' HOUSE, TOO...
HERE'S A PIRATE SHIP! YOU CAN MEET PETER PAN AND CAPTAIN HOOK AND LONG JOHN SILVER HERE, AND SEE SLAVES AND EVEN WALK THE PLANK...
THAT'S MOUNT BALDY, WITH ALL KINDS OF SCARY CREATURES, INCLUDING VAMPIRES AND WITCHES AND GHOSTS AN' TEZUKA'S CRAZY GOURD CHARACTERS.
HOW 'BOUT THIS FELLA? THEY'RE ALL ROBOTS, OF 'COURSE, *HA HA*... SPEAKING OF WHICH, LET ME SHOW YOU THE ROBOT FACTORY...
THUMP
THUMP
BANG

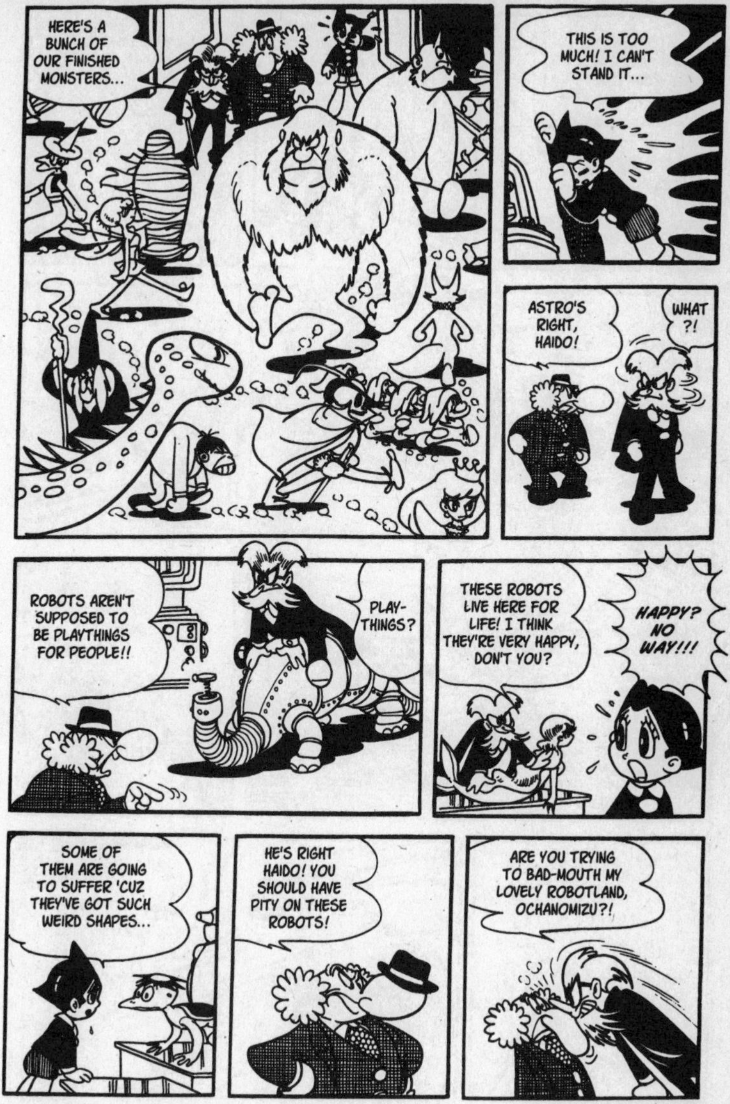
HERE'S A BUNCH OF OUR FINISHED MONSTERS...
THIS IS TOO MUCH! I CAN'T STAND IT...
ASTRO'S RIGHT, HAIDO!
WHAT ?!
ROBOTS AREN'T SUPPOSED TO BE PLAYTHINGS FOR PEOPLE!!
PLAY-THINGS?
THESE ROBOTS LIVE HERE FOR LIFE! I THINK THEY'RE VERY HAPPY, DON'T YOU?
HAPPY? NO WAY!!!
SOME OF THEM ARE GOING TO SUFFER 'CUZ THEY'VE GOT SUCH WEIRD SHAPES...
HE'S RIGHT HAIDO! YOU SHOULD HAVE PITY ON THESE ROBOTS!
ARE YOU TRYING TO BAD-MOUTH MY LOVELY ROBOTLAND, OCHANOMIZU?!

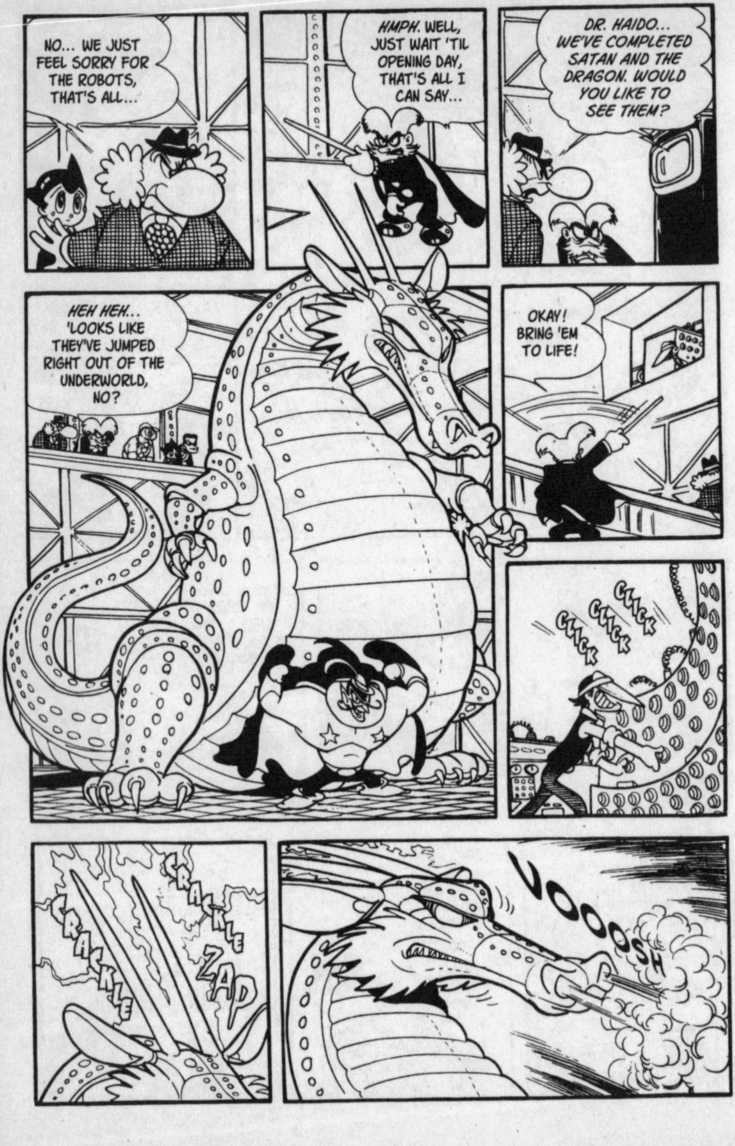
NO... WE JUST FEEL SORRY FOR THE ROBOTS, THAT'S ALL...
HMPH. WELL, JUST WAIT 'TIL OPENING DAY, THAT'S ALL I CAN SAY...
DR. HAIDO... WE'VE COMPLETED SATAN AND THE DRAGON. WOULD YOU LIKE TO SEE THEM?
HEH HEH... 'LOOKS LIKE THEY'VE JUMPED RIGHT OUT OF THE UNDERWORLD, NO?
OKAY! BRING 'EM TO LIFE!
CLICK
CLICK
CLICK
CRACKLE
CRACKLE
ZAP
VOOOOSH

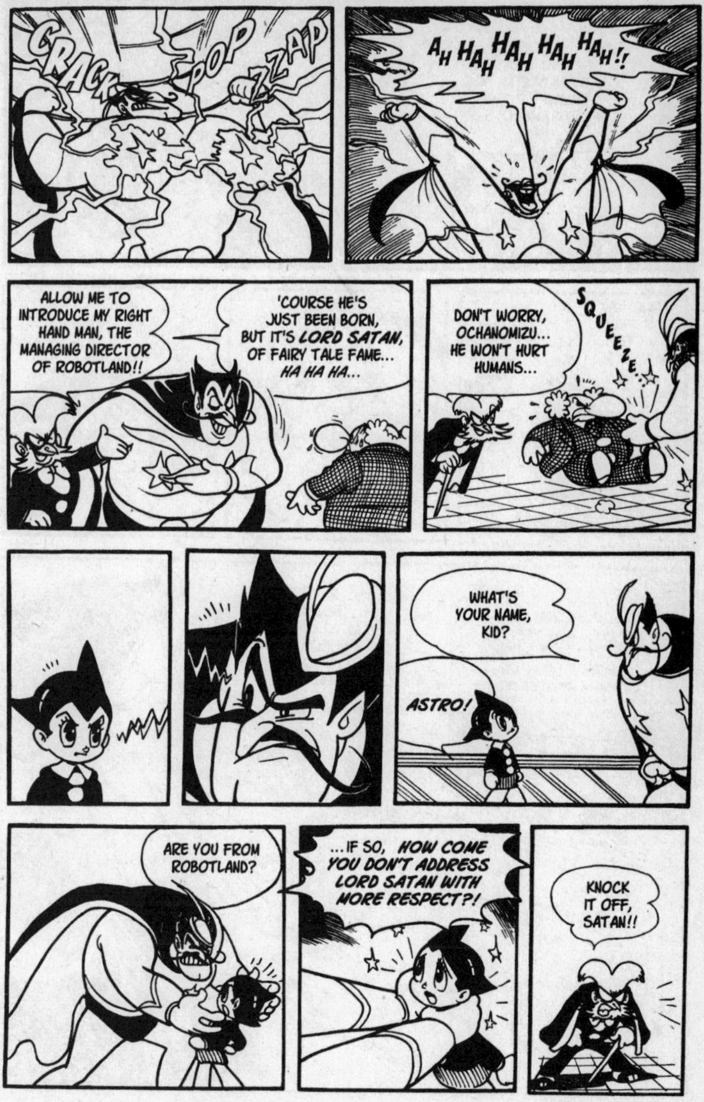

CRACK
POP
ZZAP
AH HAH HAH HAH HAH!!
ALLOW ME TO INTRODUCE MY RIGHT HAND MAN, THE MANAGING DIRECTOR OF ROBOTLAND!!
'COURSE HE'S JUST BEEN BORN, BUT IT'S LORD SATAN, OF FAIRY TALE FAME... HA HA HA...
DON'T WORRY, OCHANOMIZU... HE WON'T HURT HUMANS...
SQUEEZE...
WHAT'S YOUR NAME, KID?
ASTRO!
ARE YOU FROM ROBOTLAND?
...IF SO, HOW COME YOU DON'T ADDRESS LORD SATAN WITH MORE RESPECT?!
KNOCK IT OFF, SATAN!!

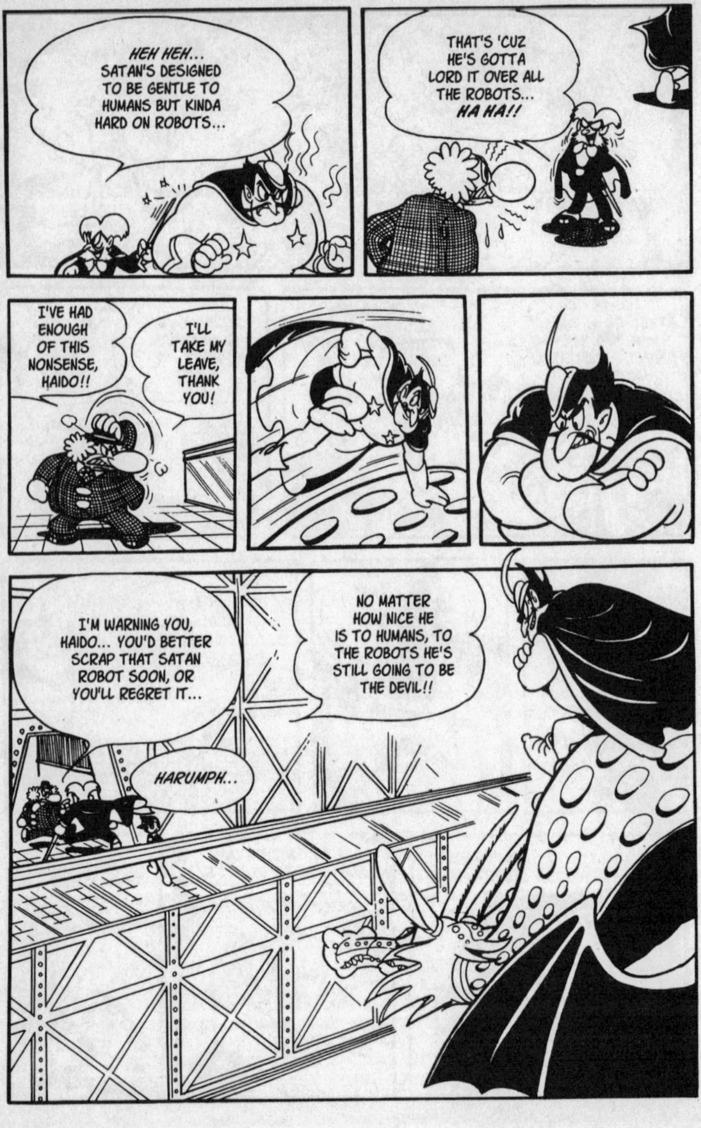

HEH HEH... SATAN'S DESIGNED TO BE GENTLE TO HUMANS BUT KINDA HARD ON ROBOTS...
THAT'S 'CUZ HE'S GOTTA LORD IT OVER ALL THE ROBOTS... HA HA!!
I'VE HAD ENOUGH OF THIS NONSENSE, HAIDO!!
I'LL TAKE MY LEAVE, THANK YOU!
I'M WARNING YOU, HAIDO... YOU'D BETTER SCRAP THAT SATAN ROBOT SOON, OR YOU'LL REGRET IT...
HARUMPH...
NO MATTER HOW NICE HE IS TO HUMANS, TO THE ROBOTS HE'S STILL GOING TO BE THE DEVIL!!

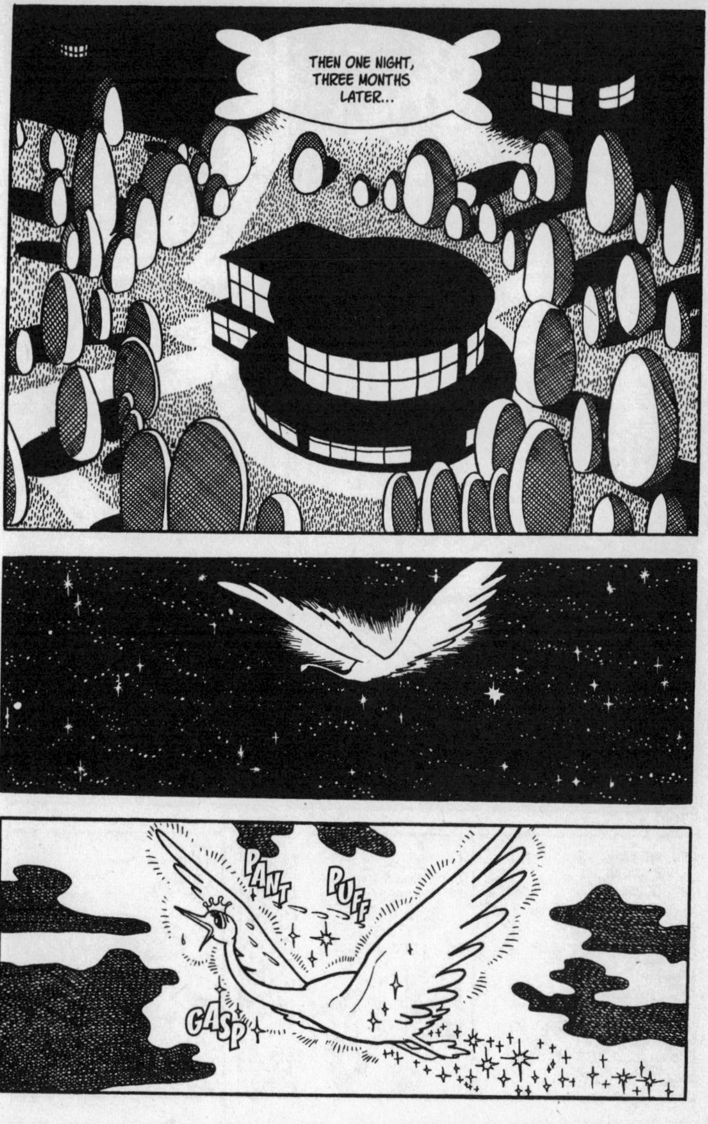
THEN ONE NIGHT, THREE MONTHS LATER...
PANT
PUFF
GASP

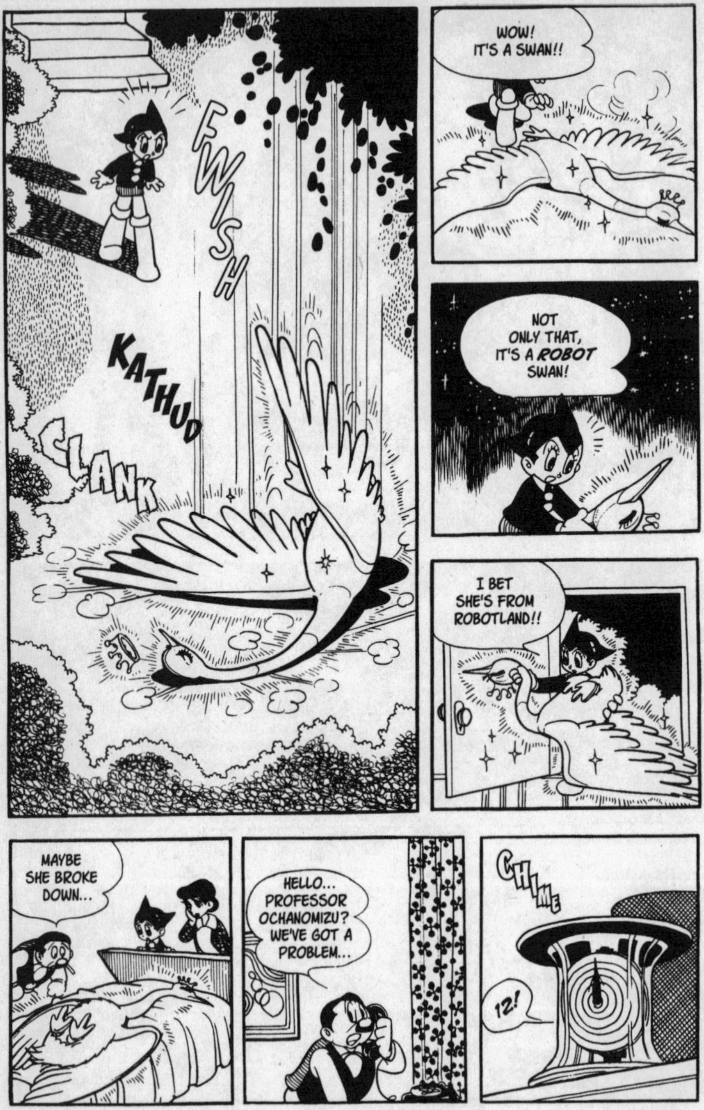
FWISH
KATHUD
CLANK
WOW! IT'S A SWAN!!
NOT ONLY THAT, IT'S A *ROBOT* SWAN!
I BET SHE'S FROM ROBOTLAND!!
MAYBE SHE BROKE DOWN...
HELLO... PROFESSOR OCHANOMIZU? WE'VE GOT A PROBLEM...
CHIME
12!

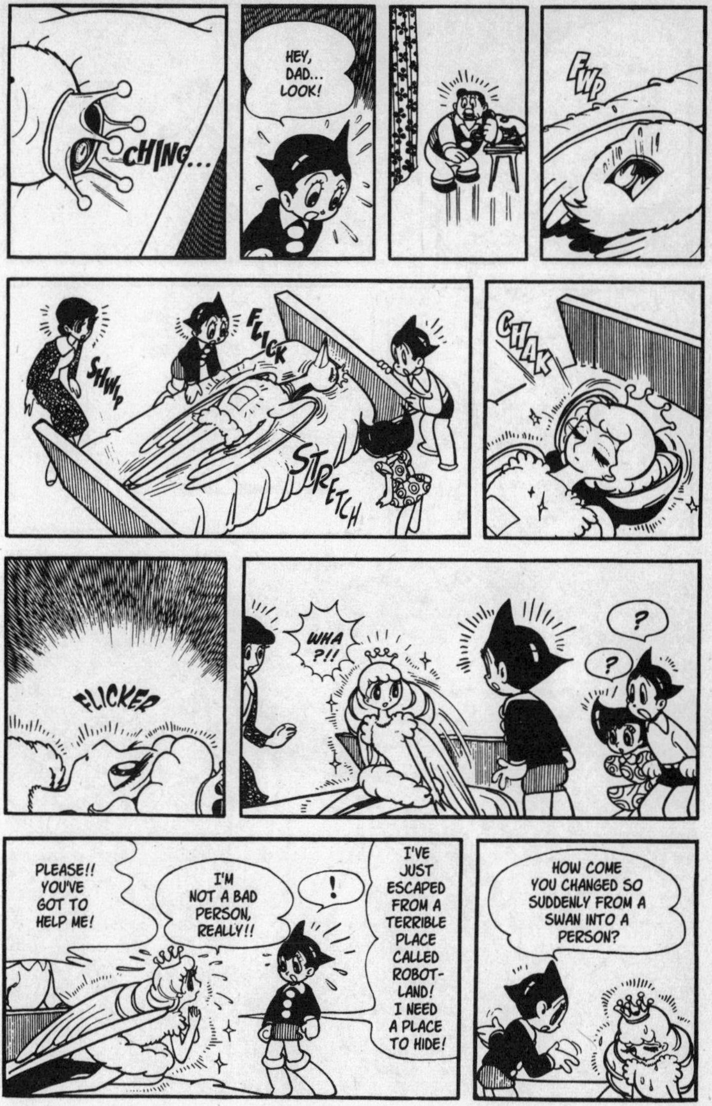
CHING...
HEY, DAD... LOOK!
FWP
SHWIP
FLICK
STRETCH
CHAK
FLICKER
WHA ?!!
?
?
PLEASE!! YOU'VE GOT TO HELP ME!
I'M NOT A BAD PERSON, REALLY!!
!
I'VE JUST ESCAPED FROM A TERRIBLE PLACE CALLED ROBOT-LAND! I NEED A PLACE TO HIDE!
HOW COME YOU CHANGED SO SUDDENLY FROM A SWAN INTO A PERSON?

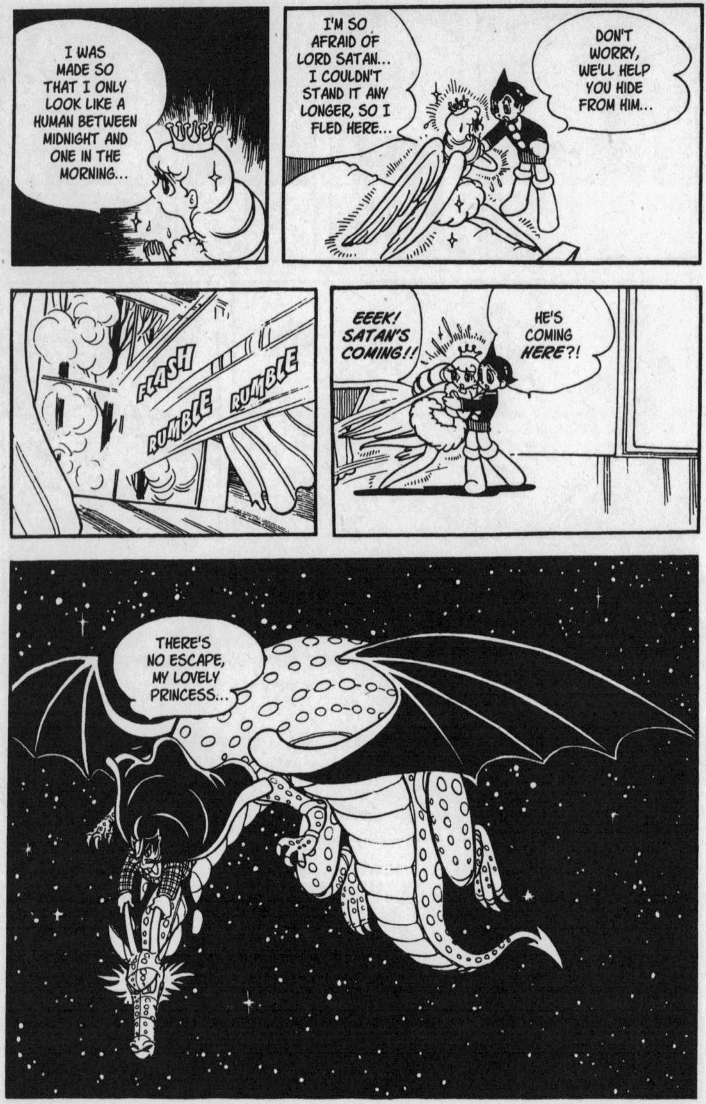
I WAS MADE SO THAT I ONLY LOOK LIKE A HUMAN BETWEEN MIDNIGHT AND ONE IN THE MORNING...
I'M SO AFRAID OF LORD SATAN... I COULDN'T STAND IT ANY LONGER, SO I FLED HERE...
DON'T WORRY, WE'LL HELP YOU HIDE FROM HIM...
FLASH
RUMBLE
RUMBLE
EEEK! SATAN'S COMING!!
HE'S COMING HERE?!
THERE'S NO ESCAPE, MY LOVELY PRINCESS...

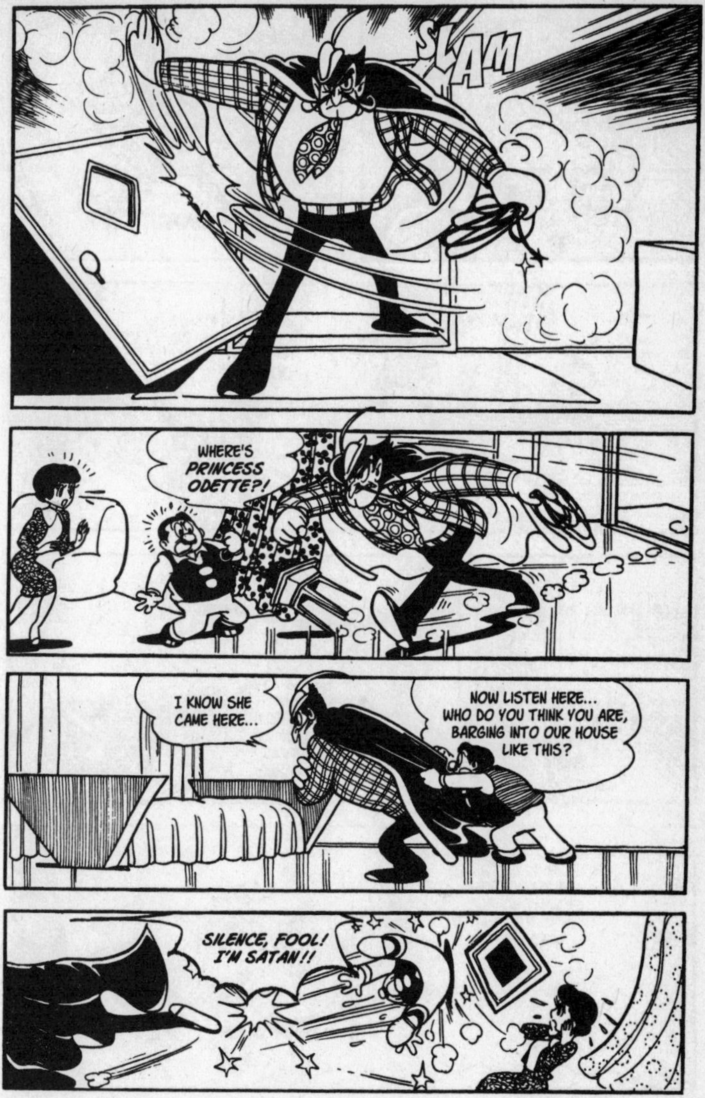
SLAM
WHERE'S PRINCESS ODETTE?!
I KNOW SHE CAME HERE...
NOW LISTEN HERE... WHO DO YOU THINK YOU ARE, BARGING INTO OUR HOUSE LIKE THIS?
SILENCE, FOOL! I'M SATAN!!

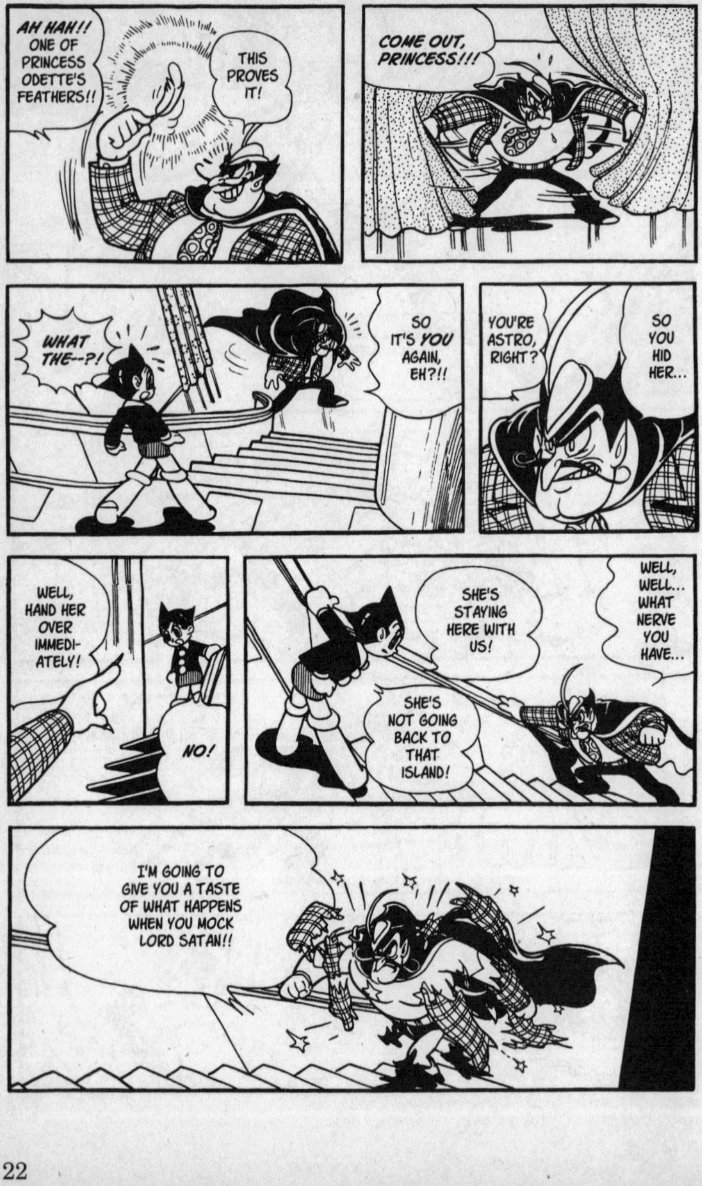

AH HAH!! ONE OF PRINCESS ODETTE'S FEATHERS!!
THIS PROVES IT!
COME OUT, PRINCESS!!!
WHAT THE--?!
SO IT'S YOU AGAIN, EH?!!
YOU'RE ASTRO, RIGHT?
SO YOU HID HER...
WELL, HAND HER OVER IMMEDI-ATELY!
NO!
SHE'S STAYING HERE WITH US!
SHE'S NOT GOING BACK TO THAT ISLAND!
WELL, WELL... WHAT NERVE YOU HAVE...
I'M GOING TO GIVE YOU A TASTE OF WHAT HAPPENS WHEN YOU MOCK LORD SATAN!!

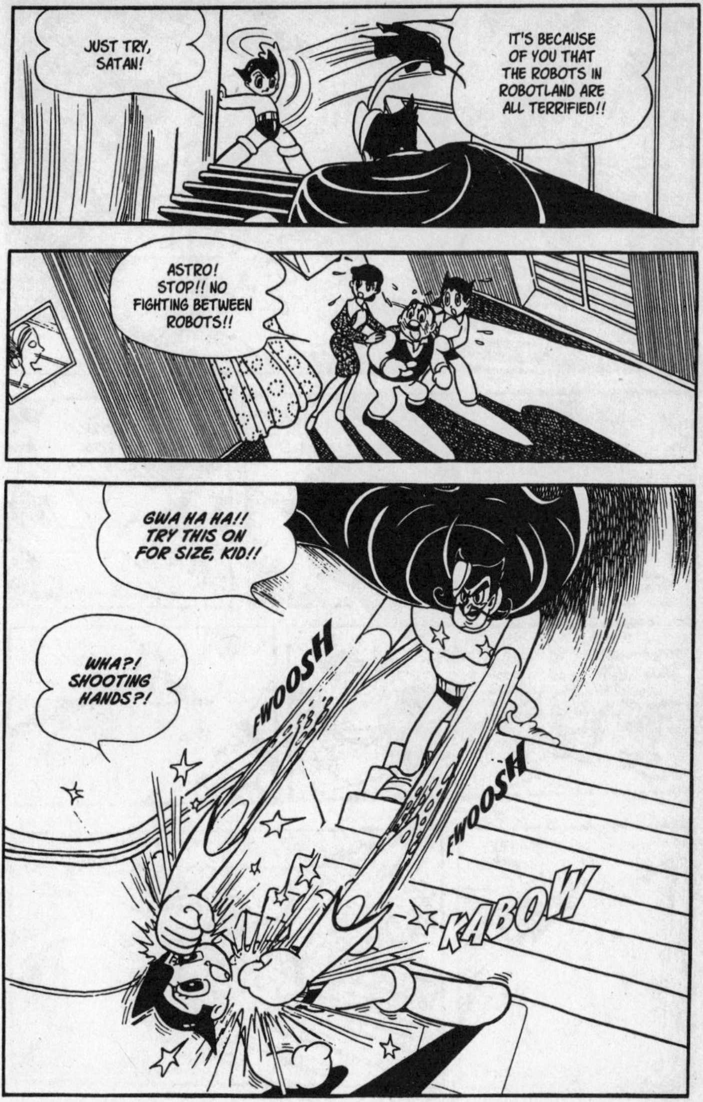
JUST TRY, SATAN!
IT'S BECAUSE OF YOU THAT THE ROBOTS IN ROBOTLAND ARE ALL TERRIFIED!!
ASTRO! STOP!! NO FIGHTING BETWEEN ROBOTS!!
GWA HA HA!! TRY THIS ON FOR SIZE, KID!!
WHA?! SHOOTING HANDS?!
FWOOSH
FWOOSH
KABOW

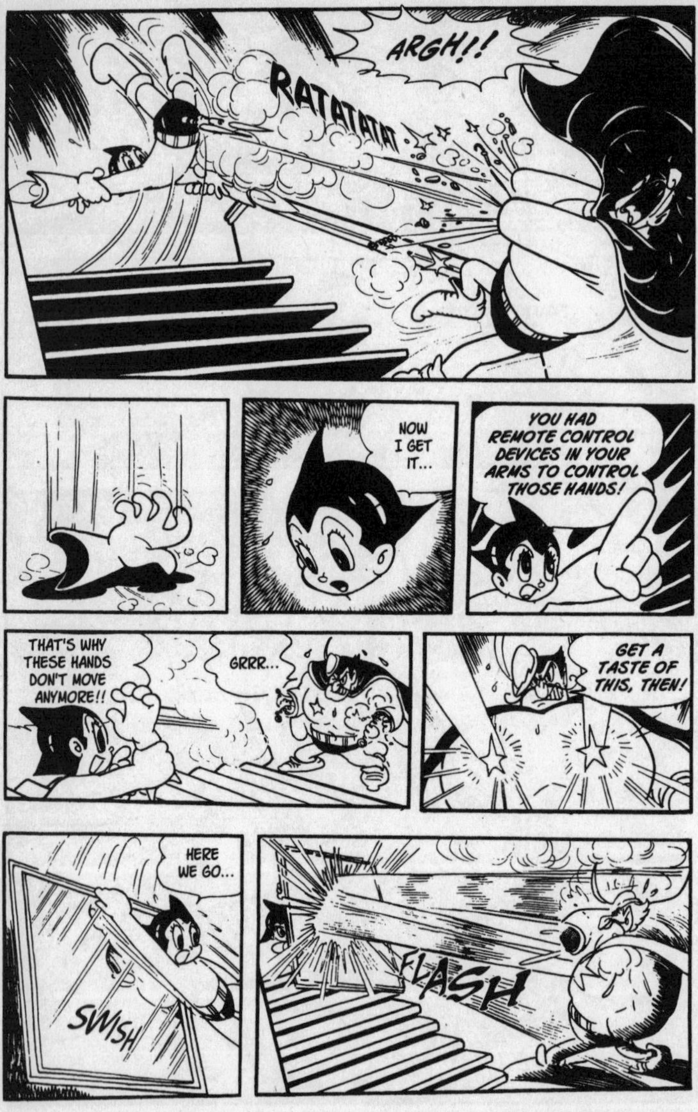
ARGH!!
RATATATAT
NOW I GET IT...
YOU HAD REMOTE CONTROL DEVICES IN YOUR ARMS TO CONTROL THOSE HANDS!
THAT'S WHY THESE HANDS DON'T MOVE ANYMORE!!
GRRR...
GET A TASTE OF THIS, THEN!
HERE WE GO...
SWISH
FLASH

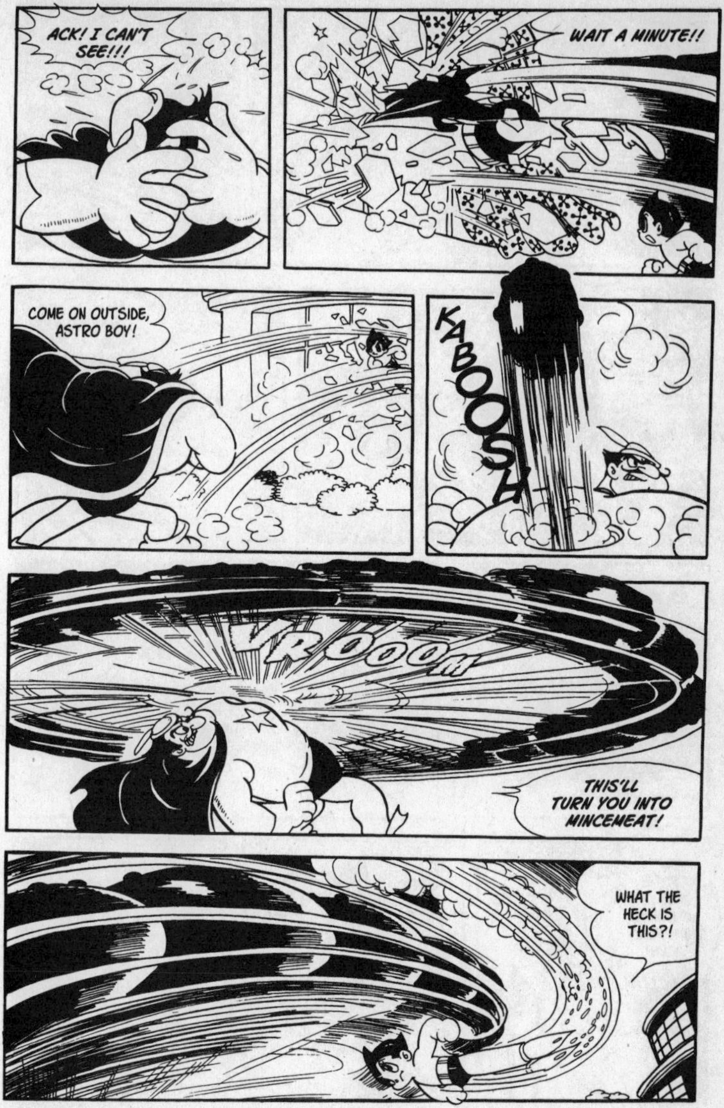
ACK! I CAN'T SEE!!!
WAIT A MINUTE!!
COME ON OUTSIDE, ASTRO BOY!
KABOOOSH
VROOOOM
THIS'LL TURN YOU INTO MINCEMEAT!
WHAT THE HECK IS THIS?!

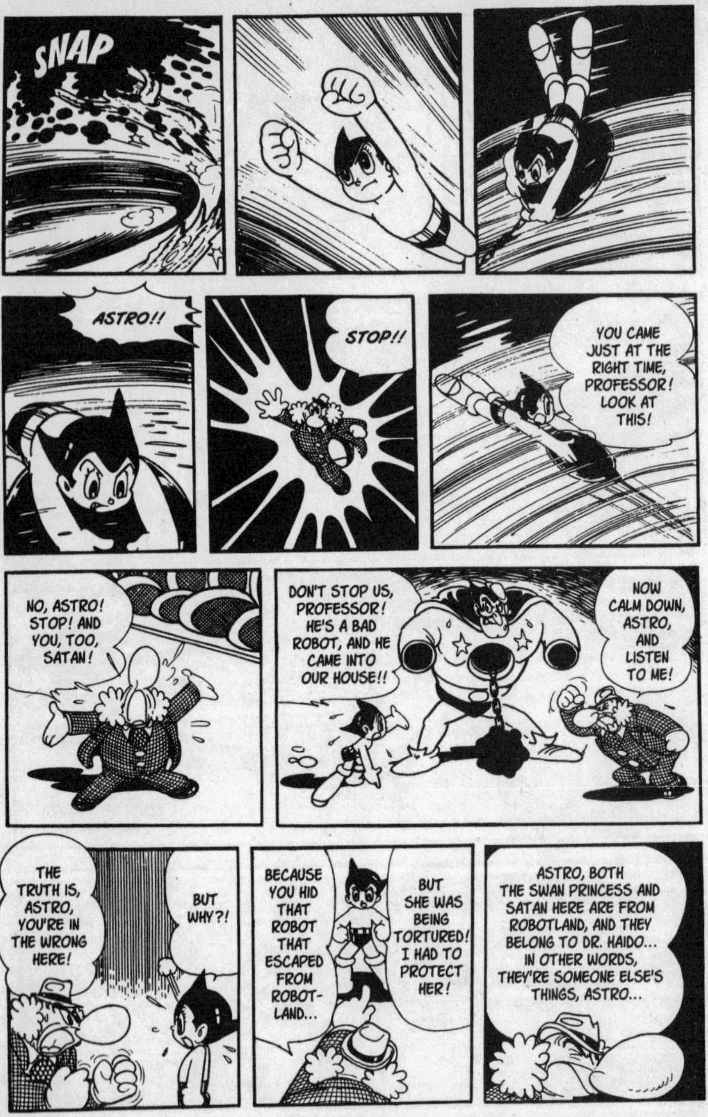
SNAP
ASTRO!!
STOP!!
YOU CAME JUST AT THE RIGHT TIME, PROFESSOR! LOOK AT THIS!
NO, ASTRO! STOP! AND YOU, TOO, SATAN!
DON'T STOP US, PROFESSOR! HE'S A BAD ROBOT, AND HE CAME INTO OUR HOUSE!!
NOW CALM DOWN, ASTRO, AND LISTEN TO ME!
THE TRUTH IS, ASTRO, YOU'RE IN THE WRONG HERE!
BUT WHY?!
BECAUSE YOU HID THAT ROBOT THAT ESCAPED FROM ROBOT-LAND...
BUT SHE WAS BEING TORTURED! I HAD TO PROTECT HER!
ASTRO, BOTH THE SWAN PRINCESS AND SATAN HERE ARE FROM ROBOTLAND, AND THEY BELONG TO DR. HAIDO... IN OTHER WORDS, THEY'RE SOMEONE ELSE'S THINGS, ASTRO...

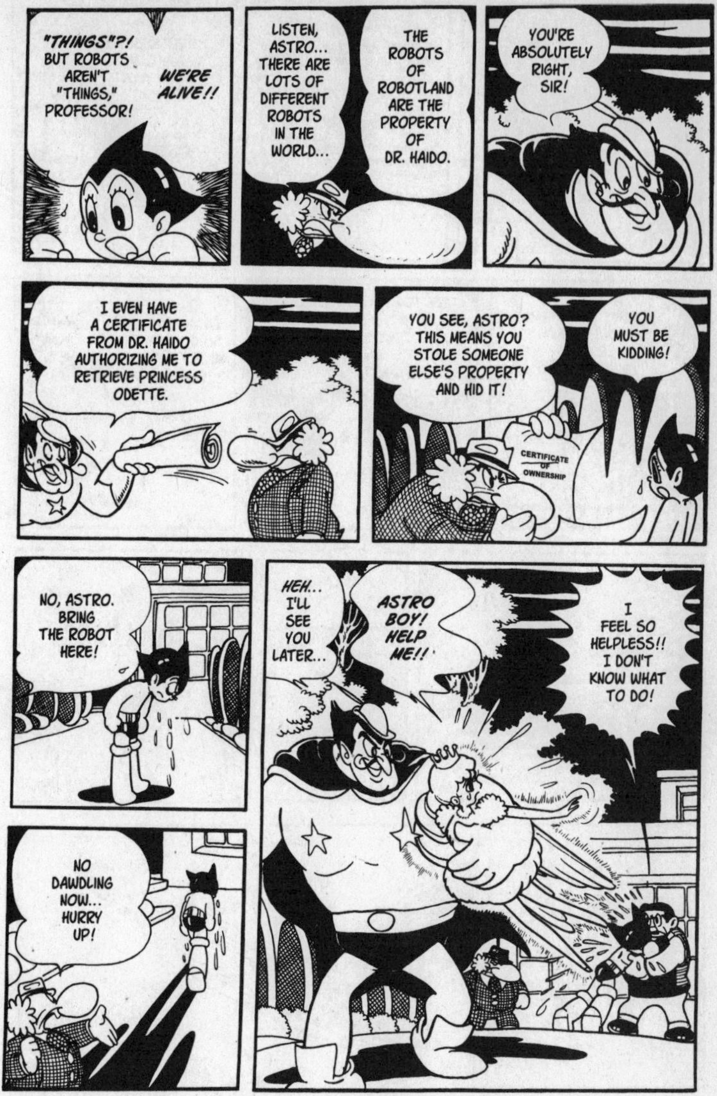
"THINGS"?! BUT ROBOTS AREN'T "THINGS," PROFESSOR!
WE'RE ALIVE!!
LISTEN, ASTRO... THERE ARE LOTS OF DIFFERENT ROBOTS IN THE WORLD...
THE ROBOTS OF ROBOTLAND ARE THE PROPERTY OF DR. HAIDO.
YOU'RE ABSOLUTELY RIGHT, SIR!
I EVEN HAVE A CERTIFICATE FROM DR. HAIDO AUTHORIZING ME TO RETRIEVE PRINCESS ODETTE.
YOU SEE, ASTRO? THIS MEANS YOU STOLE SOMEONE ELSE'S PROPERTY AND HID IT!
YOU MUST BE KIDDING!
CERTIFICATE OF OWNERSHIP
NO, ASTRO. BRING THE ROBOT HERE!
NO DAWDLING NOW... HURRY UP!
HEH... I'LL SEE YOU LATER...
ASTRO BOY! HELP ME!!
I FEEL SO HELPLESS!! I DON'T KNOW WHAT TO DO!

LISTEN, ASTRO, I KNOW EXACTLY HOW YOU FEEL!

...BUT THE PROFESSOR'S RIGHT, TOO, YOU KNOW...

YOU'VE JUST GOT TO FORGET IT... THERE'S NOTHING WE CAN DO TO HELP THE ROBOTS OF ROBOTLAND...

ARE YOU TRYING TO TELL ME I HAVE TO SIT BACK AND DO NOTHING WHILE SATAN CREATES HELL IN ROBOTLAND?!

BUT... I WANT TO DO SOMETHING TO HELP THE POOR ROBOTS...

ASTRO BOY! HELP ME!!

I KNOW!!

I'LL SNEAK INTO ROBOTLAND!

WHOOSH!

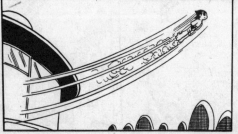

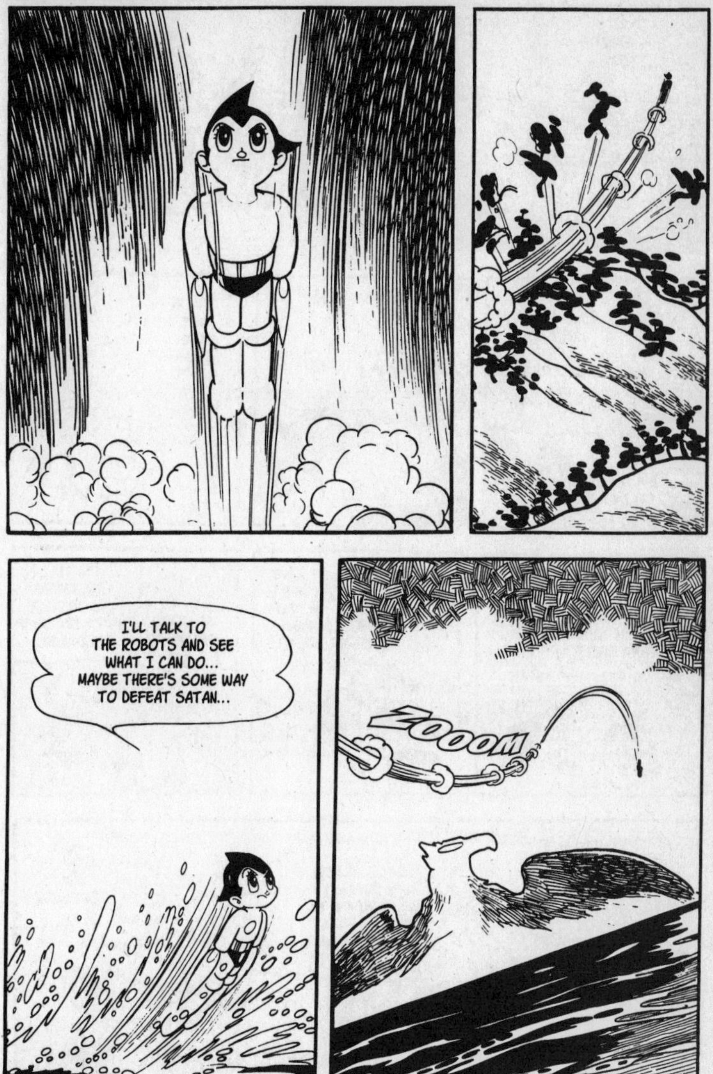
I'LL TALK TO THE ROBOTS AND SEE WHAT I CAN DO... MAYBE THERE'S SOME WAY TO DEFEAT SATAN...
ZOOOM

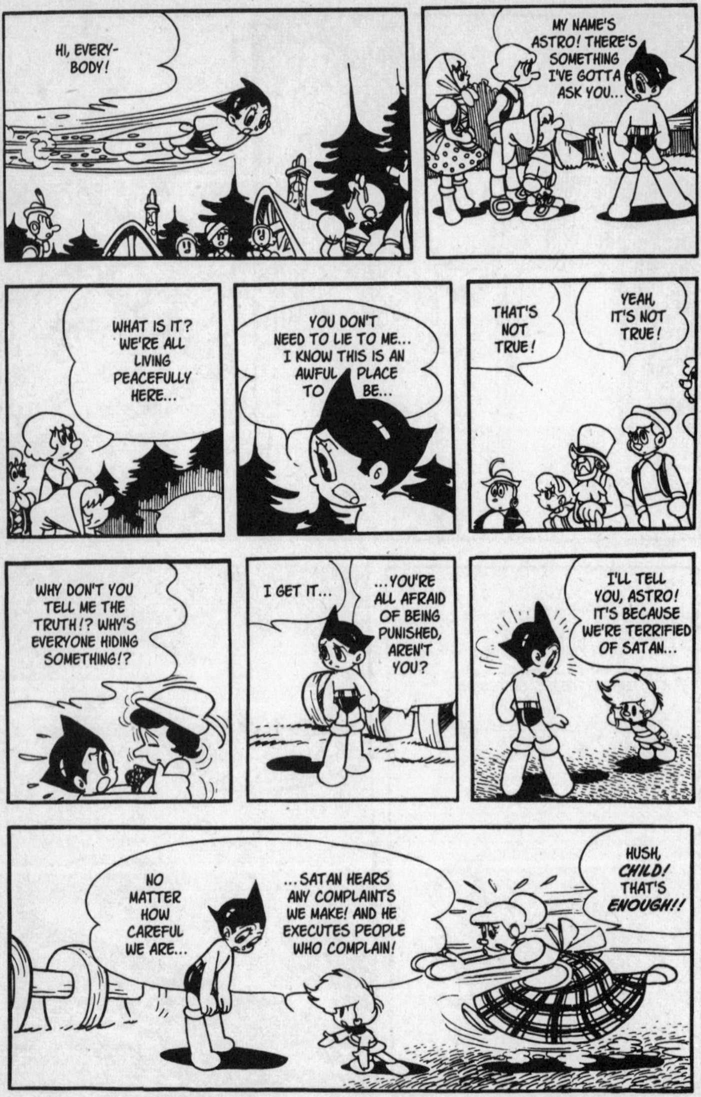

HI, EVERY-BODY!
MY NAME'S ASTRO! THERE'S SOMETHING I'VE GOTTA ASK YOU...
WHAT IS IT? WE'RE ALL LIVING PEACEFULLY HERE...
YOU DON'T NEED TO LIE TO ME... I KNOW THIS IS AN AWFUL PLACE TO BE...
THAT'S NOT TRUE!
YEAH, IT'S NOT TRUE!
WHY DON'T YOU TELL ME THE TRUTH!? WHY'S EVERYONE HIDING SOMETHING!?
I GET IT...
...YOU'RE ALL AFRAID OF BEING PUNISHED, AREN'T YOU?
I'LL TELL YOU, ASTRO! IT'S BECAUSE WE'RE TERRIFIED OF SATAN...
NO MATTER HOW CAREFUL WE ARE...
...SATAN HEARS ANY COMPLAINTS WE MAKE! AND HE EXECUTES PEOPLE WHO COMPLAIN!
HUSH, *CHILD!* THAT'S *ENOUGH!!*

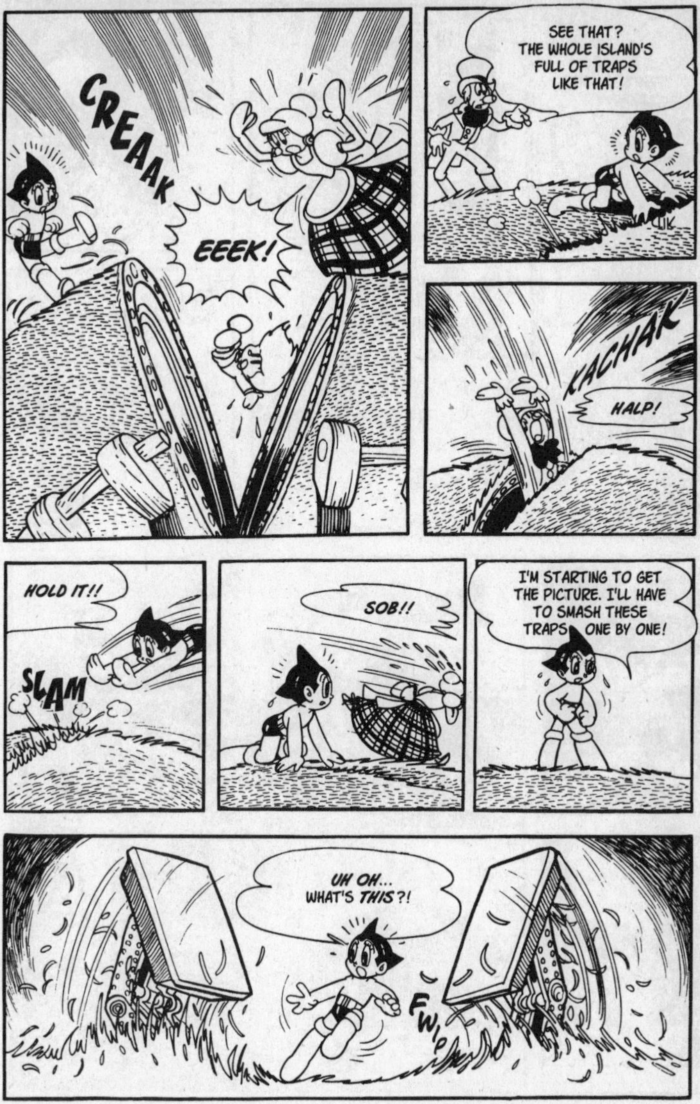
CREAAAK
EEEK!
SEE THAT? THE WHOLE ISLAND'S FULL OF TRAPS LIKE THAT!
LIK
KACHAK
HALP!
HOLD IT!!
SLAM
SOB!!
I'M STARTING TO GET THE PICTURE. I'LL HAVE TO SMASH THESE TRAPS ONE BY ONE!
UH OH... WHAT'S THIS?!
FWIP

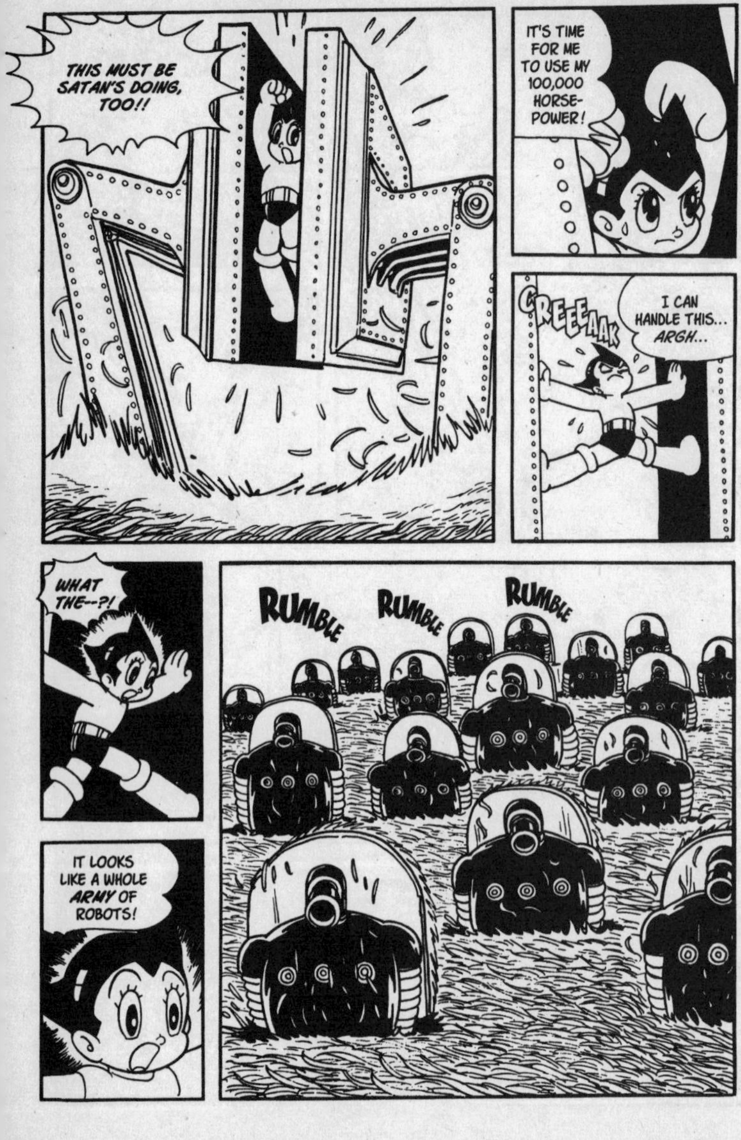
THIS MUST BE SATAN'S DOING, TOO!!
IT'S TIME FOR ME TO USE MY 100,000 HORSE-POWER!
CREEEAAK
I CAN HANDLE THIS... ARGH...
WHAT THE--?!
RUMBLE
RUMBLE
RUMBLE
IT LOOKS LIKE A WHOLE ARMY OF ROBOTS!

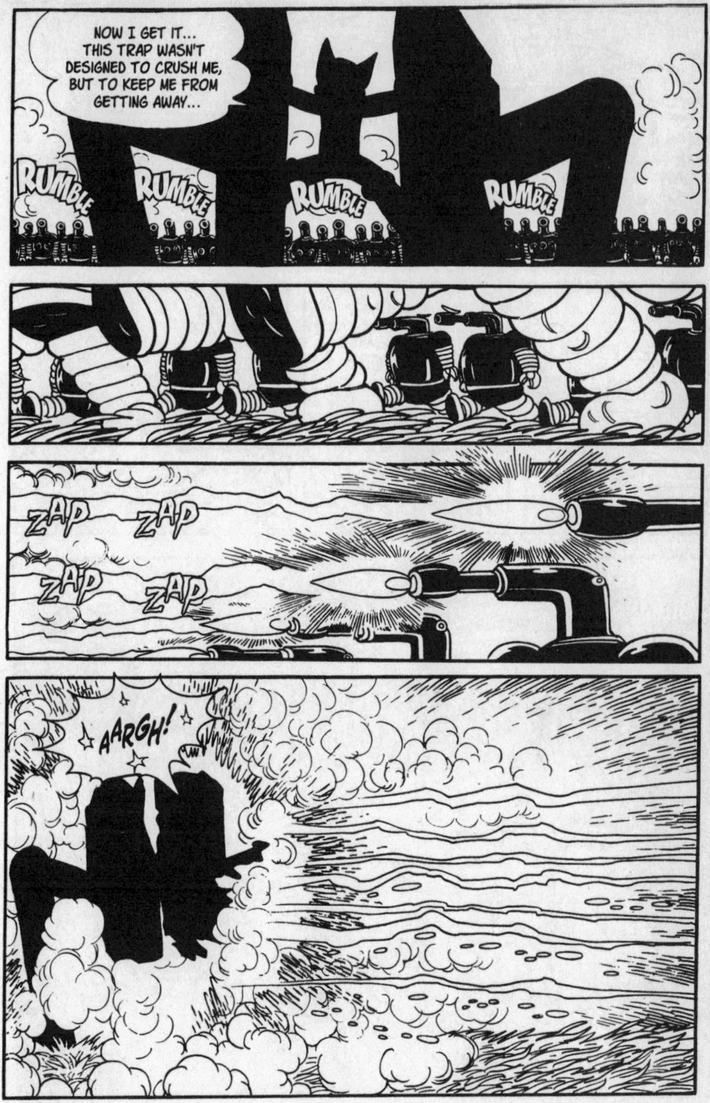

NOW I GET IT... THIS TRAP WASN'T DESIGNED TO CRUSH ME, BUT TO KEEP ME FROM GETTING AWAY...
RUMBLE
RUMBLE
RUMBLE
RUMBLE
ZAP
ZAP
ZAP
ZAP
AARGH!

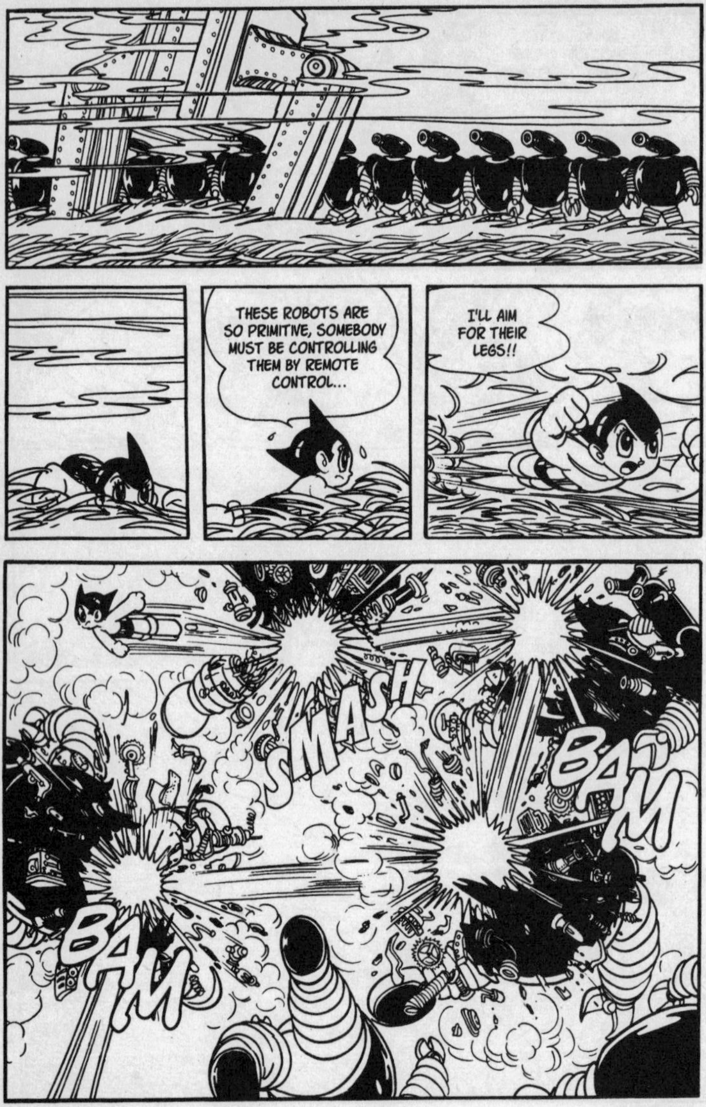
THESE ROBOTS ARE SO PRIMITIVE, SOMEBODY MUST BE CONTROLLING THEM BY REMOTE CONTROL...
I'LL AIM FOR THEIR LEGS!!
SMASH
BAM
BAM

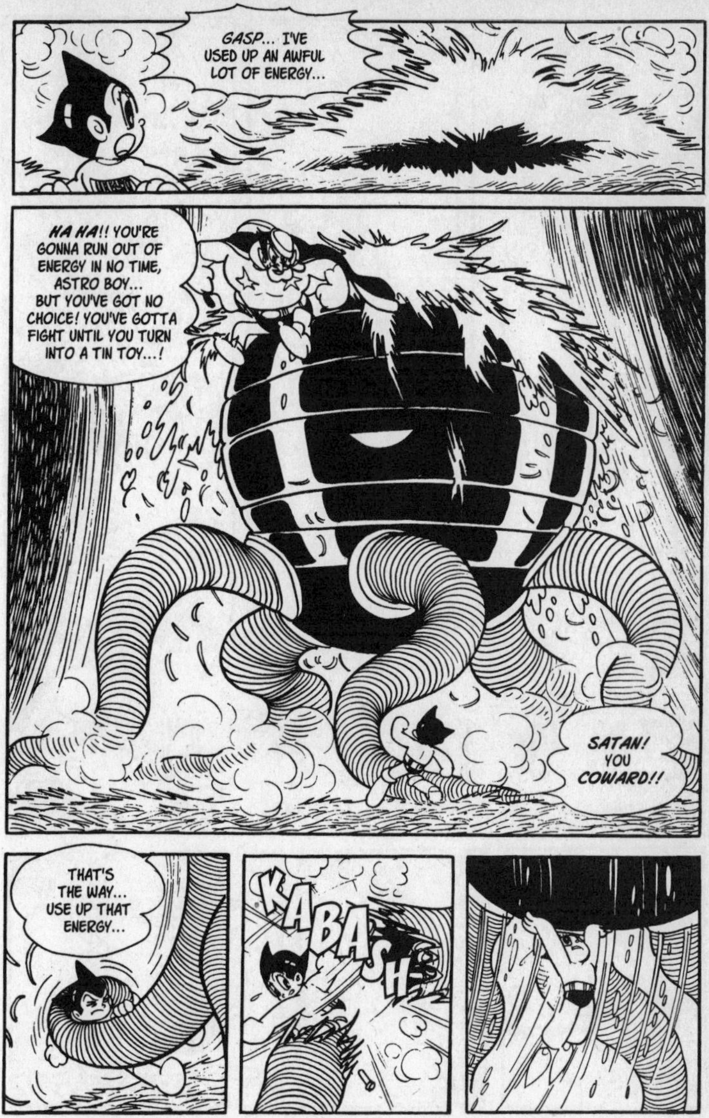
GASP... I'VE USED UP AN AWFUL LOT OF ENERGY...
HA HA!! YOU'RE GONNA RUN OUT OF ENERGY IN NO TIME, ASTRO BOY... BUT YOU'VE GOT NO CHOICE! YOU'VE GOTTA FIGHT UNTIL YOU TURN INTO A TIN TOY...!
SATAN! YOU COWARD!!
THAT'S THE WAY... USE UP THAT ENERGY...
KABASH-

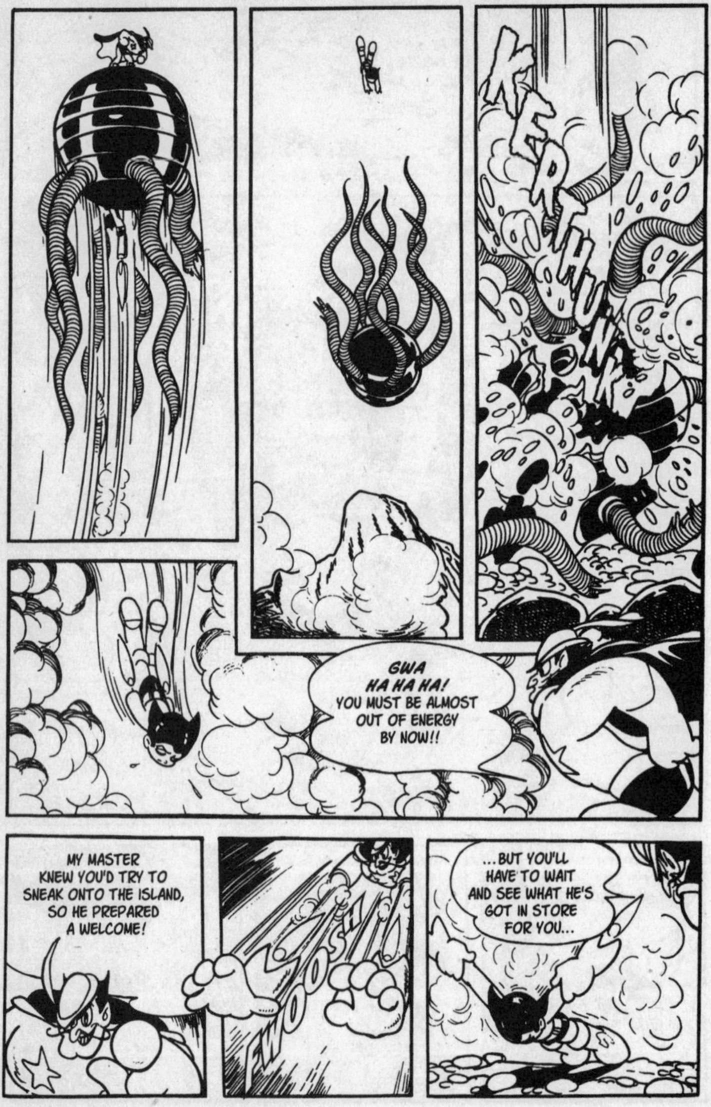
KERTHUNK!
GWA HA HA HA! YOU MUST BE ALMOST OUT OF ENERGY BY NOW!!
MY MASTER KNEW YOU'D TRY TO SNEAK ONTO THE ISLAND, SO HE PREPARED A WELCOME!
FWOOOSH
...BUT YOU'LL HAVE TO WAIT AND SEE WHAT HE'S GOT IN STORE FOR YOU...

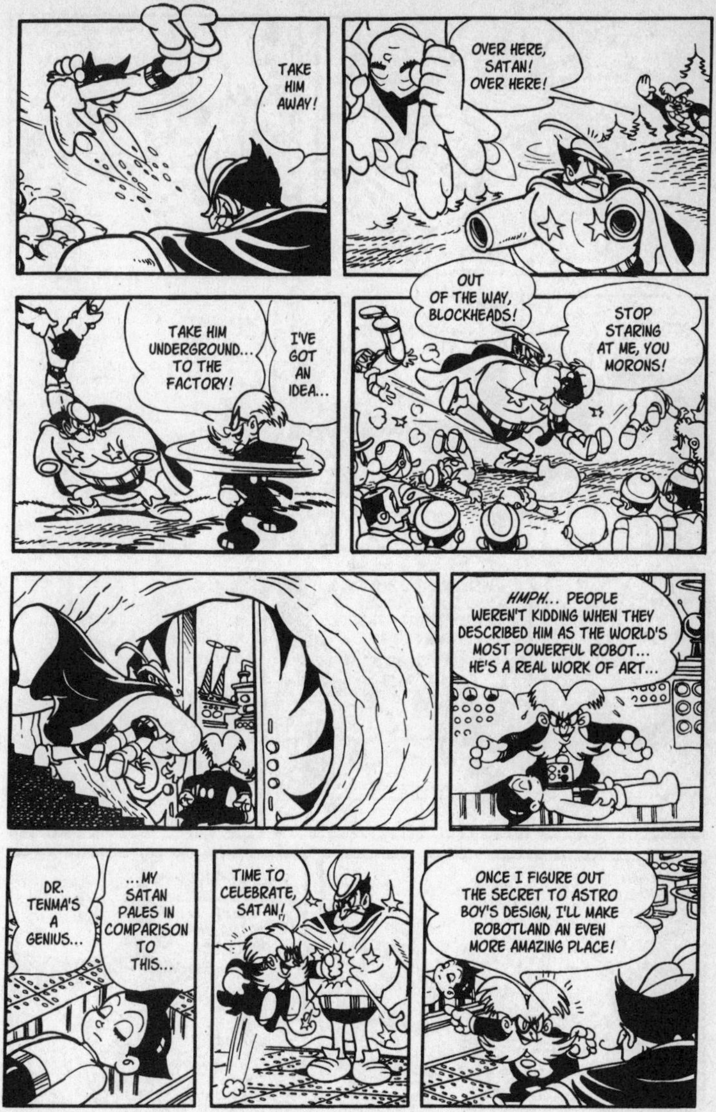
TAKE HIM AWAY!
OVER HERE, SATAN! OVER HERE!
TAKE HIM UNDERGROUND... TO THE FACTORY!
I'VE GOT AN IDEA...
OUT OF THE WAY, BLOCKHEADS!
STOP STARING AT ME, YOU MORONS!
HMPH... PEOPLE WEREN'T KIDDING WHEN THEY DESCRIBED HIM AS THE WORLD'S MOST POWERFUL ROBOT... HE'S A REAL WORK OF ART...
DR. TENMA'S A GENIUS...
...MY SATAN PALES IN COMPARISON TO THIS...
TIME TO CELEBRATE, SATAN!
ONCE I FIGURE OUT THE SECRET TO ASTRO BOY'S DESIGN, I'LL MAKE ROBOTLAND AN EVEN MORE AMAZING PLACE!

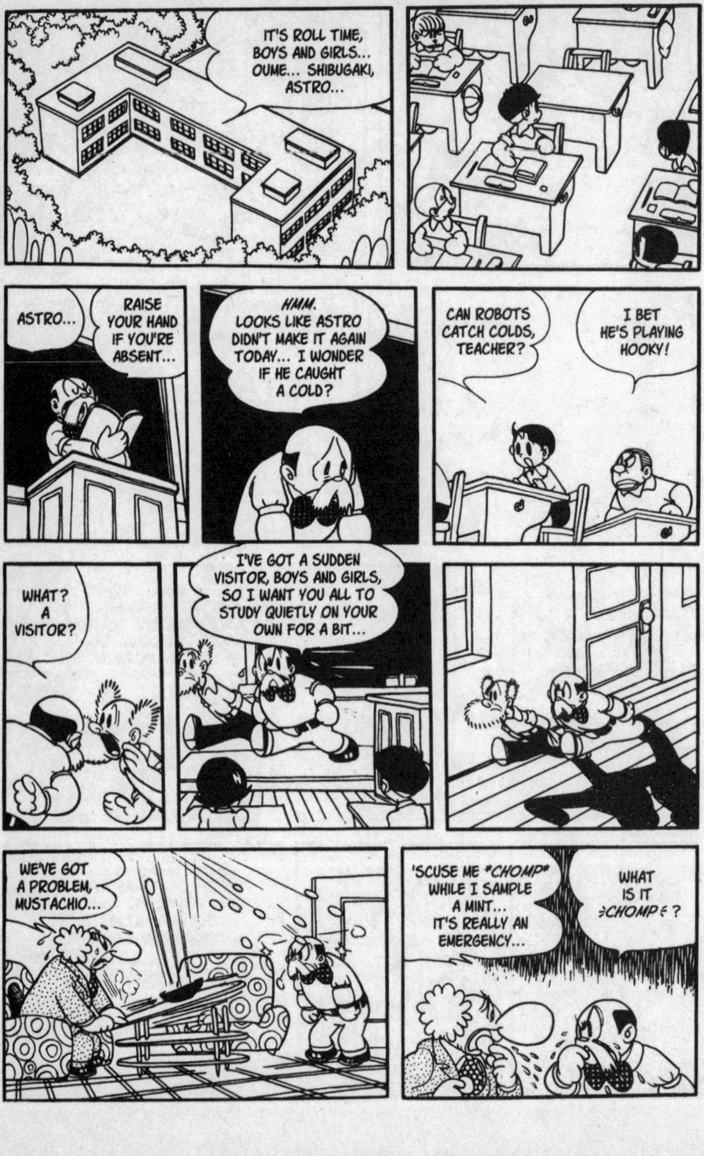
IT'S ROLL TIME, BOYS AND GIRLS... OUME... SHIBUGAKI, ASTRO...
ASTRO...
RAISE YOUR HAND IF YOU'RE ABSENT...
HMM. LOOKS LIKE ASTRO DIDN'T MAKE IT AGAIN TODAY... I WONDER IF HE CAUGHT A COLD?
CAN ROBOTS CATCH COLDS, TEACHER?
I BET HE'S PLAYING HOOKY!
WHAT? A VISITOR?
I'VE GOT A SUDDEN VISITOR, BOYS AND GIRLS, SO I WANT YOU ALL TO STUDY QUIETLY ON YOUR OWN FOR A BIT...
WE'VE GOT A PROBLEM, MUSTACHIO...
'SCUSE ME *CHOMP* WHILE I SAMPLE A MINT... IT'S REALLY AN EMERGENCY...
WHAT IS IT *CHOMP* ?

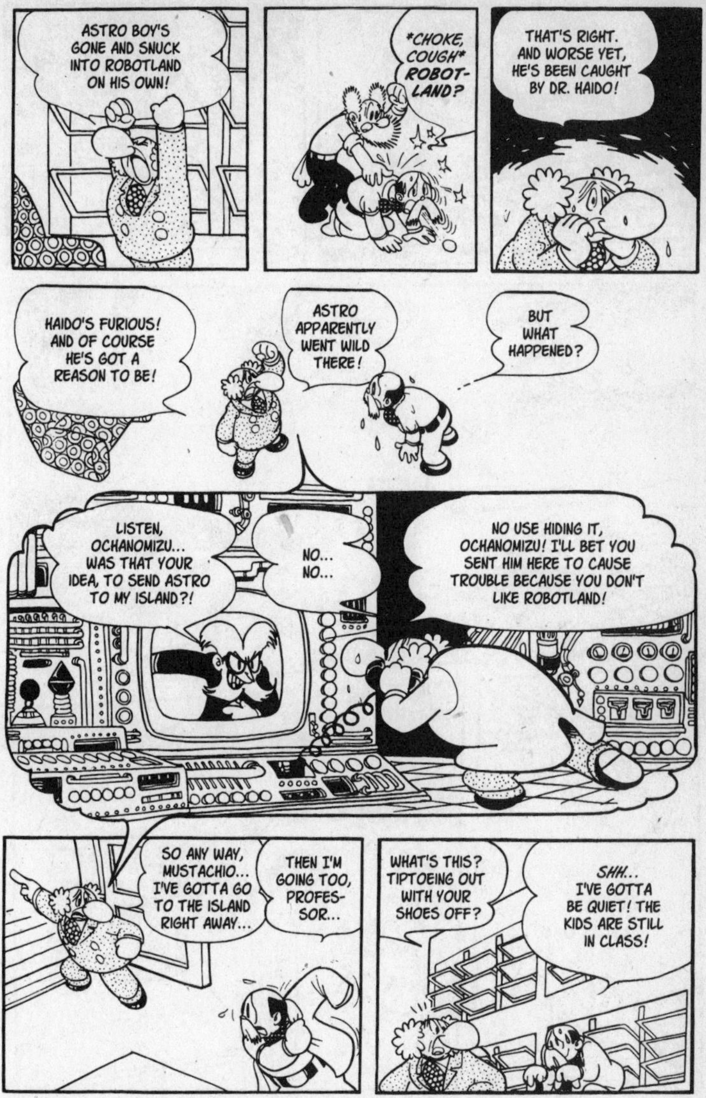
ASTRO BOY'S GONE AND SNUCK INTO ROBOTLAND ON HIS OWN!
CHOKE, COUGH ROBOT-LAND?
THAT'S RIGHT. AND WORSE YET, HE'S BEEN CAUGHT BY DR. HAIDO!
HAIDO'S FURIOUS! AND OF COURSE HE'S GOT A REASON TO BE!
ASTRO APPARENTLY WENT WILD THERE!
BUT WHAT HAPPENED?
LISTEN, OCHANOMIZU... WAS THAT YOUR IDEA, TO SEND ASTRO TO MY ISLAND?!
NO... NO...
NO USE HIDING IT, OCHANOMIZU! I'LL BET YOU SENT HIM HERE TO CAUSE TROUBLE BECAUSE YOU DON'T LIKE ROBOTLAND!
SO ANY WAY, MUSTACHIO... I'VE GOTTA GO TO THE ISLAND RIGHT AWAY...
THEN I'M GOING TOO, PROFES-SOR...
WHAT'S THIS? TIPTOEING OUT WITH YOUR SHOES OFF?
SHH... I'VE GOTTA BE QUIET! THE KIDS ARE STILL IN CLASS!

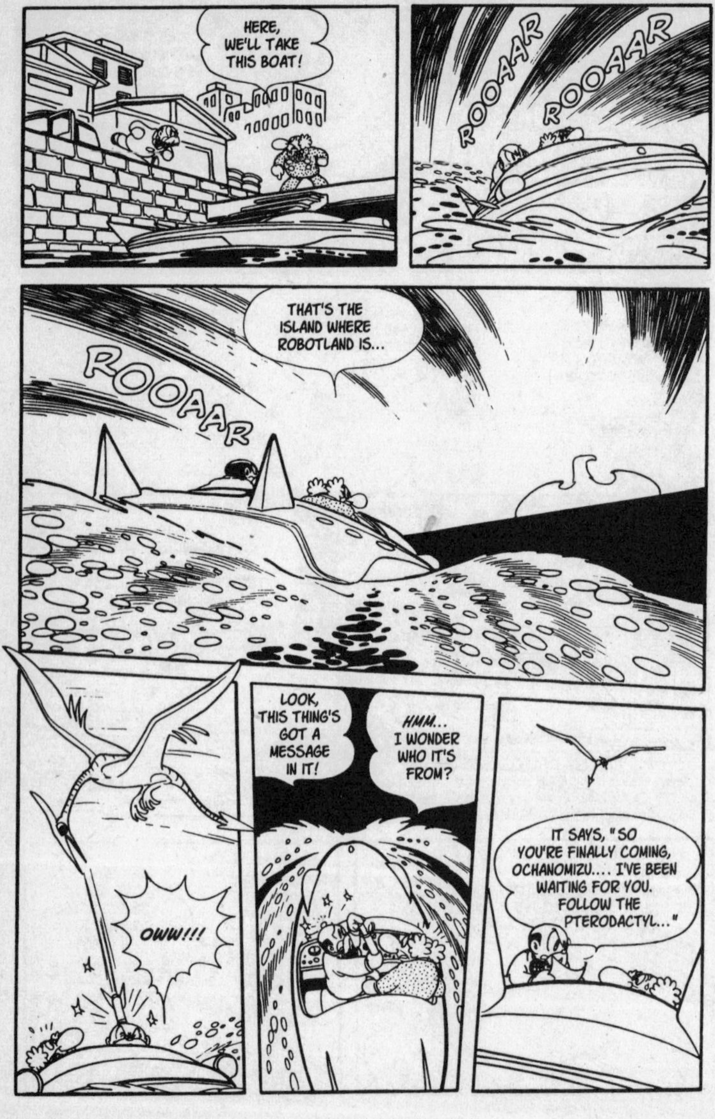
HERE, WE'LL TAKE THIS BOAT!
ROOAAR
ROOAAR
THAT'S THE ISLAND WHERE ROBOTLAND IS...
ROOAAR
OWW!!!
LOOK, THIS THING'S GOT A MESSAGE IN IT!
HMM... I WONDER WHO IT'S FROM?
IT SAYS, "SO YOU'RE FINALLY COMING, OCHANOMIZU.... I'VE BEEN WAITING FOR YOU. FOLLOW THE PTERODACTYL..."

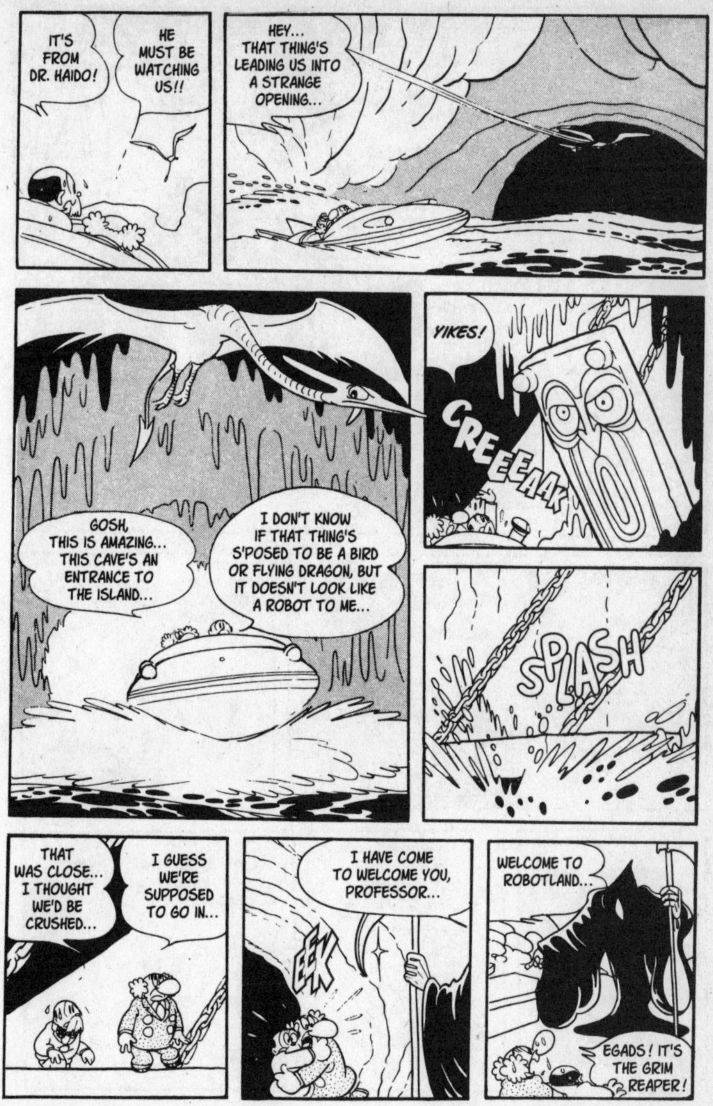
IT'S FROM DR. HAIDO!
HE MUST BE WATCHING US!!
HEY... THAT THING'S LEADING US INTO A STRANGE OPENING...
GOSH, THIS IS AMAZING... THIS CAVE'S AN ENTRANCE TO THE ISLAND...
I DON'T KNOW IF THAT THING'S S'POSED TO BE A BIRD OR FLYING DRAGON, BUT IT DOESN'T LOOK LIKE A ROBOT TO ME...
YIKES!
CREEEAAK
SPLASH
THAT WAS CLOSE... I THOUGHT WE'D BE CRUSHED...
I GUESS WE'RE SUPPOSED TO GO IN...
I HAVE COME TO WELCOME YOU, PROFESSOR...
EEK
WELCOME TO ROBOTLAND...
EGADS! IT'S THE GRIM REAPER!

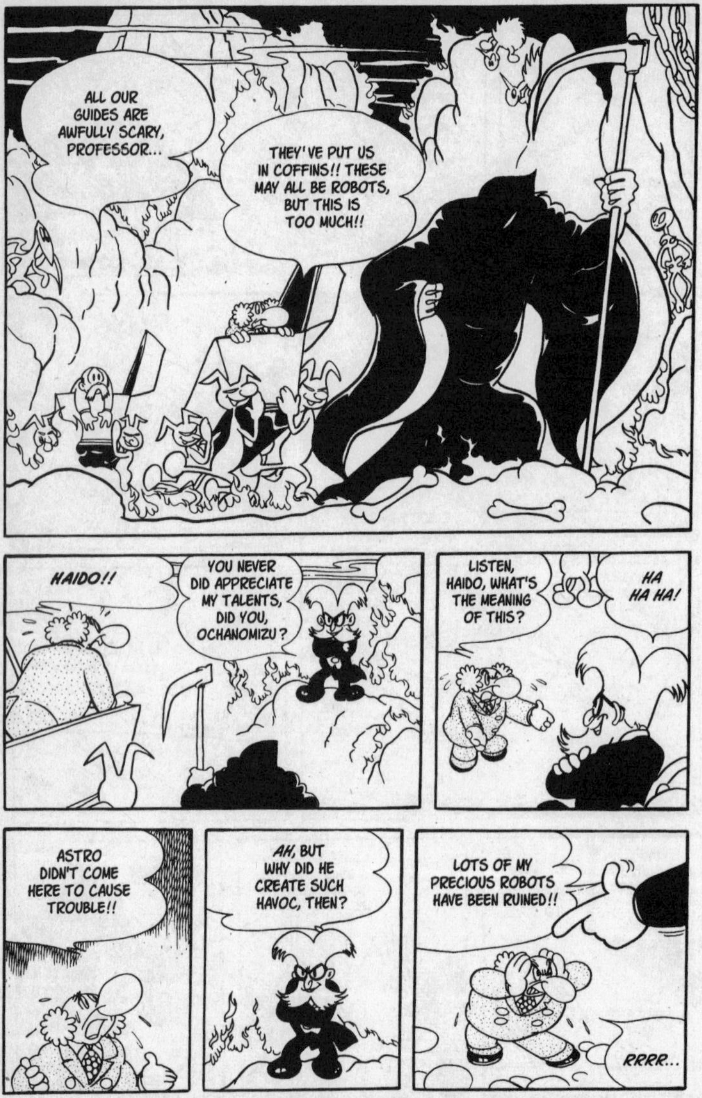
ALL OUR GUIDES ARE AWFULLY SCARY, PROFESSOR...
THEY'VE PUT US IN COFFINS!! THESE MAY ALL BE ROBOTS, BUT THIS IS TOO MUCH!!
HAIDO!!
YOU NEVER DID APPRECIATE MY TALENTS, DID YOU, OCHANOMIZU?
LISTEN, HAIDO, WHAT'S THE MEANING OF THIS?
HA HA HA!
ASTRO DIDN'T COME HERE TO CAUSE TROUBLE!!
AH, BUT WHY DID HE CREATE SUCH HAVOC, THEN?
LOTS OF MY PRECIOUS ROBOTS HAVE BEEN RUINED!!
RRRR...

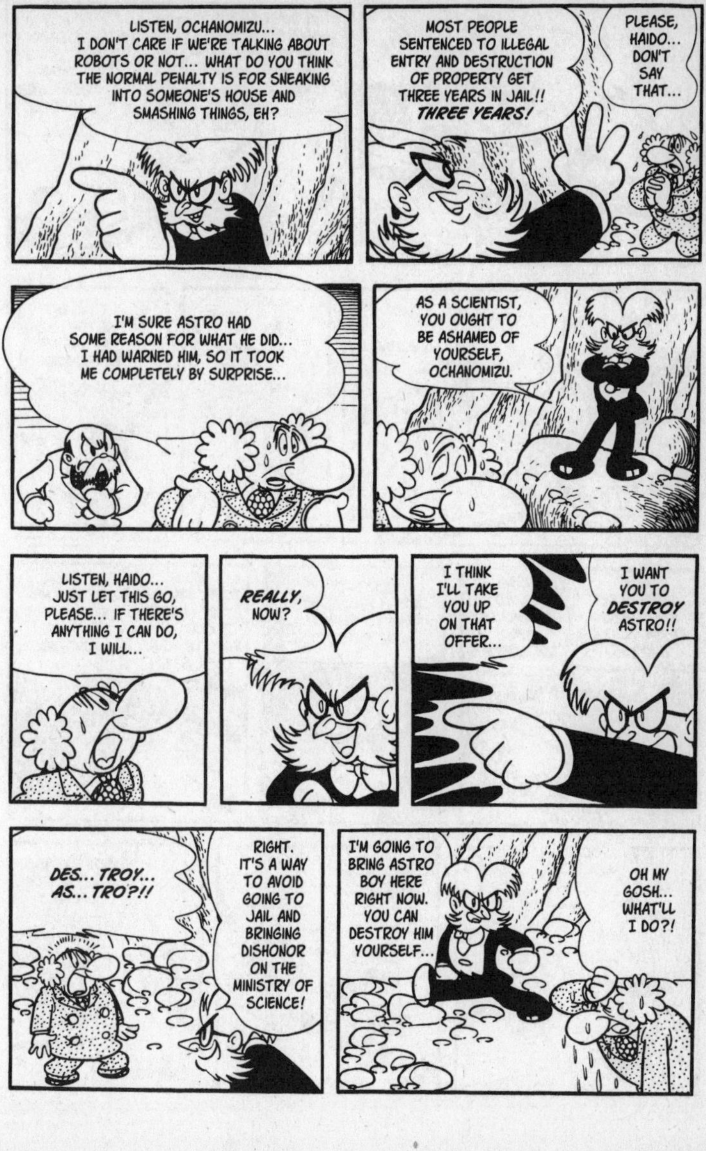
LISTEN, OCHANOMIZU... I DON'T CARE IF WE'RE TALKING ABOUT ROBOTS OR NOT... WHAT DO YOU THINK THE NORMAL PENALTY IS FOR SNEAKING INTO SOMEONE'S HOUSE AND SMASHING THINGS, EH?
MOST PEOPLE SENTENCED TO ILLEGAL ENTRY AND DESTRUCTION OF PROPERTY GET THREE YEARS IN JAIL!! *THREE YEARS!*
PLEASE, HAIDO... DON'T SAY THAT...
I'M SURE ASTRO HAD SOME REASON FOR WHAT HE DID... I HAD WARNED HIM, SO IT TOOK ME COMPLETELY BY SURPRISE...
AS A SCIENTIST, YOU OUGHT TO BE ASHAMED OF YOURSELF, OCHANOMIZU.
LISTEN, HAIDO... JUST LET THIS GO, PLEASE... IF THERE'S ANYTHING I CAN DO, I WILL...
REALLY, NOW?
I THINK I'LL TAKE YOU UP ON THAT OFFER...
I WANT YOU TO *DESTROY* ASTRO!!
DES... TROY... AS... TRO?!!
RIGHT. IT'S A WAY TO AVOID GOING TO JAIL AND BRINGING DISHONOR ON THE MINISTRY OF SCIENCE!
I'M GOING TO BRING ASTRO BOY HERE RIGHT NOW. YOU CAN DESTROY HIM YOURSELF...
OH MY GOSH... WHAT'LL I DO?!

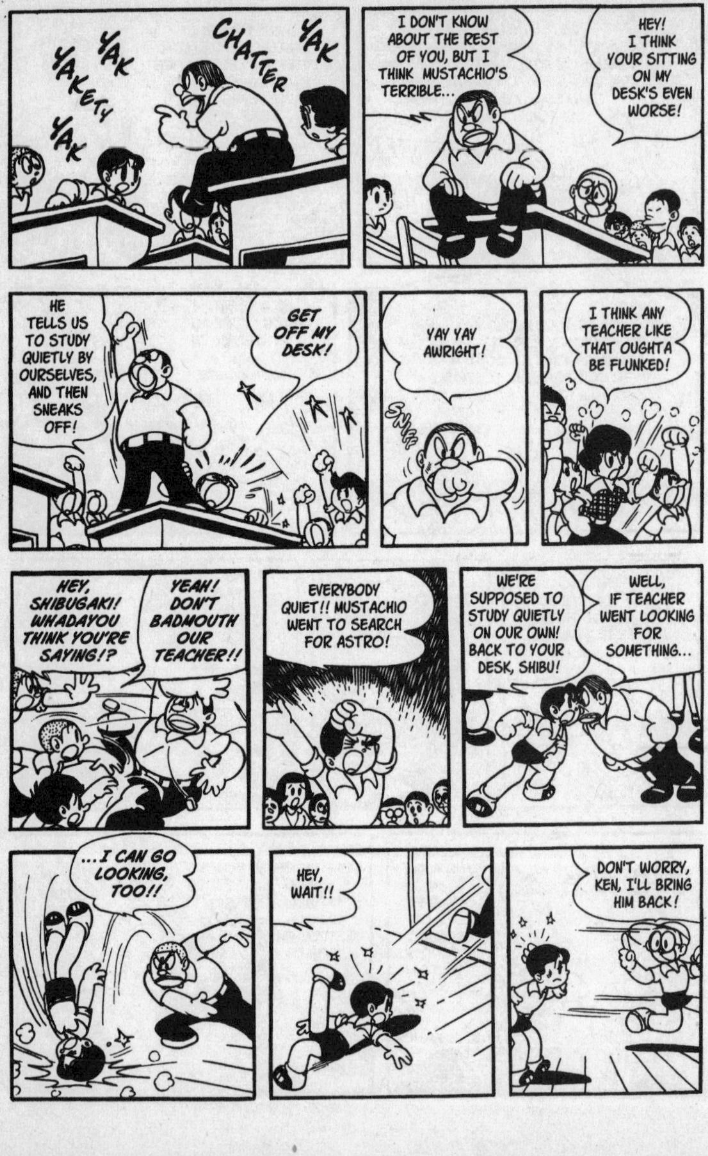
YAKETY YAK
YAK
CHATTER
YAK
I DON'T KNOW ABOUT THE REST OF YOU, BUT I THINK MUSTACHIO'S TERRIBLE...
HEY! I THINK YOUR SITTING ON MY DESK'S EVEN WORSE!
HE TELLS US TO STUDY QUIETLY BY OURSELVES, AND THEN SNEAKS OFF!
GET OFF MY DESK!
YAY YAY AWRIGHT!
I THINK ANY TEACHER LIKE THAT OUGHTA BE FLUNKED!
HEY, SHIBUGAKI! WHADAYOU THINK YOU'RE SAYING!?
YEAH! DON'T BADMOUTH OUR TEACHER!!
EVERYBODY QUIET!! MUSTACHIO WENT TO SEARCH FOR ASTRO!
WE'RE SUPPOSED TO STUDY QUIETLY ON OUR OWN! BACK TO YOUR DESK, SHIBU!
WELL, IF TEACHER WENT LOOKING FOR SOMETHING...
...I CAN GO LOOKING, TOO!!
HEY, WAIT!!
DON'T WORRY, KEN, I'LL BRING HIM BACK!

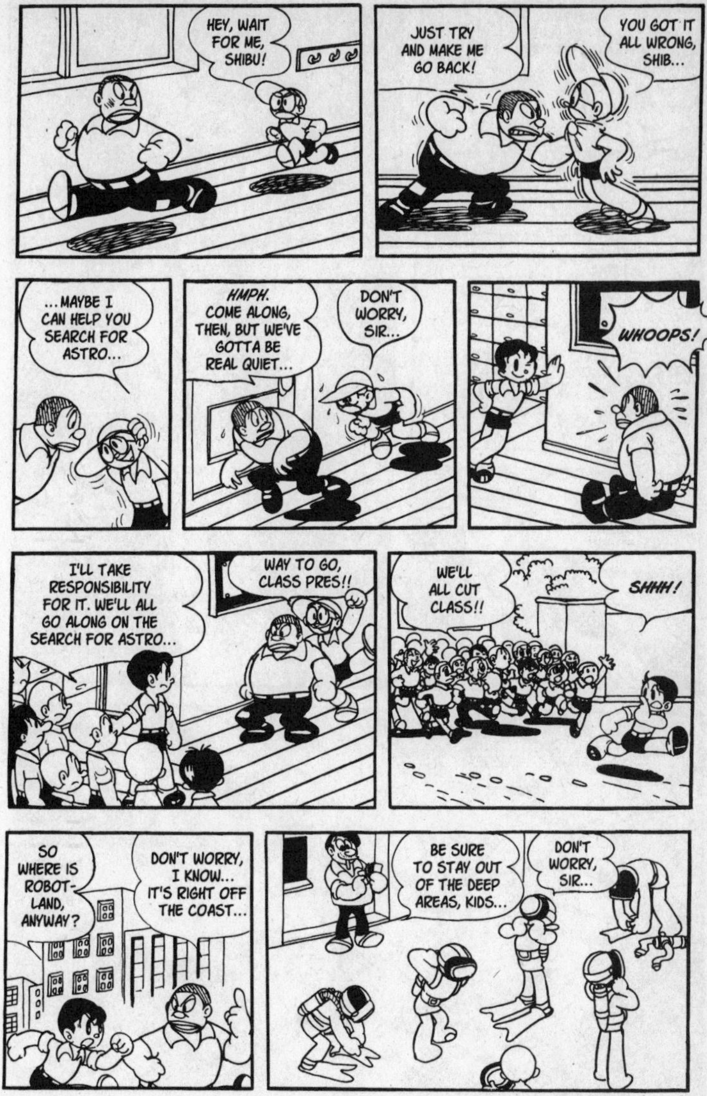
HEY, WAIT FOR ME, SHIBU!
JUST TRY AND MAKE ME GO BACK!
YOU GOT IT ALL WRONG, SHIB...
...MAYBE I CAN HELP YOU SEARCH FOR ASTRO...
HMPH. COME ALONG, THEN, BUT WE'VE GOTTA BE REAL QUIET...
DON'T WORRY, SIR...
WHOOPS!
I'LL TAKE RESPONSIBILITY FOR IT. WE'LL ALL GO ALONG ON THE SEARCH FOR ASTRO...
WAY TO GO, CLASS PRES!!
WE'LL ALL CUT CLASS!!
SHHH!
SO WHERE IS ROBOT-LAND, ANYWAY?
DON'T WORRY, I KNOW... IT'S RIGHT OFF THE COAST...
BE SURE TO STAY OUT OF THE DEEP AREAS, KIDS...
DON'T WORRY, SIR...

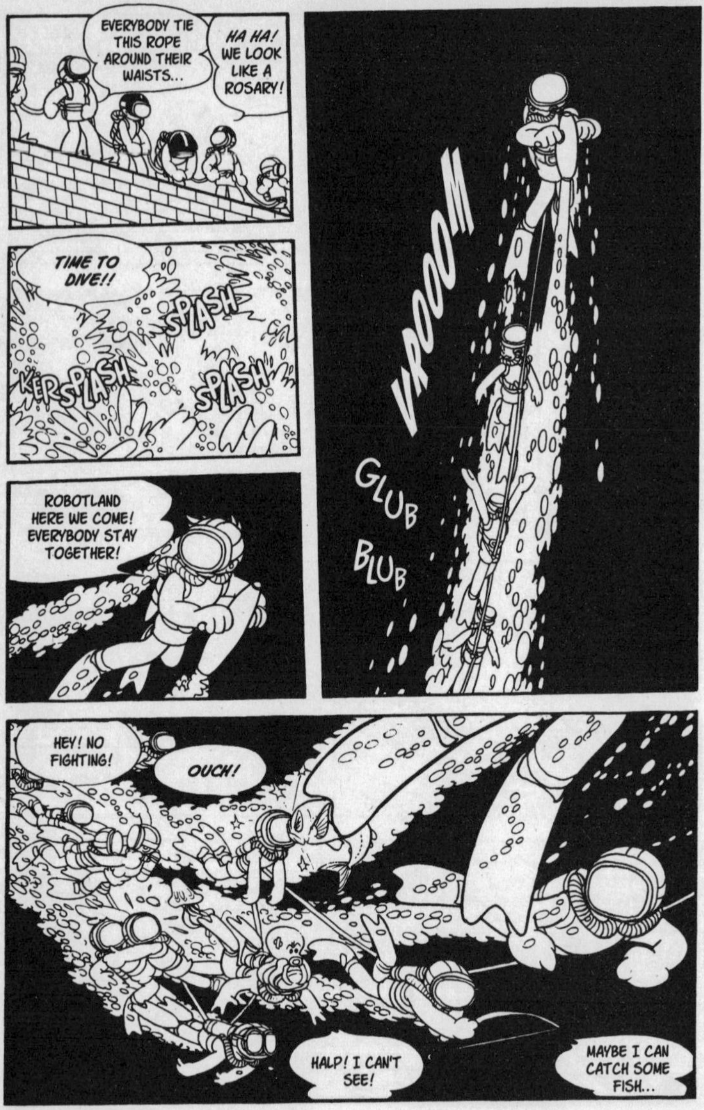
EVERYBODY TIE THIS ROPE AROUND THEIR WAISTS...
HA HA! WE LOOK LIKE A ROSARY!
VROOOM
GLUB
BLUB
TIME TO DIVE!!
SPLASH
KERSPLASH
SPLASH
ROBOTLAND HERE WE COME! EVERYBODY STAY TOGETHER!
HEY! NO FIGHTING!
OUCH!
HALP! I CAN'T SEE!
MAYBE I CAN CATCH SOME FISH...

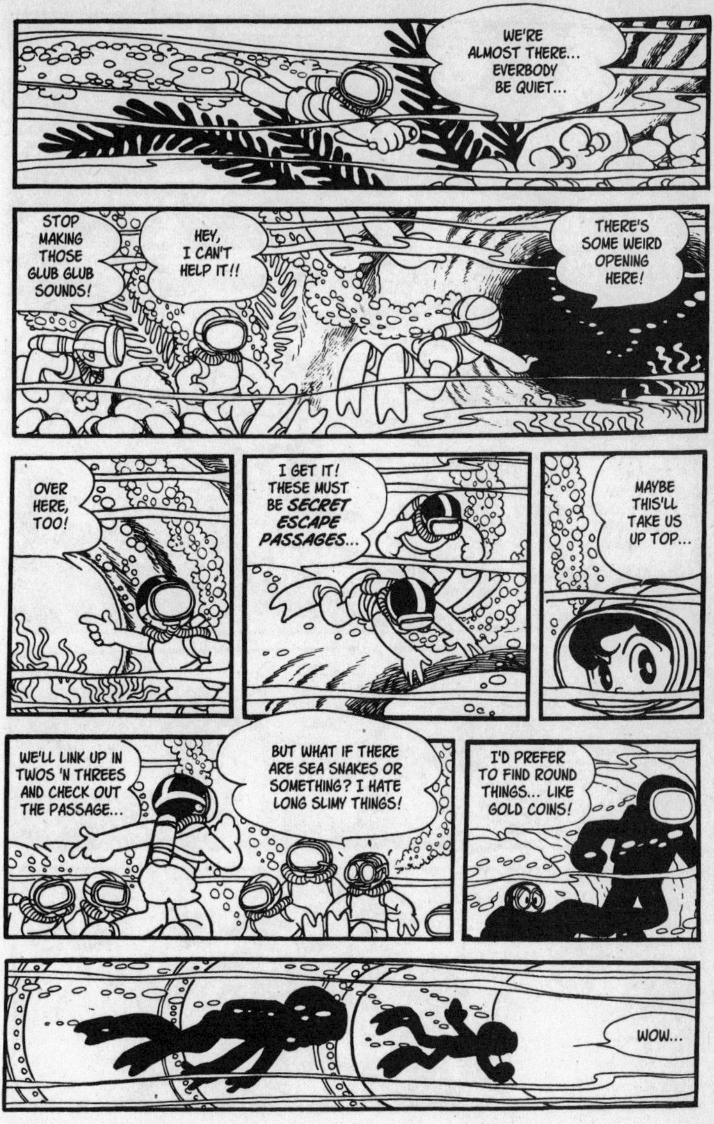
WE'RE ALMOST THERE... EVERBODY BE QUIET...
STOP MAKING THOSE GLUB GLUB SOUNDS!
HEY, I CAN'T HELP IT!!
THERE'S SOME WEIRD OPENING HERE!
OVER HERE, TOO!
I GET IT! THESE MUST BE SECRET ESCAPE PASSAGES...
MAYBE THIS'LL TAKE US UP TOP...
WE'LL LINK UP IN TWOS 'N THREES AND CHECK OUT THE PASSAGE...
BUT WHAT IF THERE ARE SEA SNAKES OR SOMETHING? I HATE LONG SLIMY THINGS!
I'D PREFER TO FIND ROUND THINGS... LIKE GOLD COINS!
WOW...

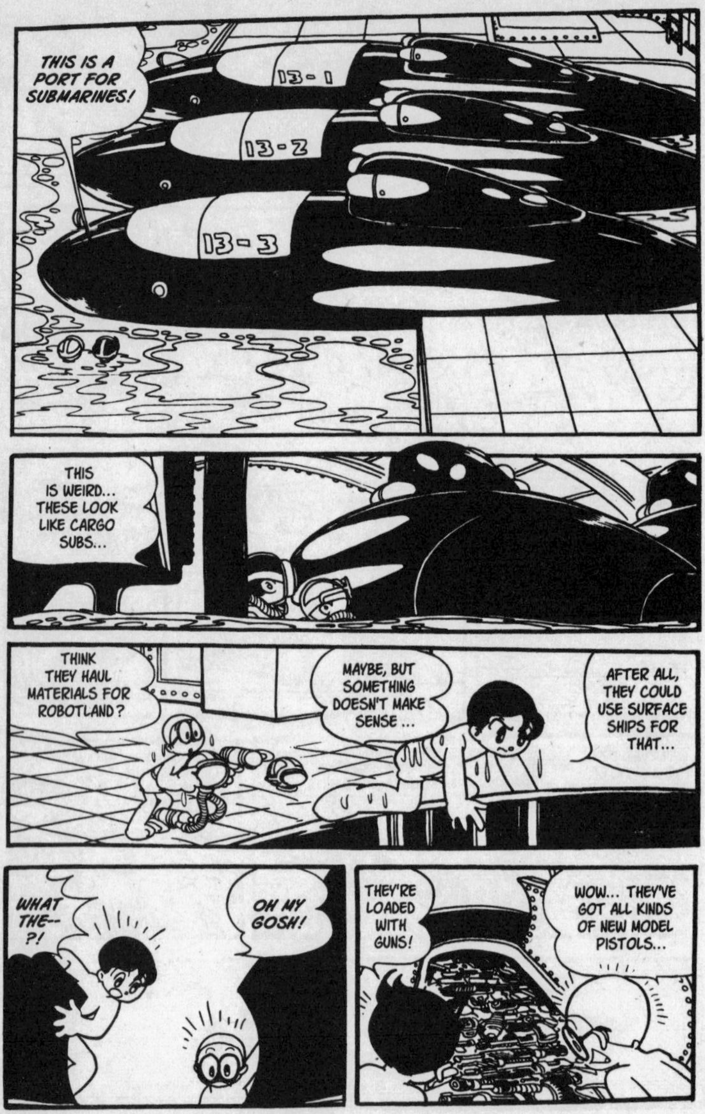
13-1
13-2
13-3
THIS IS A PORT FOR SUBMARINES!
THIS IS WEIRD... THESE LOOK LIKE CARGO SUBS...
THINK THEY HAUL MATERIALS FOR ROBOTLAND?
MAYBE, BUT SOMETHING DOESN'T MAKE SENSE ...
AFTER ALL, THEY COULD USE SURFACE SHIPS FOR THAT...
WHAT THE-- ?!
OH MY GOSH!
THEY'RE LOADED WITH GUNS!
WOW... THEY'VE GOT ALL KINDS OF NEW MODEL PISTOLS...

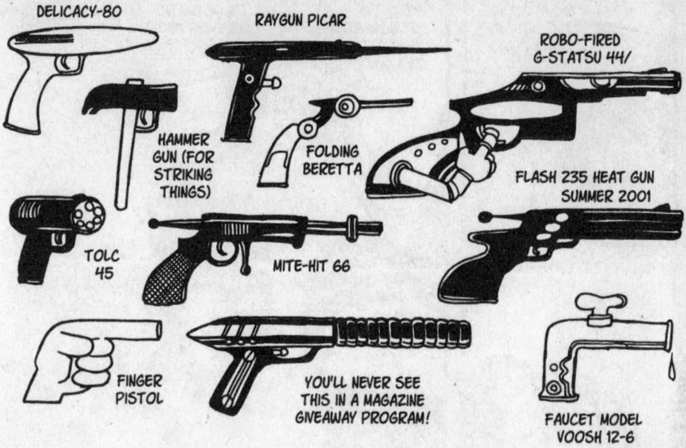
DELICACY-80
RAYGUN PICAR
ROBO-FIRED G-STATSU 44/
HAMMER GUN (FOR STRIKING THINGS)
FOLDING BERETTA
FLASH 235 HEAT GUN SUMMER 2001
TOLC 45
MITE-HIT 66
FINGER PISTOL
YOU'LL NEVER SEE THIS IN A MAGAZINE GIVEAWAY PROGRAM!
FAUCET MODEL VOOSH 12-6

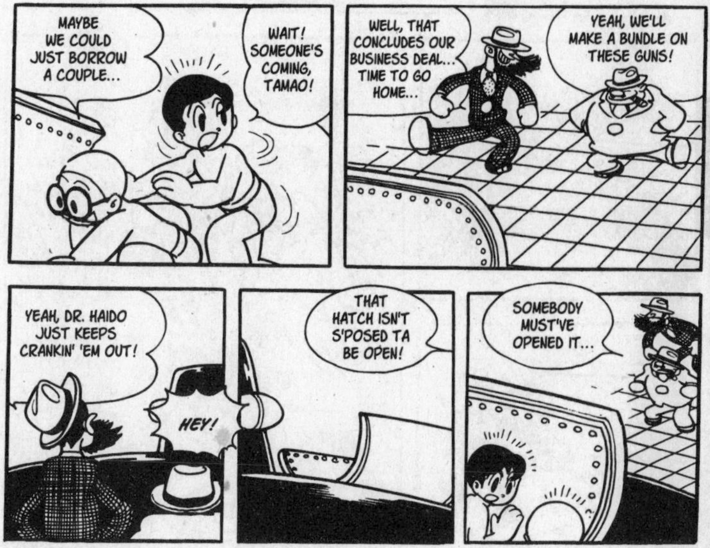
MAYBE WE COULD JUST BORROW A COUPLE...
WAIT! SOMEONE'S COMING, TAMAO!
WELL, THAT CONCLUDES OUR BUSINESS DEAL... TIME TO GO HOME...
YEAH, WE'LL MAKE A BUNDLE ON THESE GUNS!
YEAH, DR. HAIDO JUST KEEPS CRANKIN' 'EM OUT!
HEY!
THAT HATCH ISN'T S'POSED TA BE OPEN!
SOMEBODY MUST'VE OPENED IT...

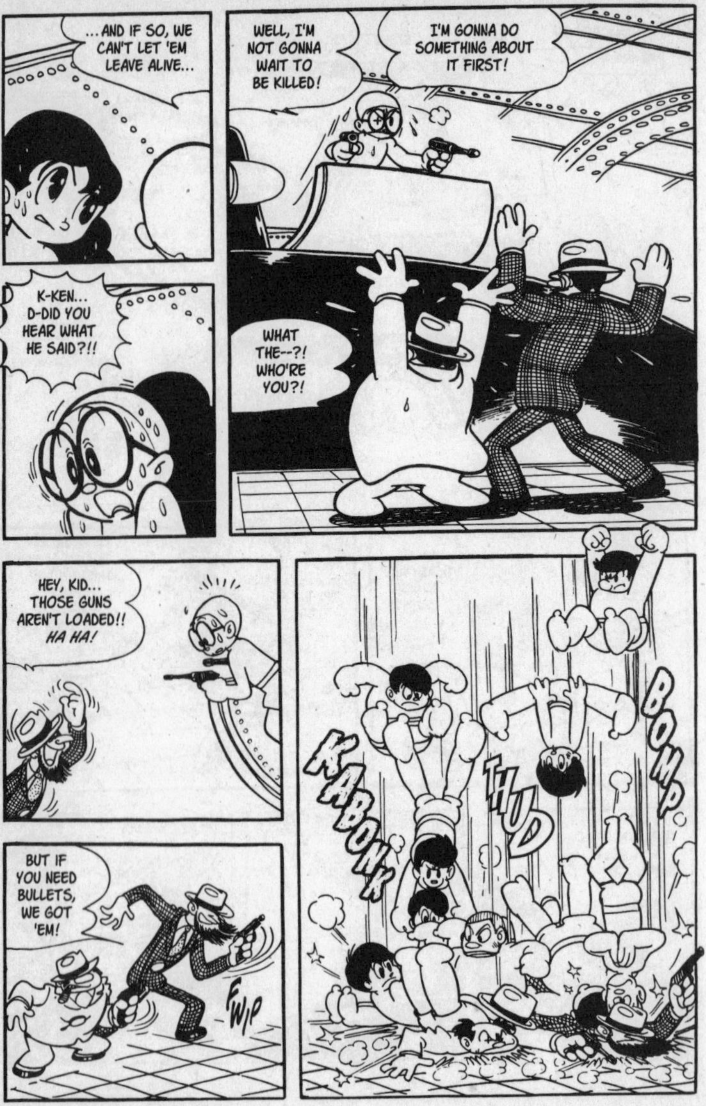
...AND IF SO, WE CAN'T LET 'EM LEAVE ALIVE...
WELL, I'M NOT GONNA WAIT TO BE KILLED!
I'M GONNA DO SOMETHING ABOUT IT FIRST!
K-KEN... D-DID YOU HEAR WHAT HE SAID?!!
WHAT THE--?! WHO'RE YOU?!
HEY, KID... THOSE GUNS AREN'T LOADED!! HA HA!
BUT IF YOU NEED BULLETS, WE GOT 'EM!
FWIP
KABONK
THUD
BOMP

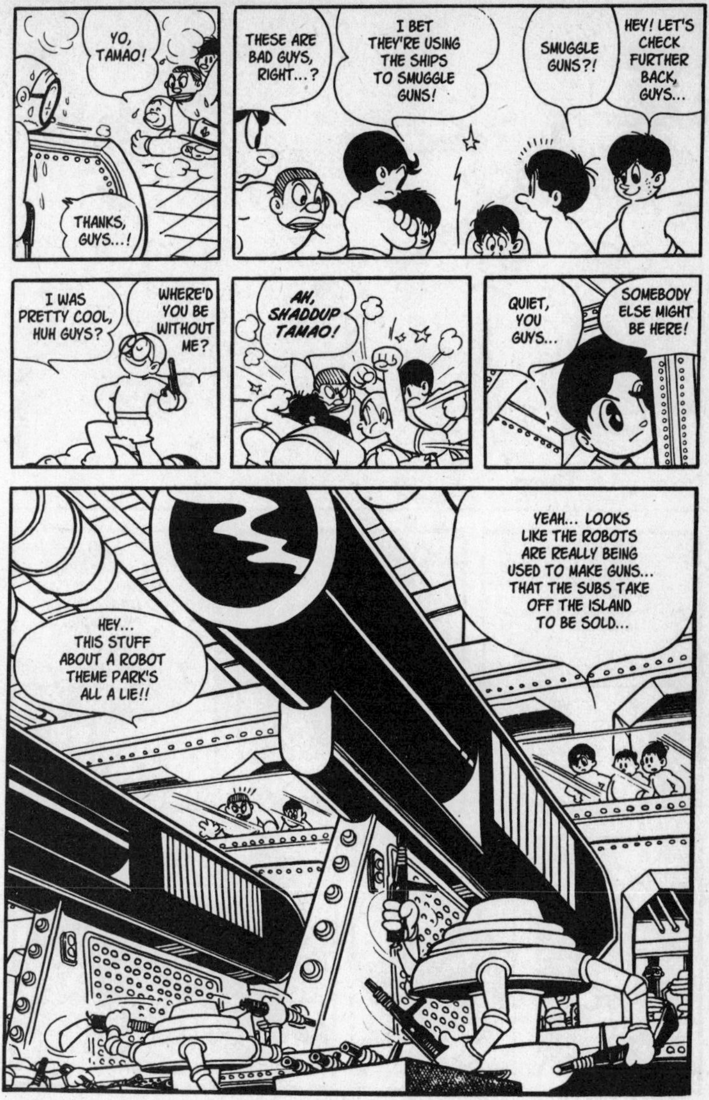
YO, TAMAO!
THANKS, GUYS...!
THESE ARE BAD GUYS, RIGHT...?
I BET THEY'RE USING THE SHIPS TO SMUGGLE GUNS!
SMUGGLE GUNS?!
HEY! LET'S CHECK FURTHER BACK, GUYS...
I WAS PRETTY COOL, HUH GUYS?
WHERE'D YOU BE WITHOUT ME?
AH, SHADDUP TAMAO!
QUIET, YOU GUYS...
SOMEBODY ELSE MIGHT BE HERE!
HEY... THIS STUFF ABOUT A ROBOT THEME PARK'S ALL A LIE!!
YEAH... LOOKS LIKE THE ROBOTS ARE REALLY BEING USED TO MAKE GUNS... THAT THE SUBS TAKE OFF THE ISLAND TO BE SOLD...

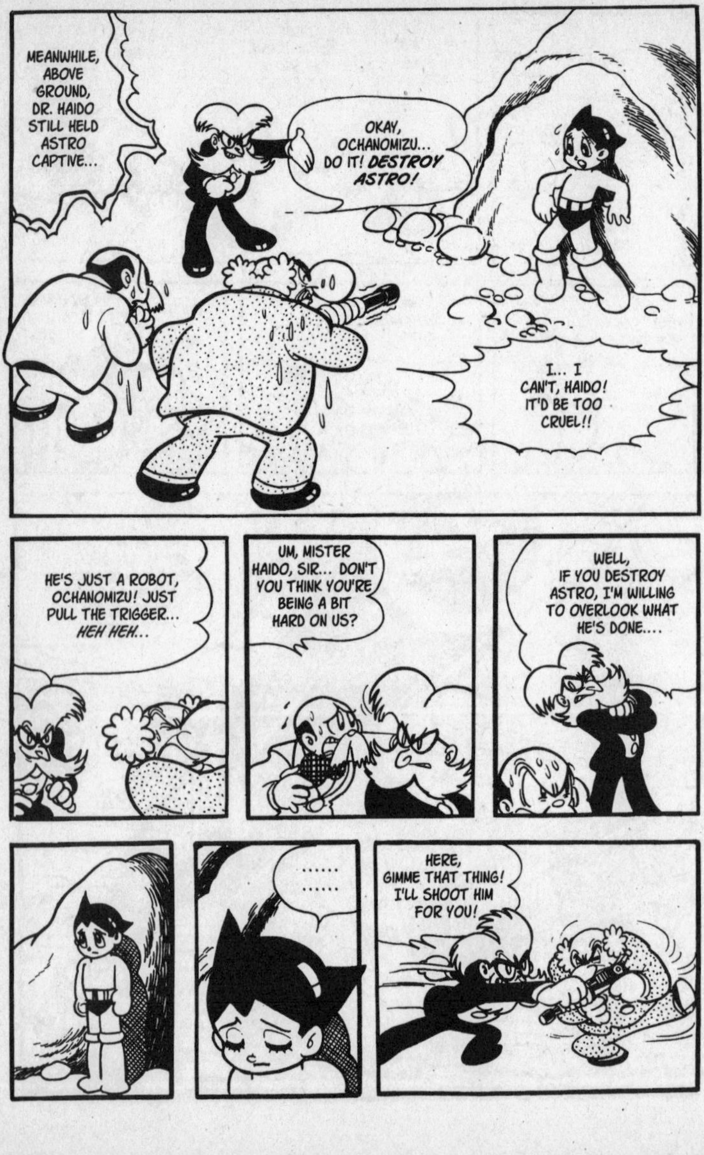
MEANWHILE, ABOVE GROUND, DR. HAIDO STILL HELD ASTRO CAPTIVE...
OKAY, OCHANOMIZU... DO IT! DESTROY ASTRO!
I... I CAN'T, HAIDO! IT'D BE TOO CRUEL!!
HE'S JUST A ROBOT, OCHANOMIZU! JUST PULL THE TRIGGER... HEH HEH...
UM, MISTER HAIDO, SIR... DON'T YOU THINK YOU'RE BEING A BIT HARD ON US?
WELL, IF YOU DESTROY ASTRO, I'M WILLING TO OVERLOOK WHAT HE'S DONE....
......
......
HERE, GIMME THAT THING! I'LL SHOOT HIM FOR YOU!

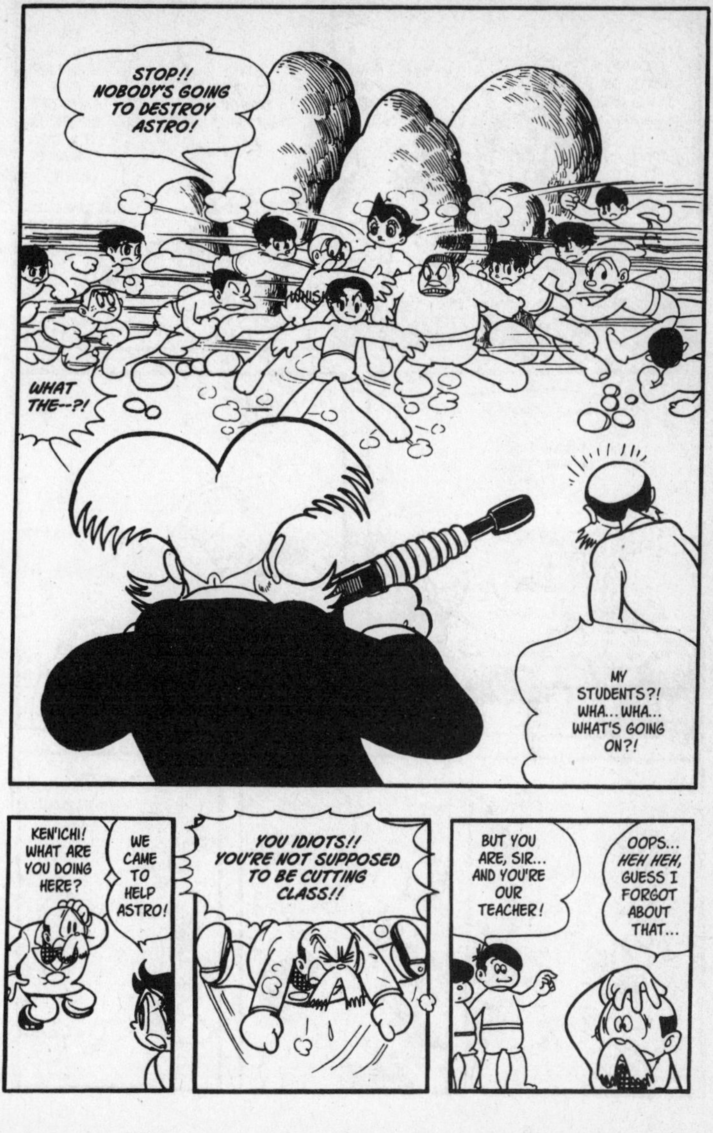
STOP!! NOBODY'S GOING TO DESTROY ASTRO!
WHAT THE--?!
MY STUDENTS?! WHA... WHA... WHAT'S GOING ON?!
KEN'ICHI! WHAT ARE YOU DOING HERE?
WE CAME TO HELP ASTRO!
YOU IDIOTS!! YOU'RE NOT SUPPOSED TO BE CUTTING CLASS!!
BUT YOU ARE, SIR... AND YOU'RE OUR TEACHER!
OOPS... HEH HEH, GUESS I FORGOT ABOUT THAT...

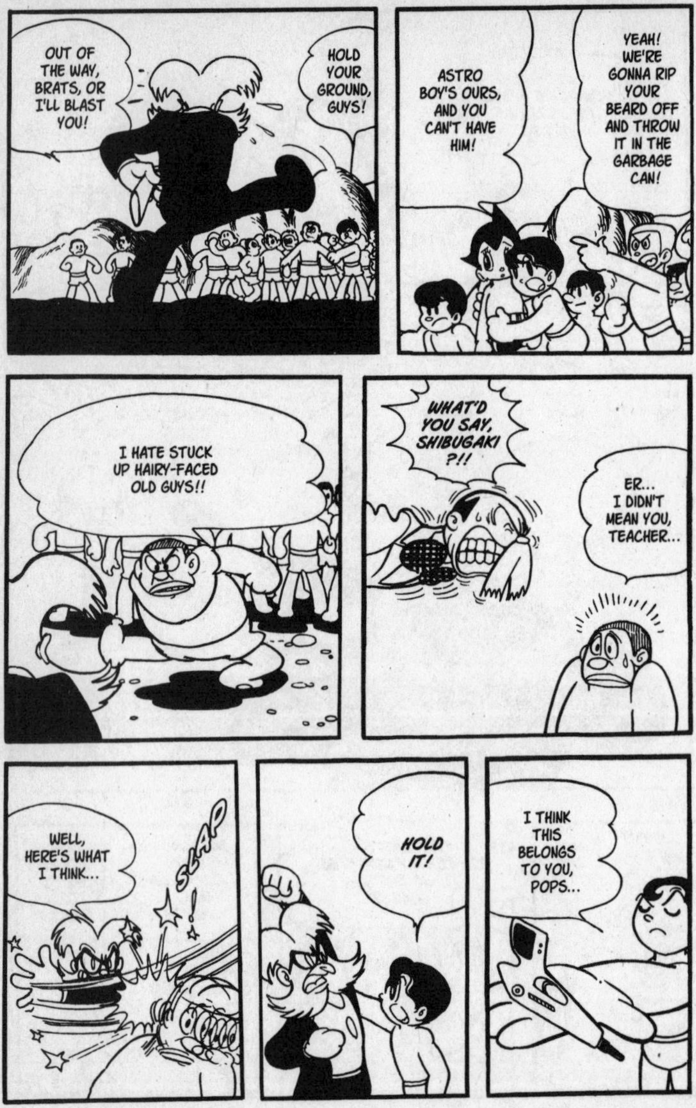
OUT OF THE WAY, BRATS, OR I'LL BLAST YOU!
HOLD YOUR GROUND, GUYS!
ASTRO BOY'S OURS, AND YOU CAN'T HAVE HIM!
YEAH! WE'RE GONNA RIP YOUR BEARD OFF AND THROW IT IN THE GARBAGE CAN!
I HATE STUCK UP HAIRY-FACED OLD GUYS!!
WHAT'D YOU SAY, SHIBUGAKI ?!!
ER... I DIDN'T MEAN YOU, TEACHER...
WELL, HERE'S WHAT I THINK...
SLAP
HOLD IT!
I THINK THIS BELONGS TO YOU, POPS...

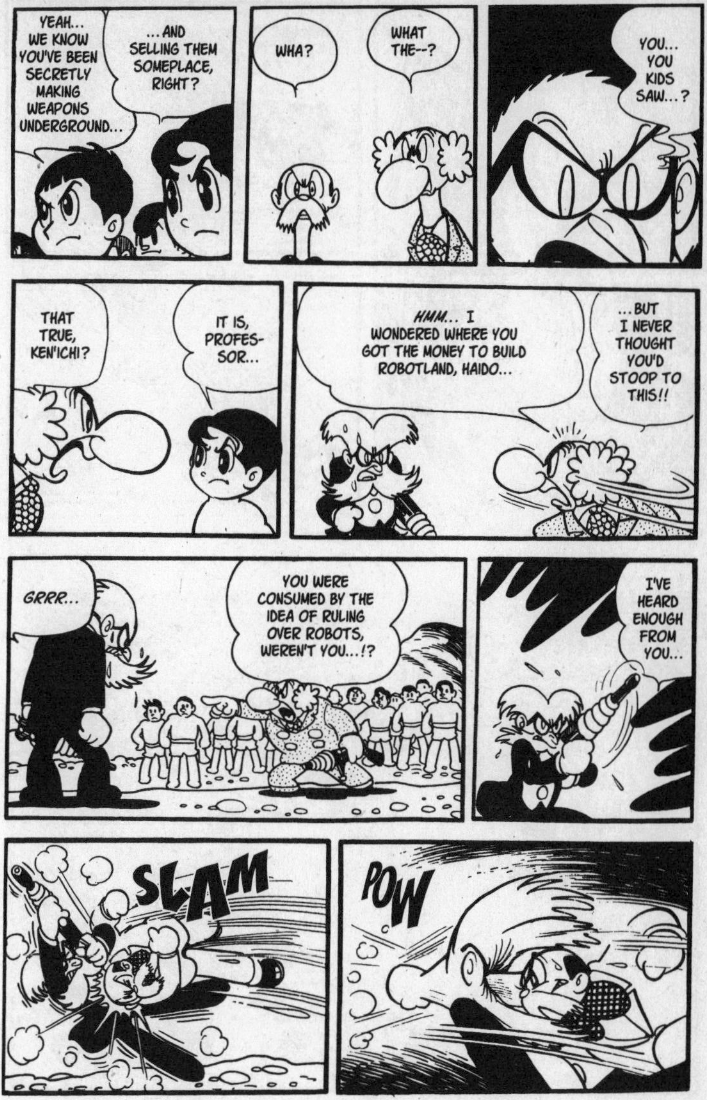
YEAH... WE KNOW YOU'VE BEEN SECRETLY MAKING WEAPONS UNDERGROUND...
...AND SELLING THEM SOMEPLACE, RIGHT?
WHA?
WHAT THE--?
YOU... YOU KIDS SAW...?
THAT TRUE, KEN'ICHI?
IT IS, PROFES-SOR...
HMM... I WONDERED WHERE YOU GOT THE MONEY TO BUILD ROBOTLAND, HAIDO...
...BUT I NEVER THOUGHT YOU'D STOOP TO THIS!!
GRRR...
YOU WERE CONSUMED BY THE IDEA OF RULING OVER ROBOTS, WEREN'T YOU...!?
I'VE HEARD ENOUGH FROM YOU...
SLAM
POW

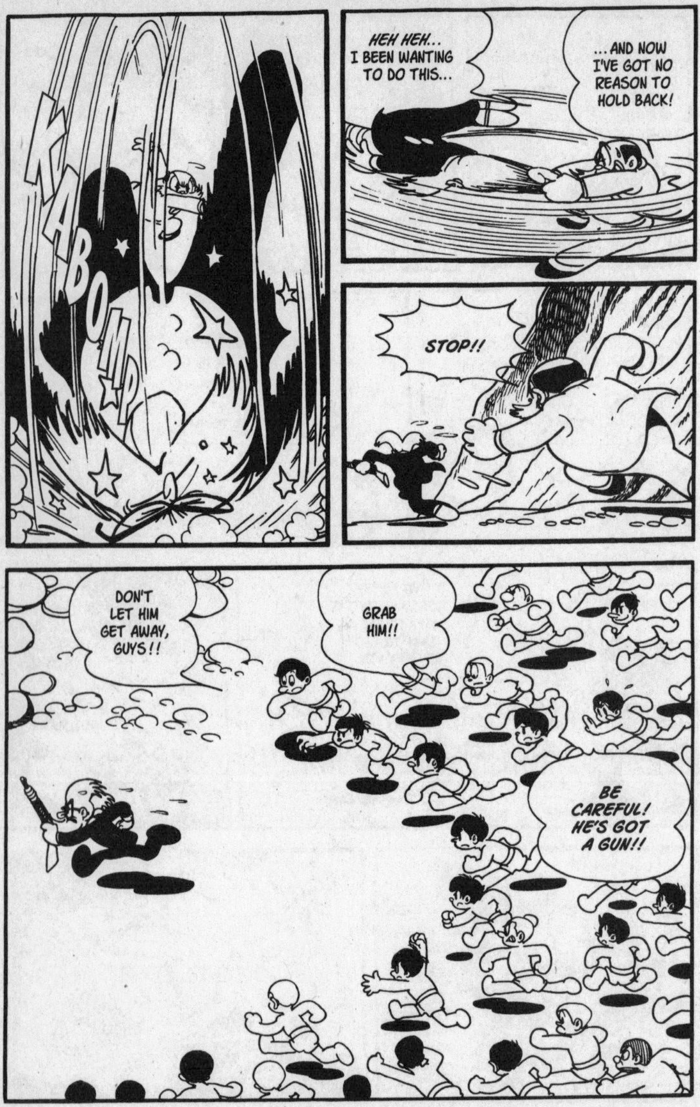
KABOMP
HEH HEH... I BEEN WANTING TO DO THIS...
...AND NOW I'VE GOT NO REASON TO HOLD BACK!
STOP!!
DON'T LET HIM GET AWAY, GUYS!!
GRAB HIM!!
BE CAREFUL! HE'S GOT A GUN!!

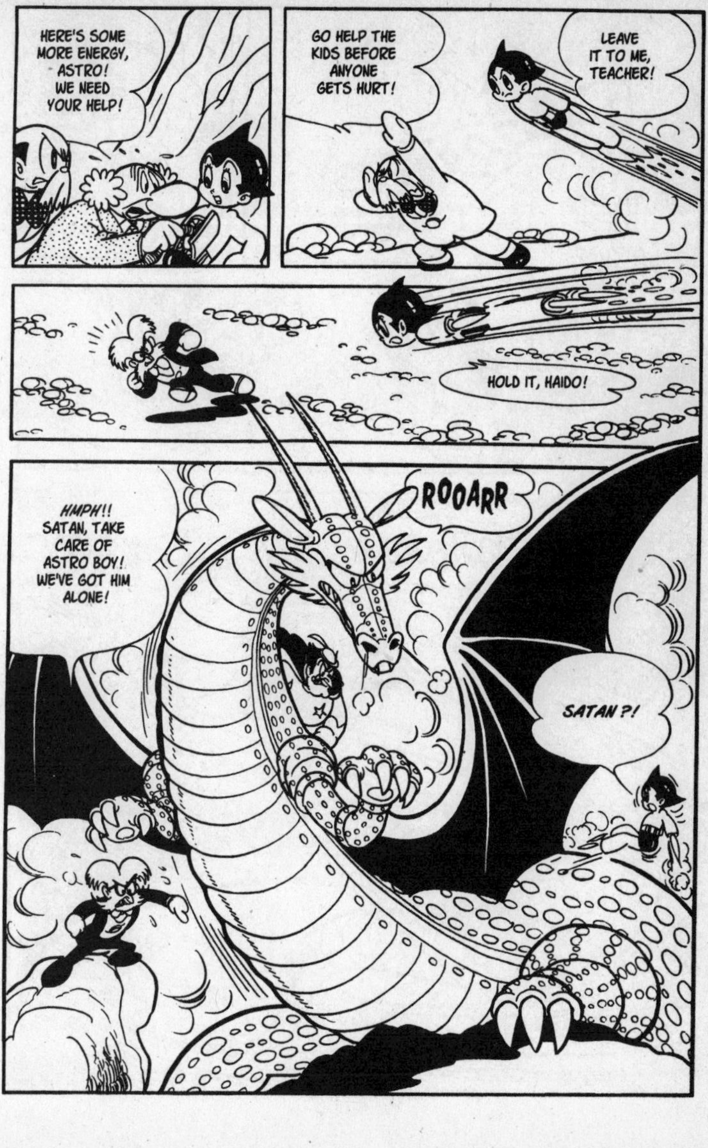
HERE'S SOME MORE ENERGY, ASTRO! WE NEED YOUR HELP!
GO HELP THE KIDS BEFORE ANYONE GETS HURT!
LEAVE IT TO ME, TEACHER!
HOLD IT, HAIDO!
HMPH!! SATAN, TAKE CARE OF ASTRO BOY! WE'VE GOT HIM ALONE!
ROOARR
SATAN?!

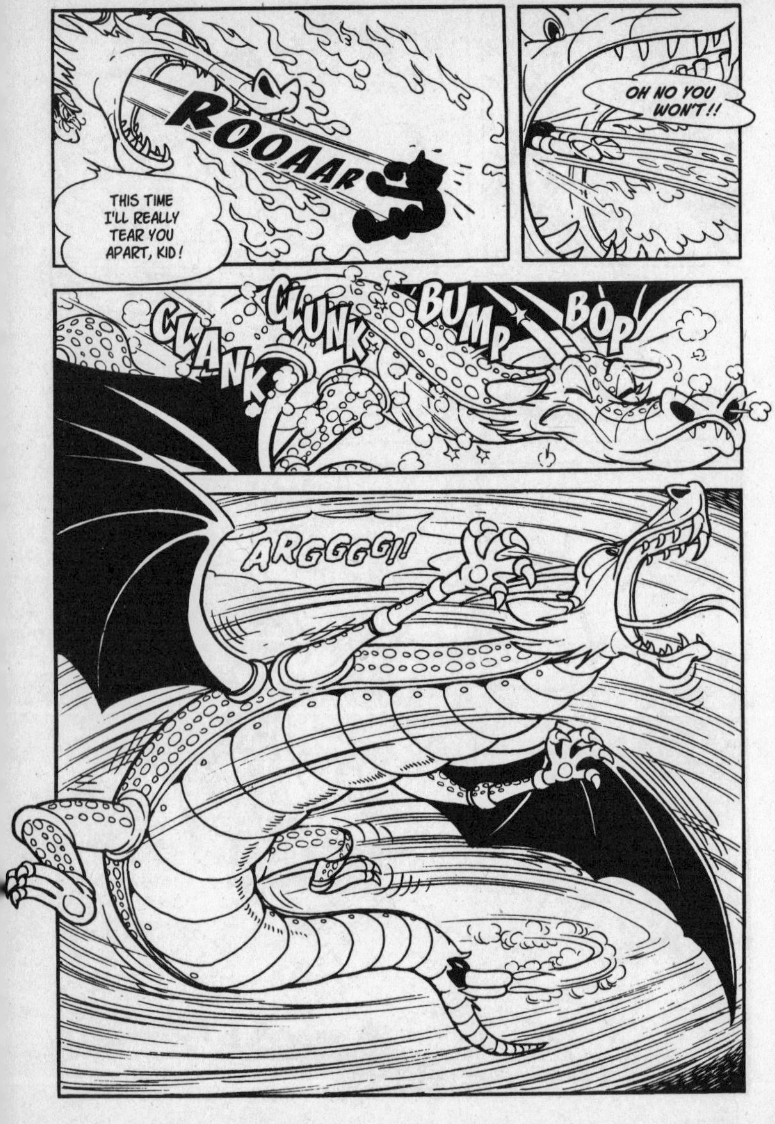
ROOOAAAR
THIS TIME I'LL REALLY TEAR YOU APART, KID!
OH NO YOU WON'T!!
CLANK
CLUNK
BUMP
BOP
ARGGGG!!

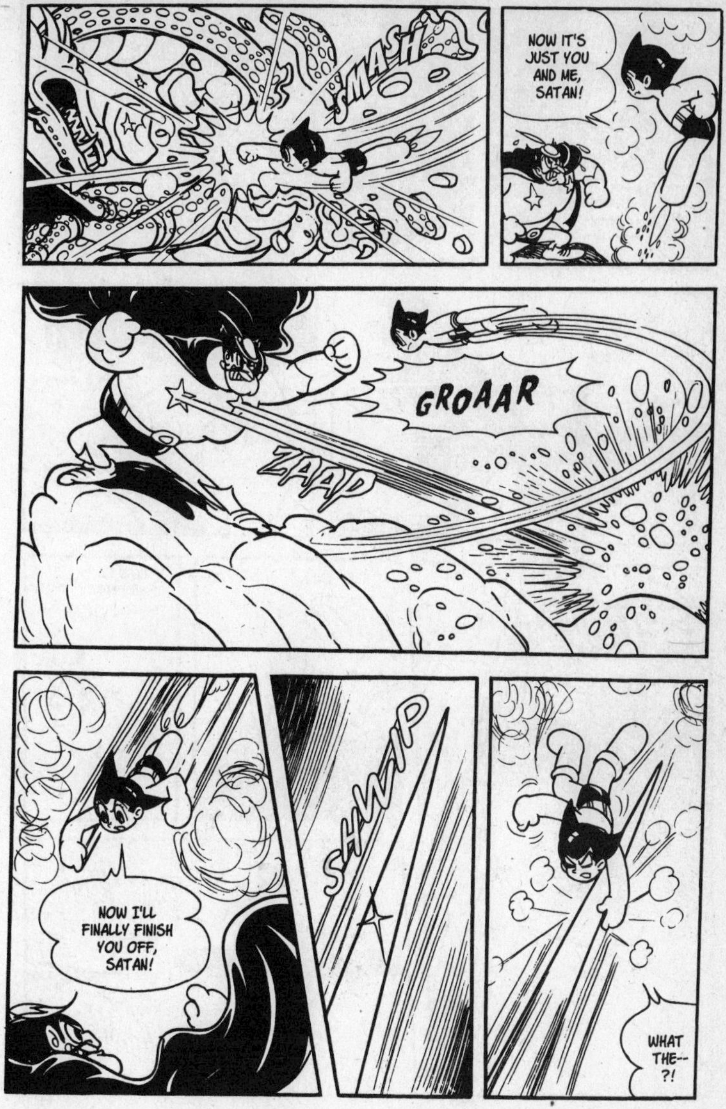
SMASH
NOW IT'S JUST YOU AND ME, SATAN!
GROAAR
ZAAP
NOW I'LL FINALLY FINISH YOU OFF, SATAN!
SHWIP
WHAT THE-- ?!

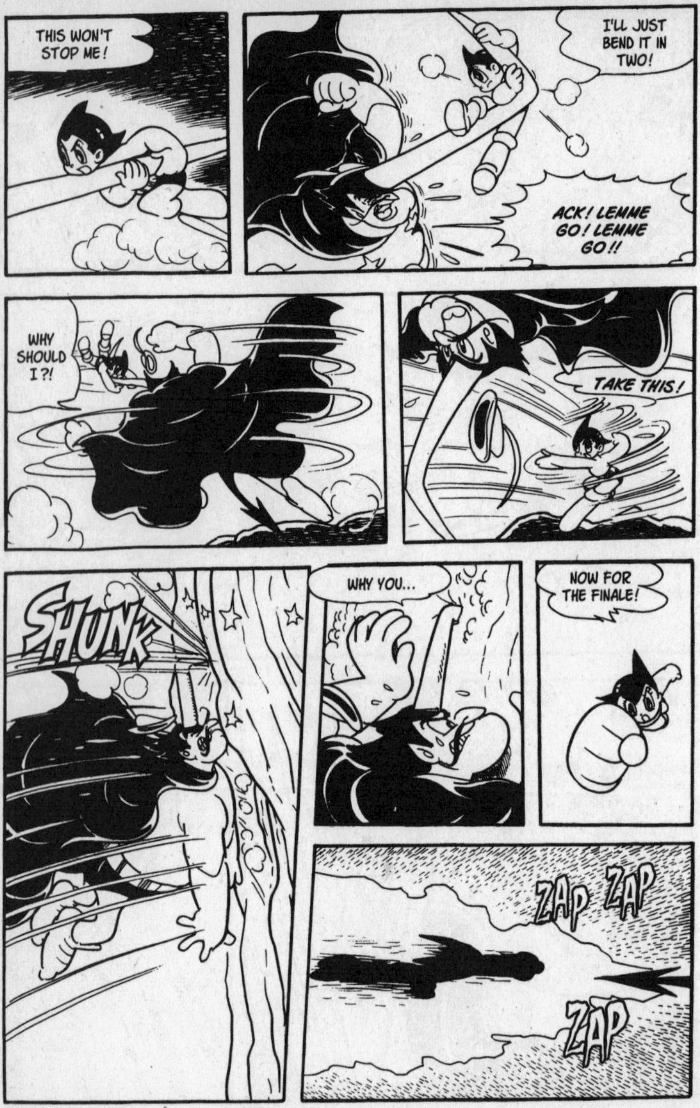
THIS WON'T STOP ME!
I'LL JUST BEND IT IN TWO!
ACK! LEMME GO! LEMME GO!!
WHY SHOULD I?!
TAKE THIS!
SHUNK
WHY YOU...
NOW FOR THE FINALE!
ZAP ZAP
ZAP

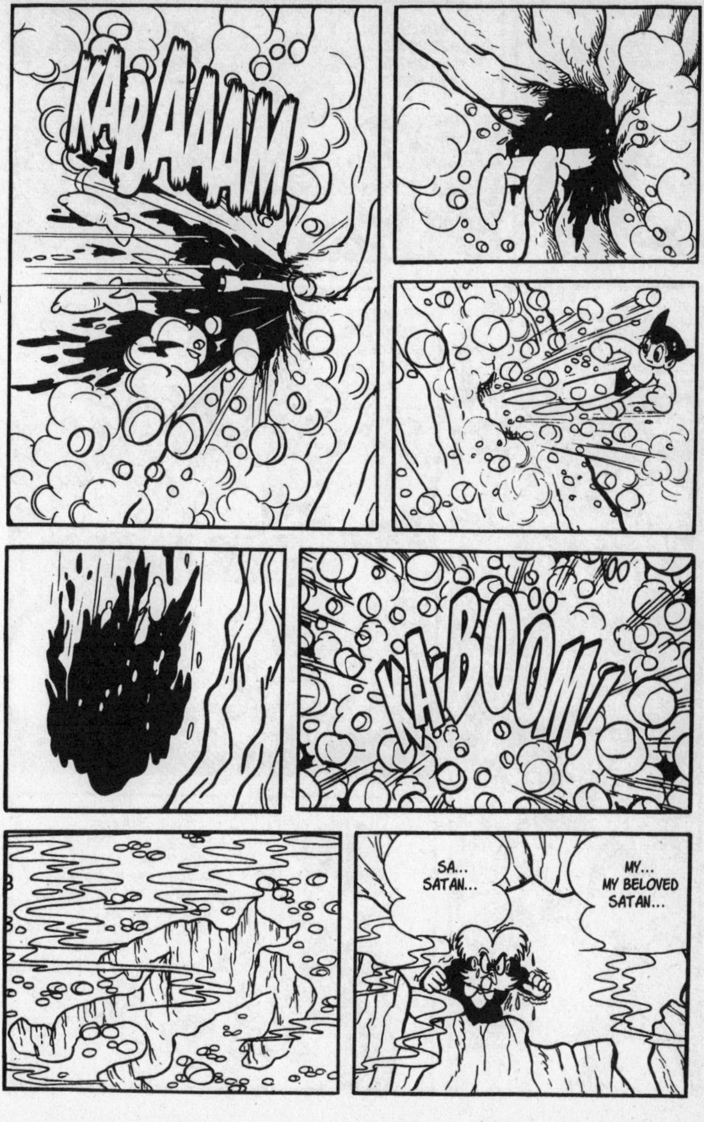
KABAAAM
KA-BOOM!
SA... SATAN...
MY... MY BELOVED SATAN...

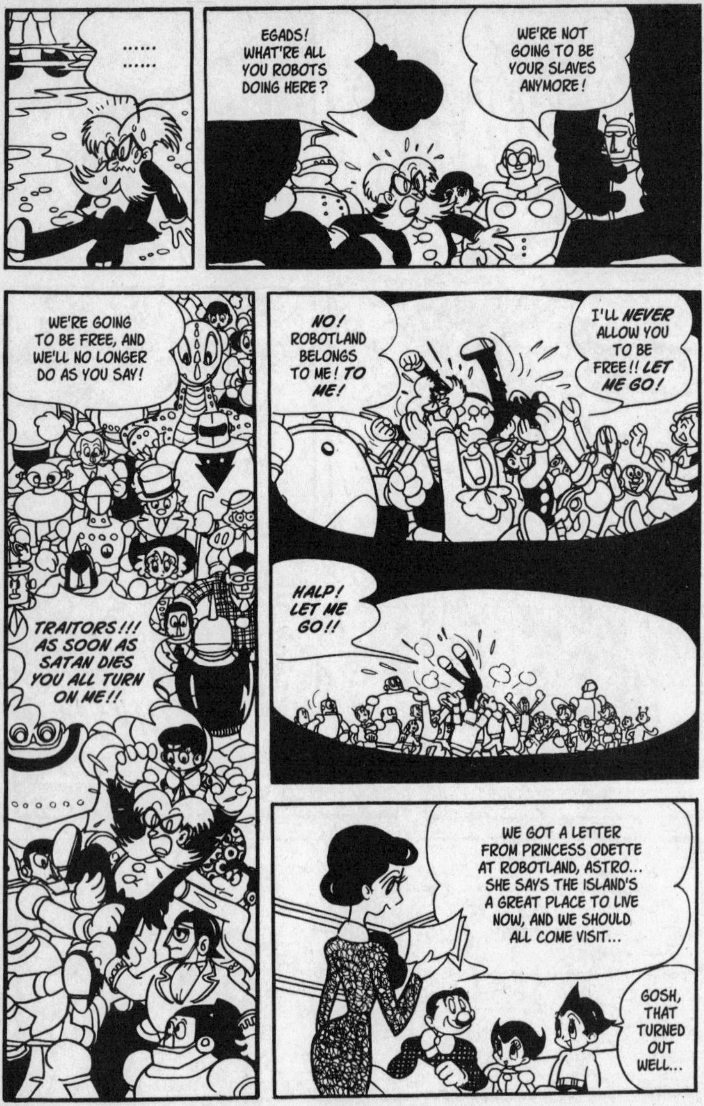
......
......
EGADS! WHAT'RE ALL YOU ROBOTS DOING HERE?
WE'RE NOT GOING TO BE YOUR SLAVES ANYMORE!
WE'RE GOING TO BE FREE, AND WE'LL NO LONGER DO AS YOU SAY!
TRAITORS!!! AS SOON AS SATAN DIES YOU ALL TURN ON ME!!
....
NO! ROBOTLAND BELONGS TO ME! TO ME!
I'LL NEVER ALLOW YOU TO BE FREE!! LET ME GO!
HALP! LET ME GO!!
WE GOT A LETTER FROM PRINCESS ODETTE AT ROBOTLAND, ASTRO... SHE SAYS THE ISLAND'S A GREAT PLACE TO LIVE NOW, AND WE SHOULD ALL COME VISIT...
GOSH, THAT TURNED OUT WELL...

IVAN THE FOOL

First serialized between February and March 1959 in *Shonen* magazine.

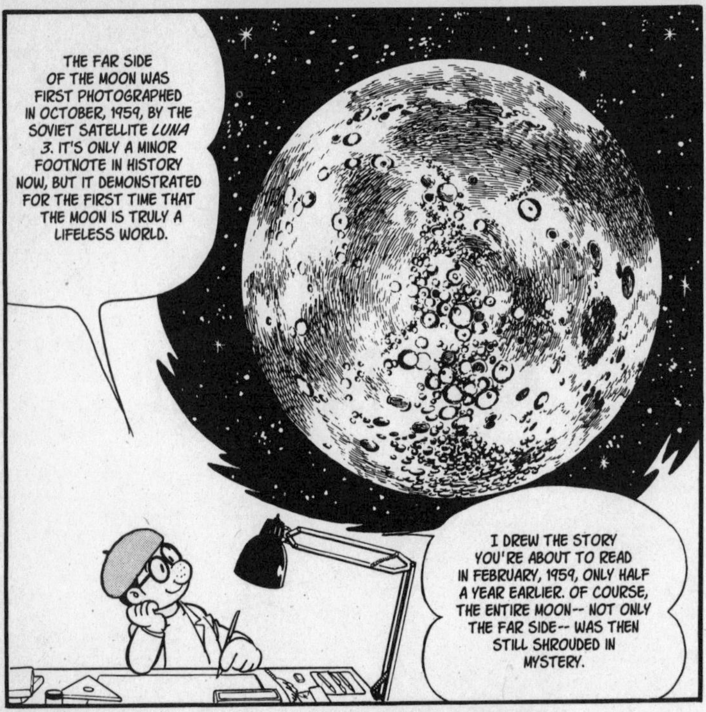
THE FAR SIDE OF THE MOON WAS FIRST PHOTOGRAPHED IN OCTOBER, 1959, BY THE SOVIET SATELLITE *LUNA 3*. IT'S ONLY A MINOR FOOTNOTE IN HISTORY NOW, BUT IT DEMONSTRATED FOR THE FIRST TIME THAT THE MOON IS TRULY A LIFELESS WORLD.
I DREW THE STORY YOU'RE ABOUT TO READ IN FEBRUARY, 1959, ONLY HALF A YEAR EARLIER. OF COURSE, THE ENTIRE MOON-- NOT ONLY THE FAR SIDE-- WAS THEN STILL SHROUDED IN MYSTERY.

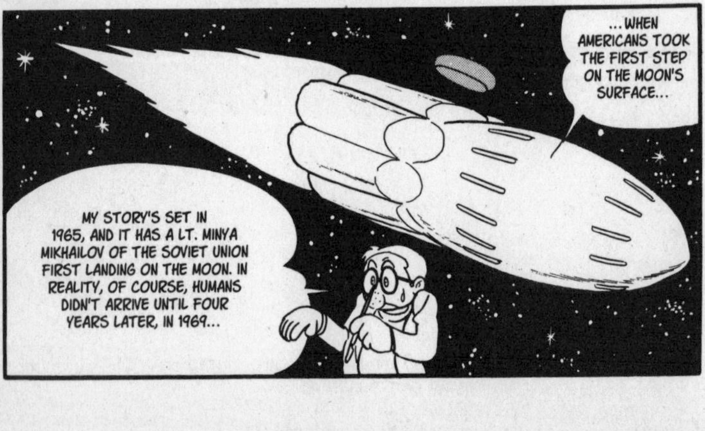
MY STORY'S SET IN 1965, AND IT HAS A LT. MINYA MIKHAILOV OF THE SOVIET UNION FIRST LANDING ON THE MOON. IN REALITY, OF COURSE, HUMANS DIDN'T ARRIVE UNTIL FOUR YEARS LATER, IN 1969...
...WHEN AMERICANS TOOK THE FIRST STEP ON THE MOON'S SURFACE...

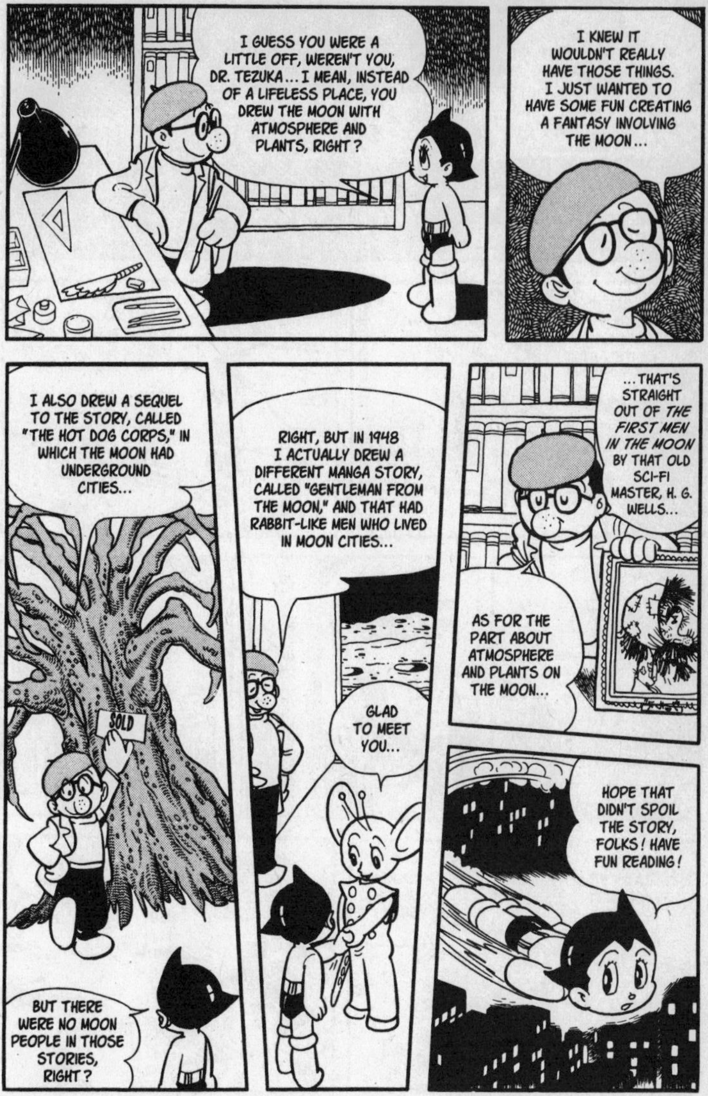
I GUESS YOU WERE A LITTLE OFF, WEREN'T YOU, DR. TEZUKA... I MEAN, INSTEAD OF A LIFELESS PLACE, YOU DREW THE MOON WITH ATMOSPHERE AND PLANTS, RIGHT?
I KNEW IT WOULDN'T REALLY HAVE THOSE THINGS. I JUST WANTED TO HAVE SOME FUN CREATING A FANTASY INVOLVING THE MOON...
I ALSO DREW A SEQUEL TO THE STORY, CALLED "THE HOT DOG CORPS," IN WHICH THE MOON HAD UNDERGROUND CITIES...
SOLD
BUT THERE WERE NO MOON PEOPLE IN THOSE STORIES, RIGHT?
RIGHT, BUT IN 1948 I ACTUALLY DREW A DIFFERENT MANGA STORY, CALLED "GENTLEMAN FROM THE MOON," AND THAT HAD RABBIT-LIKE MEN WHO LIVED IN MOON CITIES...
GLAD TO MEET YOU...
...THAT'S STRAIGHT OUT OF *THE FIRST MEN IN THE MOON* BY THAT OLD SCI-FI MASTER, H. G. WELLS...
AS FOR THE PART ABOUT ATMOSPHERE AND PLANTS ON THE MOON...
HOPE THAT DIDN'T SPOIL THE STORY, FOLKS! HAVE FUN READING!

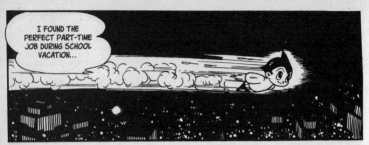

I FOUND THE PERFECT PART-TIME JOB DURING SCHOOL VACATION...

HERE IT IS... WORKING IN A SERVICE STATION AT A SPACEPORT...

FOR YOUR NEXT SPACE TRIP, TAKE THE TITAN!

A ROUND-TRIP TOUR OF THE PLANETS!

THE SPACE TRAVEL ASSOCIATION

HEHEMM. SO YOU WANT TO WORK AS A STEWARD ON OUR SPACE CRUISE SHIP, EH? GOT ANY REFERENCES?

PROFESSOR OCHANOMIZU, EH? AH, HE'LL DO FINE...

THAT'S THE SHIP YOU'LL BE ON...BEST IN THE WORLD!

DO YOU CHECK ALL YOUR PASSENGERS, SIR?

OF COURSE! WHY DO YOU ASK?

WELL, YOU'VE GOT SOME STRANGE ONES BOARDING...

...THAT MAN THERE SEEMS AWFULLY FISHY...

66

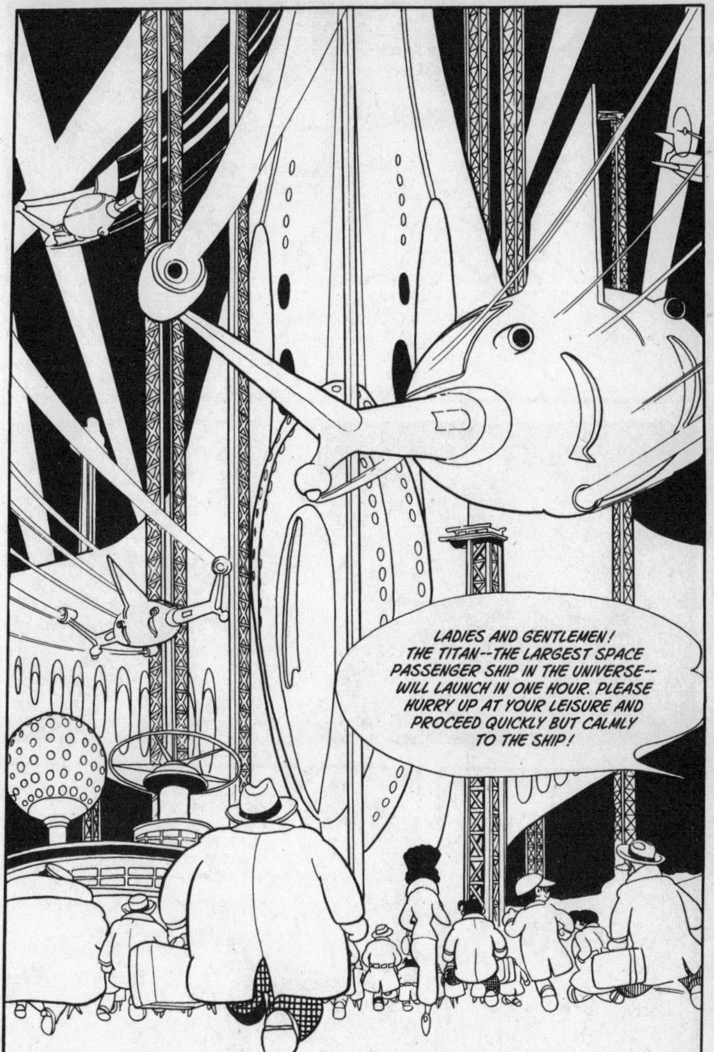
LADIES AND GENTLEMEN! THE TITAN--THE LARGEST SPACE PASSENGER SHIP IN THE UNIVERSE--WILL LAUNCH IN ONE HOUR. PLEASE HURRY UP AT YOUR LEISURE AND PROCEED QUICKLY BUT CALMLY TO THE SHIP!

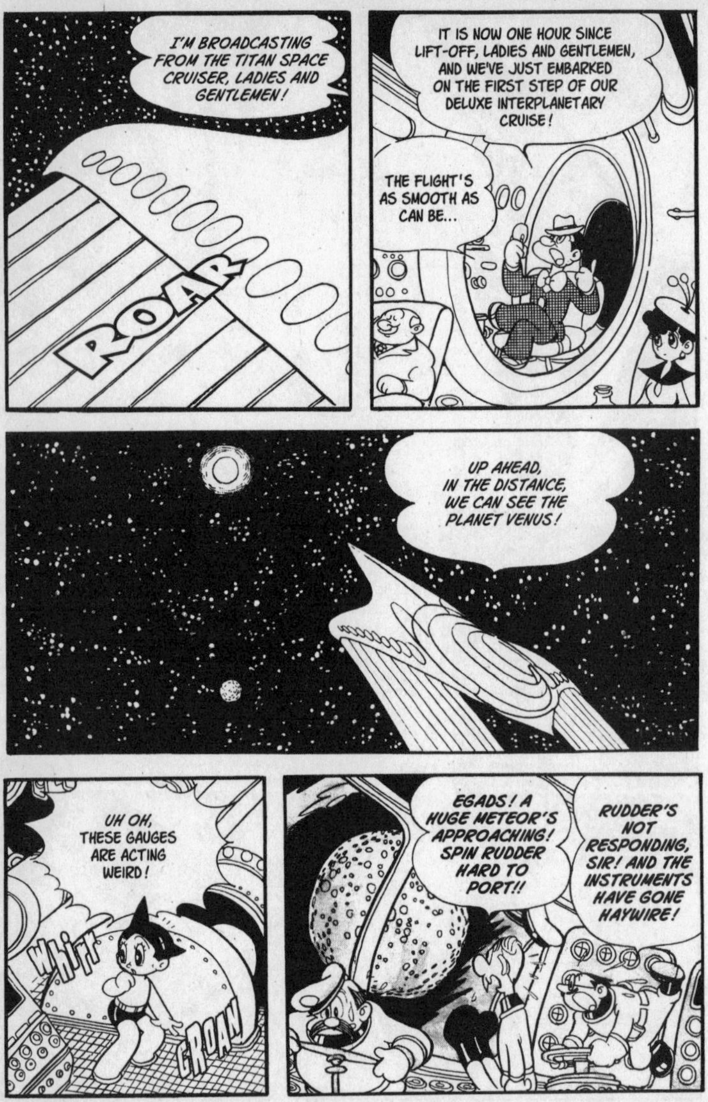
I'M BROADCASTING FROM THE TITAN SPACE CRUISER, LADIES AND GENTLEMEN!
ROAR
IT IS NOW ONE HOUR SINCE LIFT-OFF, LADIES AND GENTLEMEN, AND WE'VE JUST EMBARKED ON THE FIRST STEP OF OUR DELUXE INTERPLANETARY CRUISE!
THE FLIGHT'S AS SMOOTH AS CAN BE...
UP AHEAD, IN THE DISTANCE, WE CAN SEE THE PLANET VENUS!
UH OH, THESE GAUGES ARE ACTING WEIRD!
WHIRR
GROAN
EGADS! A HUGE METEOR'S APPROACHING! SPIN RUDDER HARD TO PORT!!
RUDDER'S NOT RESPONDING, SIR! AND THE INSTRUMENTS HAVE GONE HAYWIRE!

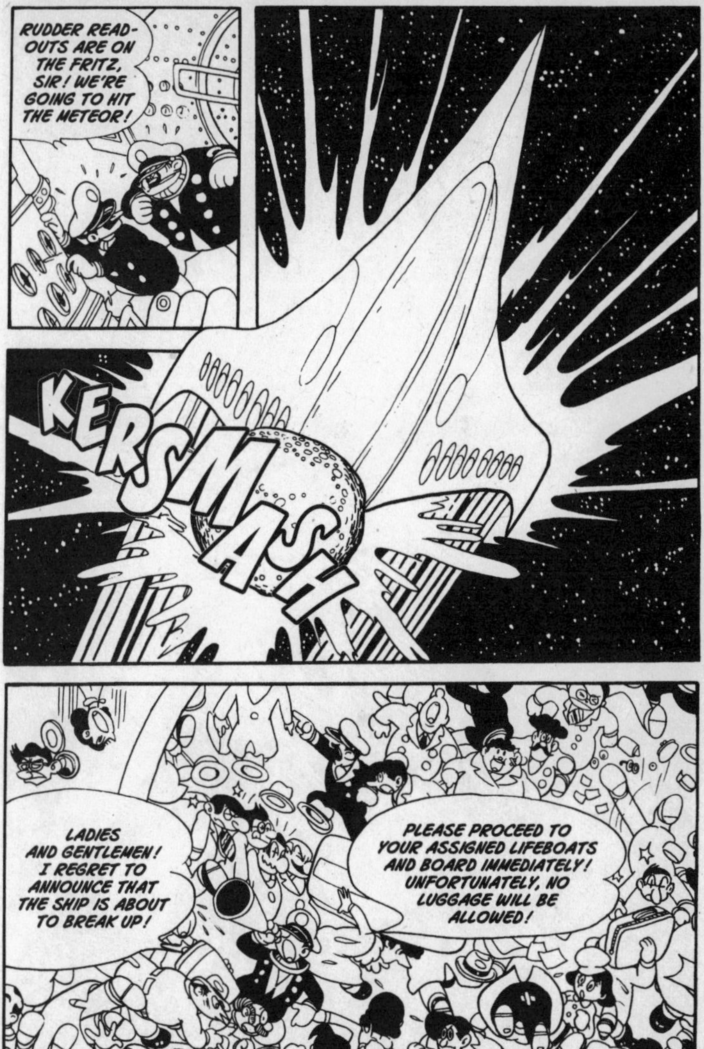
RUDDER READ-OUTS ARE ON THE FRITZ, SIR! WE'RE GOING TO HIT THE METEOR!
KERSMASH
LADIES AND GENTLEMEN! I REGRET TO ANNOUNCE THAT THE SHIP IS ABOUT TO BREAK UP!
PLEASE PROCEED TO YOUR ASSIGNED LIFEBOATS AND BOARD IMMEDIATELY! UNFORTUNATELY, NO LUGGAGE WILL BE ALLOWED!

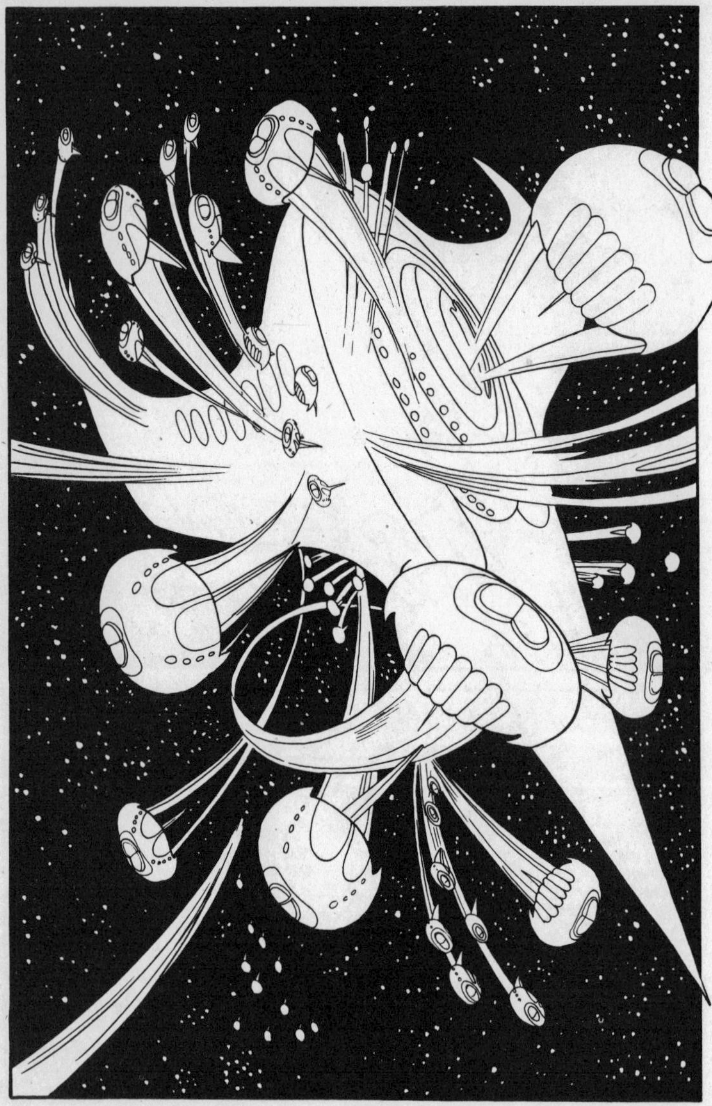

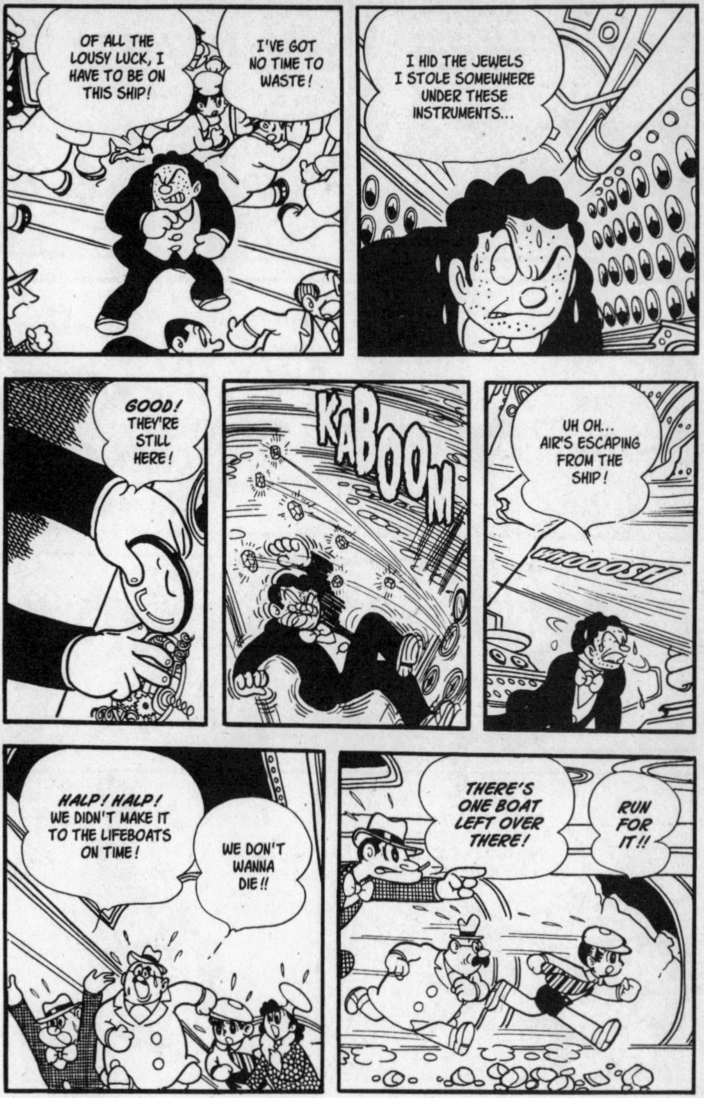

OF ALL THE LOUSY LUCK, I HAVE TO BE ON THIS SHIP!
I'VE GOT NO TIME TO WASTE!
I HID THE JEWELS I STOLE SOMEWHERE UNDER THESE INSTRUMENTS...
GOOD! THEY'RE STILL HERE!
KABOOM
UH OH... AIR'S ESCAPING FROM THE SHIP!
WHOOOSH
HALP! HALP! WE DIDN'T MAKE IT TO THE LIFEBOATS ON TIME!
WE DON'T WANNA DIE!!
THERE'S ONE BOAT LEFT OVER THERE!
RUN FOR IT!!

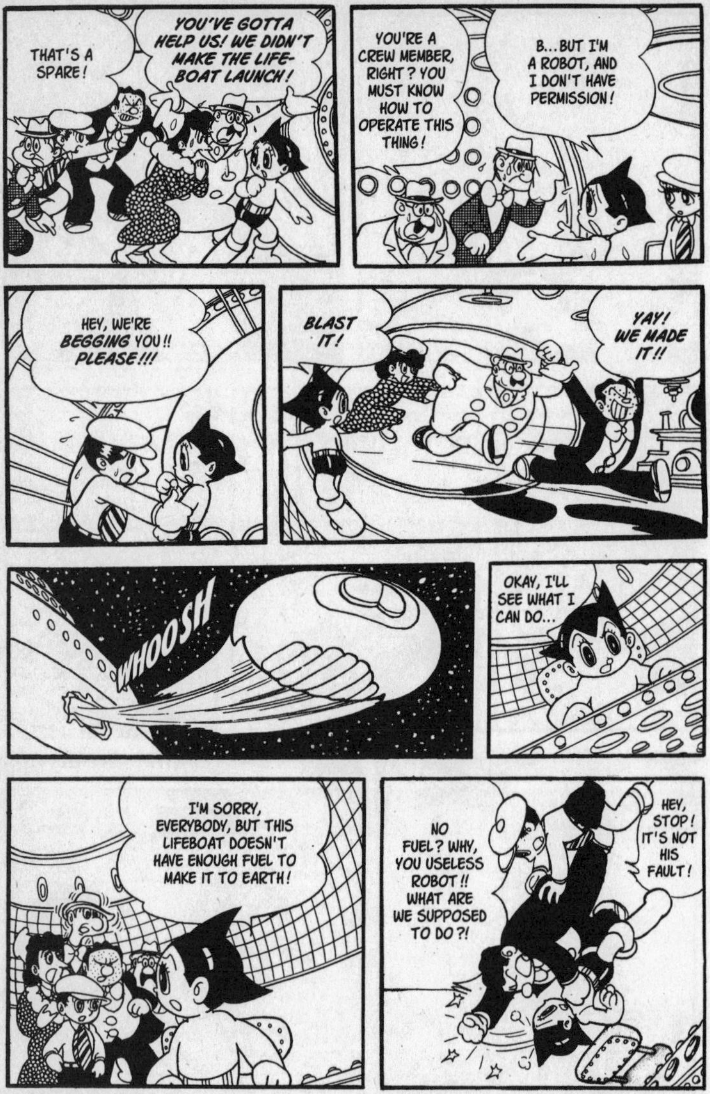
THAT'S A SPARE!
YOU'VE GOTTA HELP US! WE DIDN'T MAKE THE LIFE-BOAT LAUNCH!
YOU'RE A CREW MEMBER, RIGHT? YOU MUST KNOW HOW TO OPERATE THIS THING!
B...BUT I'M A ROBOT, AND I DON'T HAVE PERMISSION!
HEY, WE'RE BEGGING YOU!! PLEASE!!!
BLAST IT!
YAY! WE MADE IT!!
WHOOSH
OKAY, I'LL SEE WHAT I CAN DO...
I'M SORRY, EVERYBODY, BUT THIS LIFEBOAT DOESN'T HAVE ENOUGH FUEL TO MAKE IT TO EARTH!
NO FUEL? WHY, YOU USELESS ROBOT!! WHAT ARE WE SUPPOSED TO DO?!
HEY, STOP! IT'S NOT HIS FAULT!

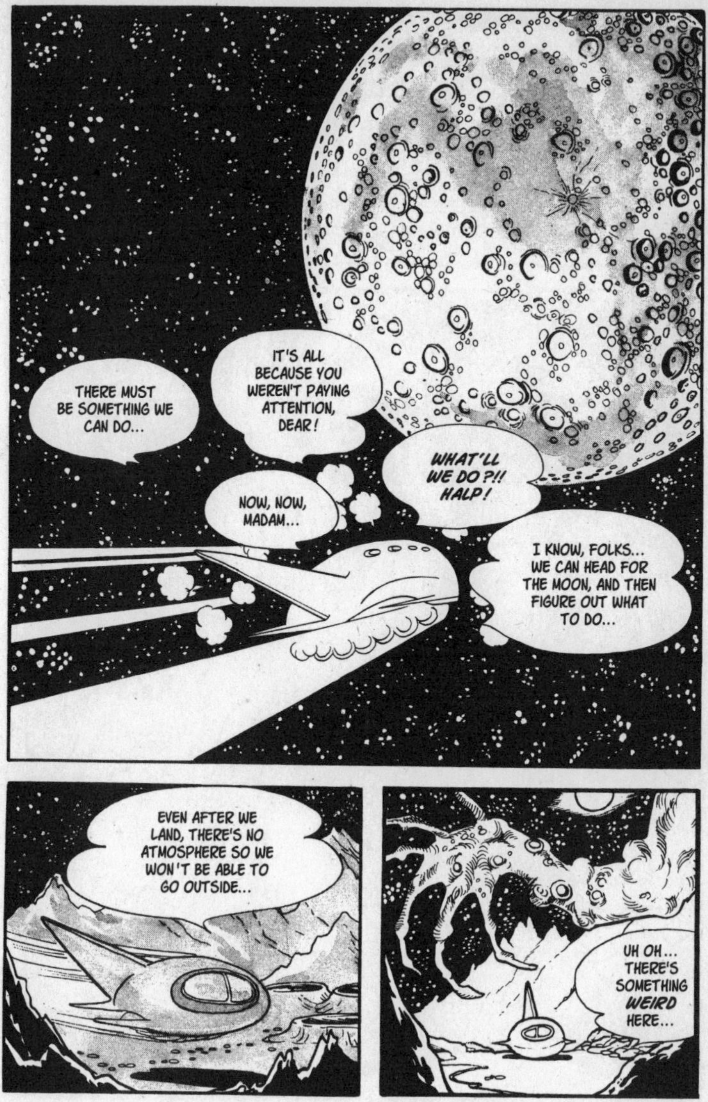
THERE MUST BE SOMETHING WE CAN DO...
IT'S ALL BECAUSE YOU WEREN'T PAYING ATTENTION, DEAR!
NOW, NOW, MADAM...
WHAT'LL WE DO?!! HALP!
I KNOW, FOLKS... WE CAN HEAD FOR THE MOON, AND THEN FIGURE OUT WHAT TO DO...
EVEN AFTER WE LAND, THERE'S NO ATMOSPHERE SO WE WON'T BE ABLE TO GO OUTSIDE...
UH OH... THERE'S SOMETHING *WEIRD* HERE...

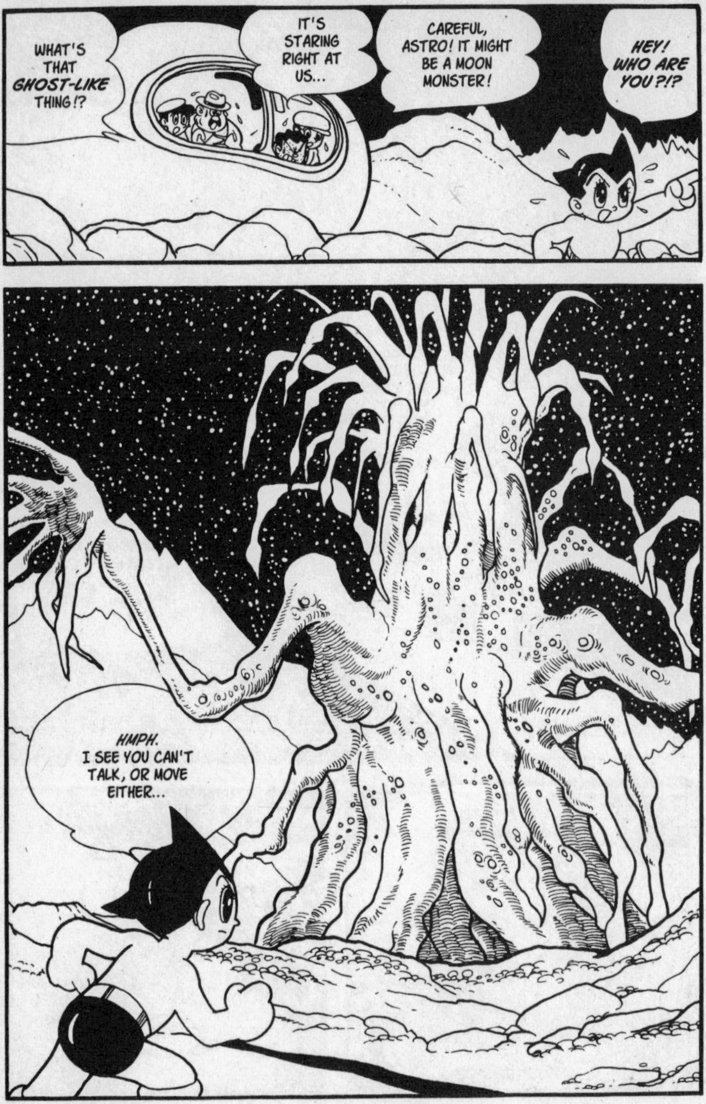
WHAT'S THAT *GHOST-LIKE* THING!?
IT'S STARING RIGHT AT US...
CAREFUL, ASTRO! IT MIGHT BE A MOON MONSTER!
HEY! WHO ARE YOU?!?
HMPH. I SEE YOU CAN'T TALK, OR MOVE EITHER...

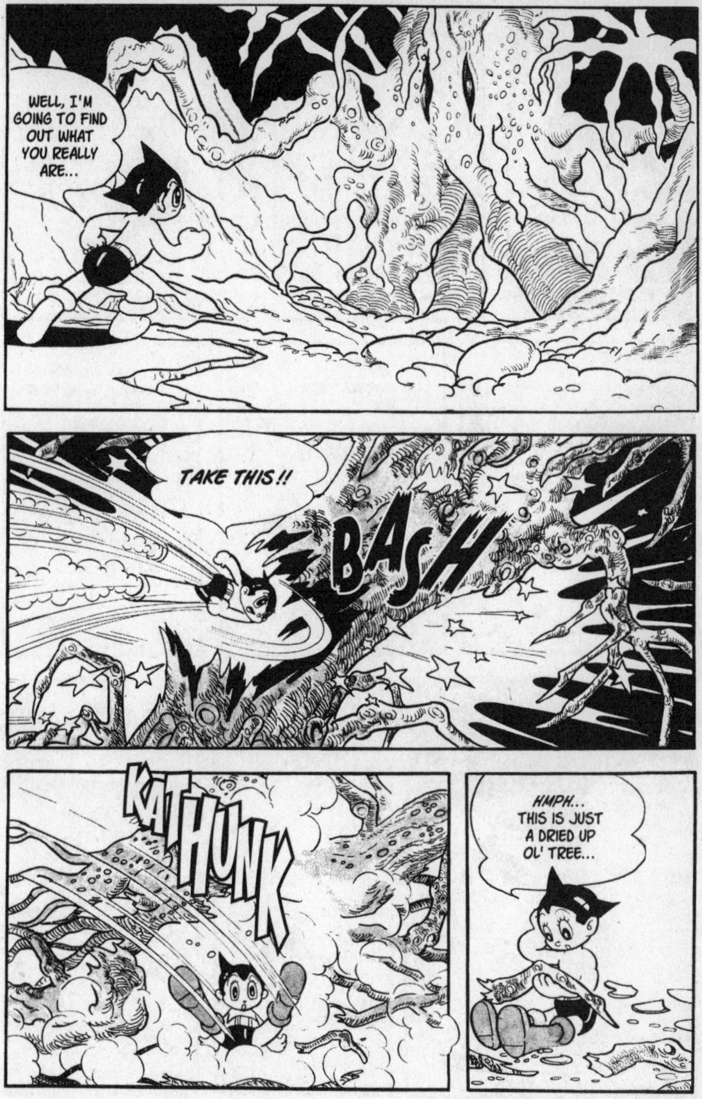
WELL, I'M GOING TO FIND OUT WHAT YOU REALLY ARE...
TAKE THIS!!
BASH
KATHUNK
HMPH... THIS IS JUST A DRIED UP OL' TREE...

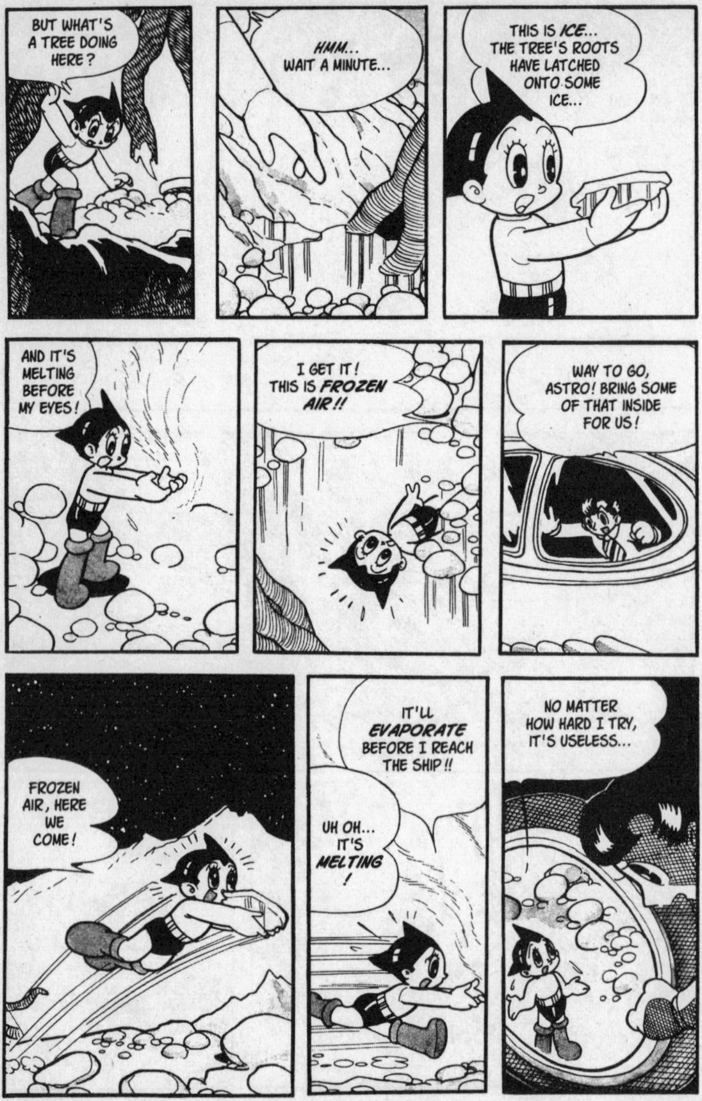
BUT WHAT'S A TREE DOING HERE?
HMM... WAIT A MINUTE...
THIS IS ICE... THE TREE'S ROOTS HAVE LATCHED ONTO SOME ICE...
AND IT'S MELTING BEFORE MY EYES!
I GET IT! THIS IS FROZEN AIR!!
WAY TO GO, ASTRO! BRING SOME OF THAT INSIDE FOR US!
FROZEN AIR, HERE WE COME!
IT'LL EVAPORATE BEFORE I REACH THE SHIP!!
UH OH... IT'S MELTING!
NO MATTER HOW HARD I TRY, IT'S USELESS...

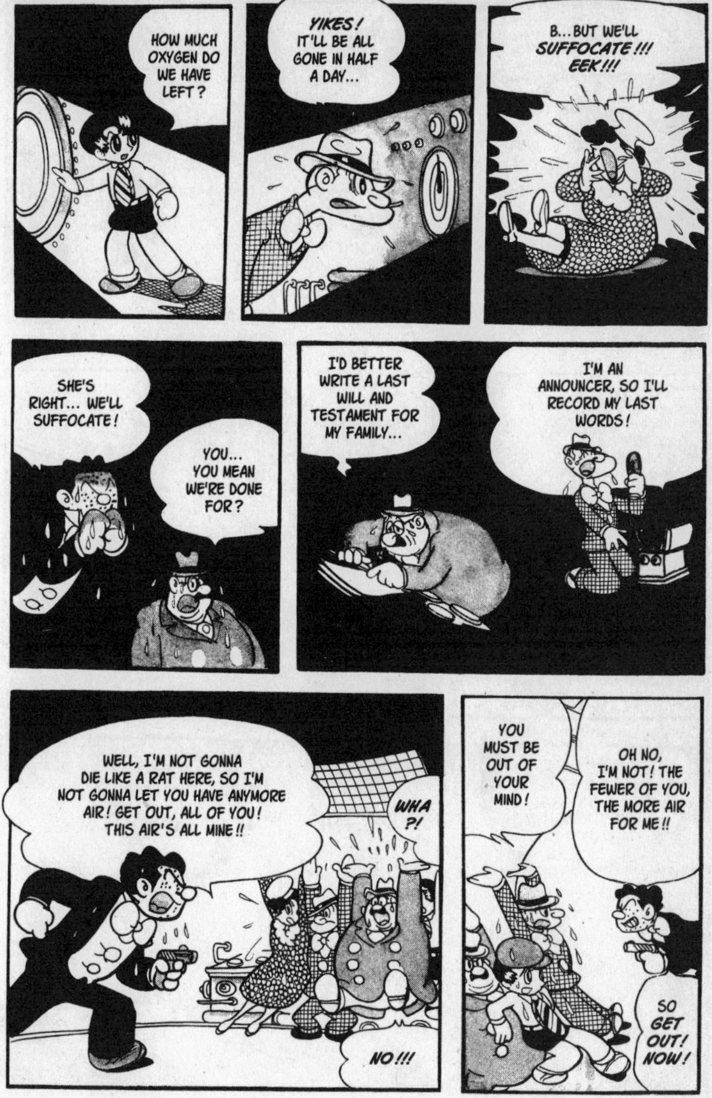
HOW MUCH OXYGEN DO WE HAVE LEFT?
YIKES! IT'LL BE ALL GONE IN HALF A DAY...
B...BUT WE'LL SUFFOCATE!!! EEK!!!
SHE'S RIGHT... WE'LL SUFFOCATE!
YOU... YOU MEAN WE'RE DONE FOR?
I'D BETTER WRITE A LAST WILL AND TESTAMENT FOR MY FAMILY...
I'M AN ANNOUNCER, SO I'LL RECORD MY LAST WORDS!
WELL, I'M NOT GONNA DIE LIKE A RAT HERE, SO I'M NOT GONNA LET YOU HAVE ANYMORE AIR! GET OUT, ALL OF YOU! THIS AIR'S ALL MINE!!
WHA?!
NO!!!
YOU MUST BE OUT OF YOUR MIND!
OH NO, I'M NOT! THE FEWER OF YOU, THE MORE AIR FOR ME!!
SO GET OUT! NOW!

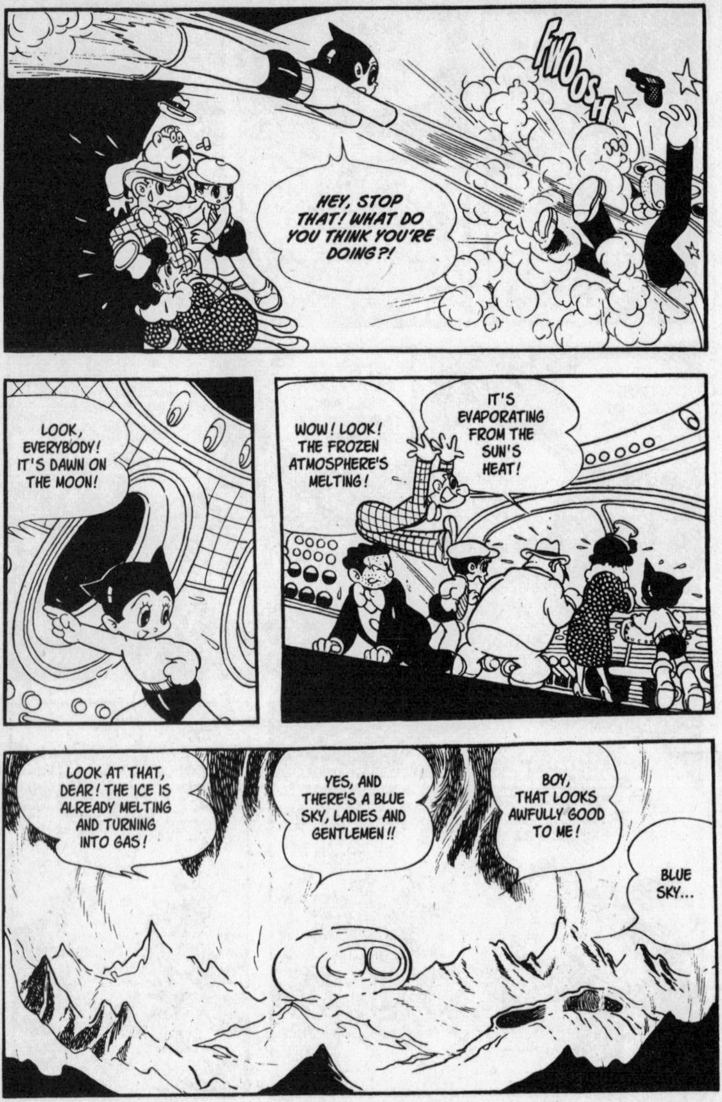
FWOOSH
HEY, STOP THAT! WHAT DO YOU THINK YOU'RE DOING?!
LOOK, EVERYBODY! IT'S DAWN ON THE MOON!
WOW! LOOK! THE FROZEN ATMOSPHERE'S MELTING!
IT'S EVAPORATING FROM THE SUN'S HEAT!
LOOK AT THAT, DEAR! THE ICE IS ALREADY MELTING AND TURNING INTO GAS!
YES, AND THERE'S A BLUE SKY, LADIES AND GENTLEMEN!!
BOY, THAT LOOKS AWFULLY GOOD TO ME!
BLUE SKY...

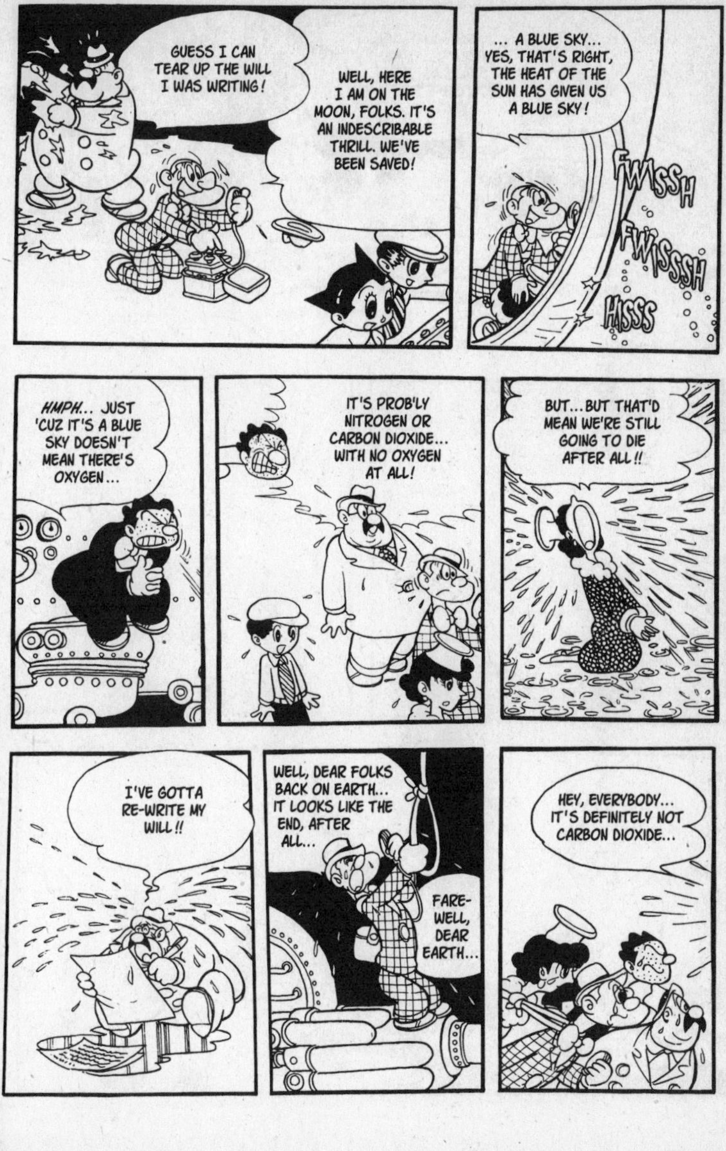
GUESS I CAN TEAR UP THE WILL I WAS WRITING!
WELL, HERE I AM ON THE MOON, FOLKS. IT'S AN INDESCRIBABLE THRILL. WE'VE BEEN SAVED!
... A BLUE SKY... YES, THAT'S RIGHT, THE HEAT OF THE SUN HAS GIVEN US A BLUE SKY!
FWISSH
FWISSSH
HISSS
HMPH... JUST 'CUZ IT'S A BLUE SKY DOESN'T MEAN THERE'S OXYGEN...
IT'S PROB'LY NITROGEN OR CARBON DIOXIDE... WITH NO OXYGEN AT ALL!
BUT...BUT THAT'D MEAN WE'RE STILL GOING TO DIE AFTER ALL!!
I'VE GOTTA RE-WRITE MY WILL!!
WELL, DEAR FOLKS BACK ON EARTH... IT LOOKS LIKE THE END, AFTER ALL...
FARE-WELL, DEAR EARTH...
HEY, EVERYBODY... IT'S DEFINITELY NOT CARBON DIOXIDE...

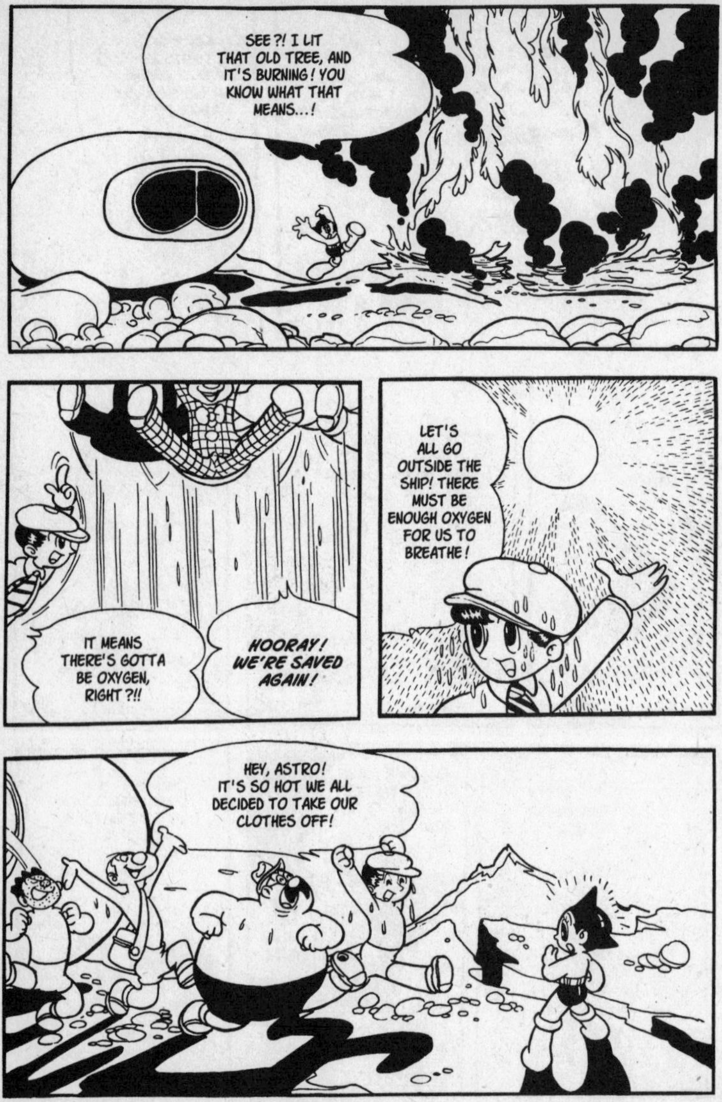
SEE?! I LIT THAT OLD TREE, AND IT'S BURNING! YOU KNOW WHAT THAT MEANS...!
IT MEANS THERE'S GOTTA BE OXYGEN, RIGHT?!!
HOORAY! WE'RE SAVED AGAIN!
LET'S ALL GO OUTSIDE THE SHIP! THERE MUST BE ENOUGH OXYGEN FOR US TO BREATHE!
HEY, ASTRO! IT'S SO HOT WE ALL DECIDED TO TAKE OUR CLOTHES OFF!

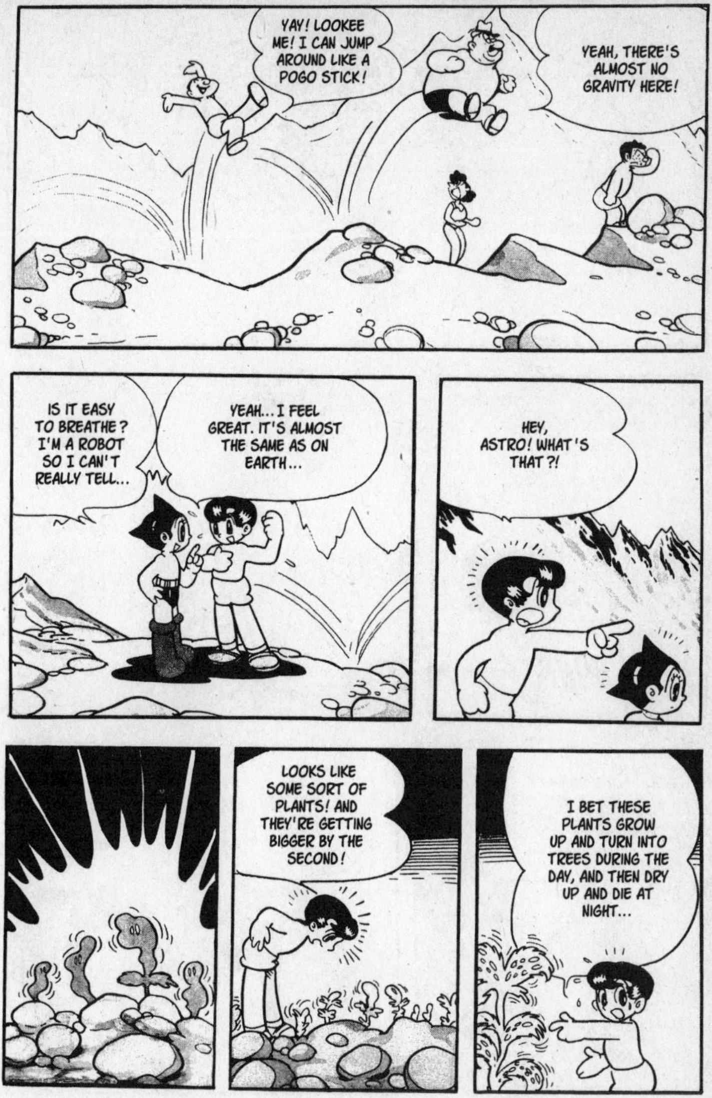
YAY! LOOKEE ME! I CAN JUMP AROUND LIKE A POGO STICK!
YEAH, THERE'S ALMOST NO GRAVITY HERE!
IS IT EASY TO BREATHE? I'M A ROBOT SO I CAN'T REALLY TELL...
YEAH... I FEEL GREAT. IT'S ALMOST THE SAME AS ON EARTH...
HEY, ASTRO! WHAT'S THAT?!
LOOKS LIKE SOME SORT OF PLANTS! AND THEY'RE GETTING BIGGER BY THE SECOND!
I BET THESE PLANTS GROW UP AND TURN INTO TREES DURING THE DAY, AND THEN DRY UP AND DIE AT NIGHT...

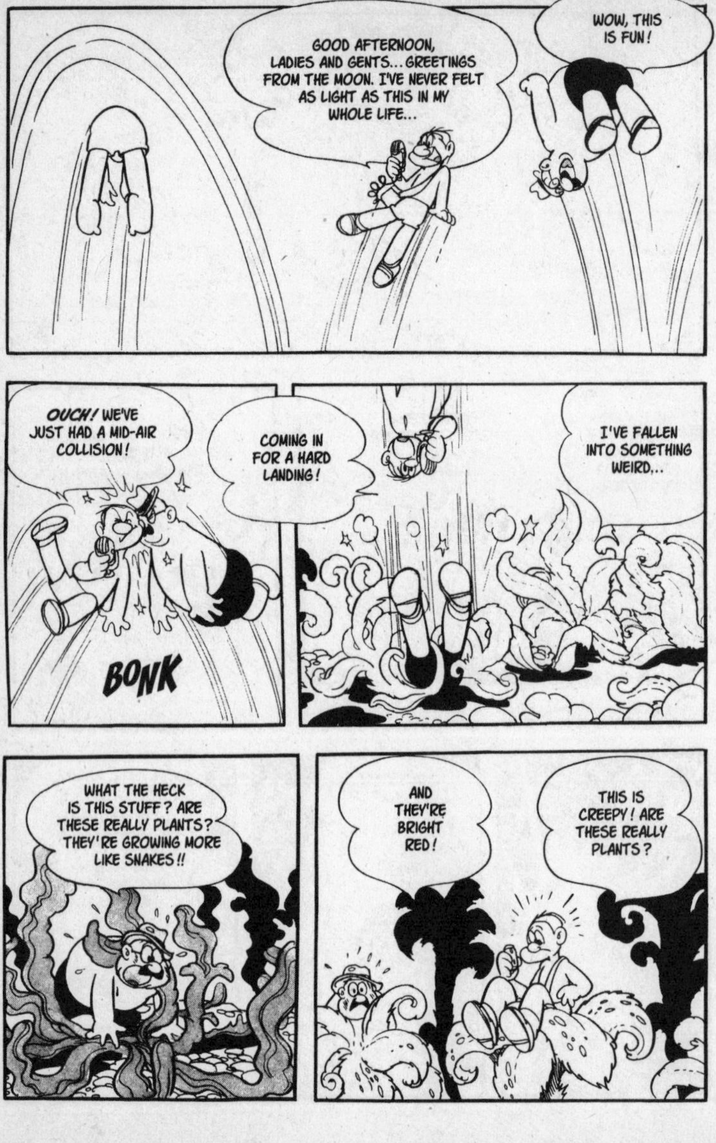
GOOD AFTERNOON, LADIES AND GENTS... GREETINGS FROM THE MOON. I'VE NEVER FELT AS LIGHT AS THIS IN MY WHOLE LIFE...
WOW, THIS IS FUN!
OUCH! WE'VE JUST HAD A MID-AIR COLLISION!
BONK
COMING IN FOR A HARD LANDING!
I'VE FALLEN INTO SOMETHING WEIRD...
WHAT THE HECK IS THIS STUFF? ARE THESE REALLY PLANTS? THEY'RE GROWING MORE LIKE SNAKES!!
AND THEY'RE BRIGHT RED!
THIS IS CREEPY! ARE THESE REALLY PLANTS?

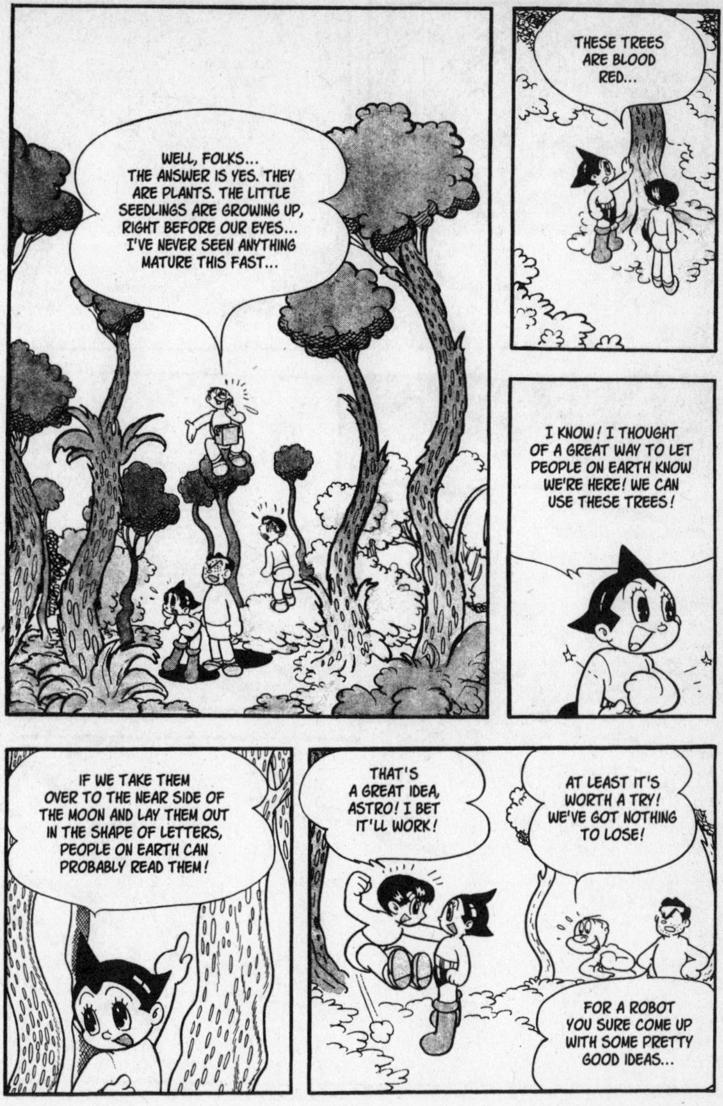
WELL, FOLKS... THE ANSWER IS YES. THEY ARE PLANTS. THE LITTLE SEEDLINGS ARE GROWING UP, RIGHT BEFORE OUR EYES... I'VE NEVER SEEN ANYTHING MATURE THIS FAST...
THESE TREES ARE BLOOD RED...
I KNOW! I THOUGHT OF A GREAT WAY TO LET PEOPLE ON EARTH KNOW WE'RE HERE! WE CAN USE THESE TREES!
IF WE TAKE THEM OVER TO THE NEAR SIDE OF THE MOON AND LAY THEM OUT IN THE SHAPE OF LETTERS, PEOPLE ON EARTH CAN PROBABLY READ THEM!
THAT'S A GREAT IDEA, ASTRO! I BET IT'LL WORK!
AT LEAST IT'S WORTH A TRY! WE'VE GOT NOTHING TO LOSE!
FOR A ROBOT YOU SURE COME UP WITH SOME PRETTY GOOD IDEAS...

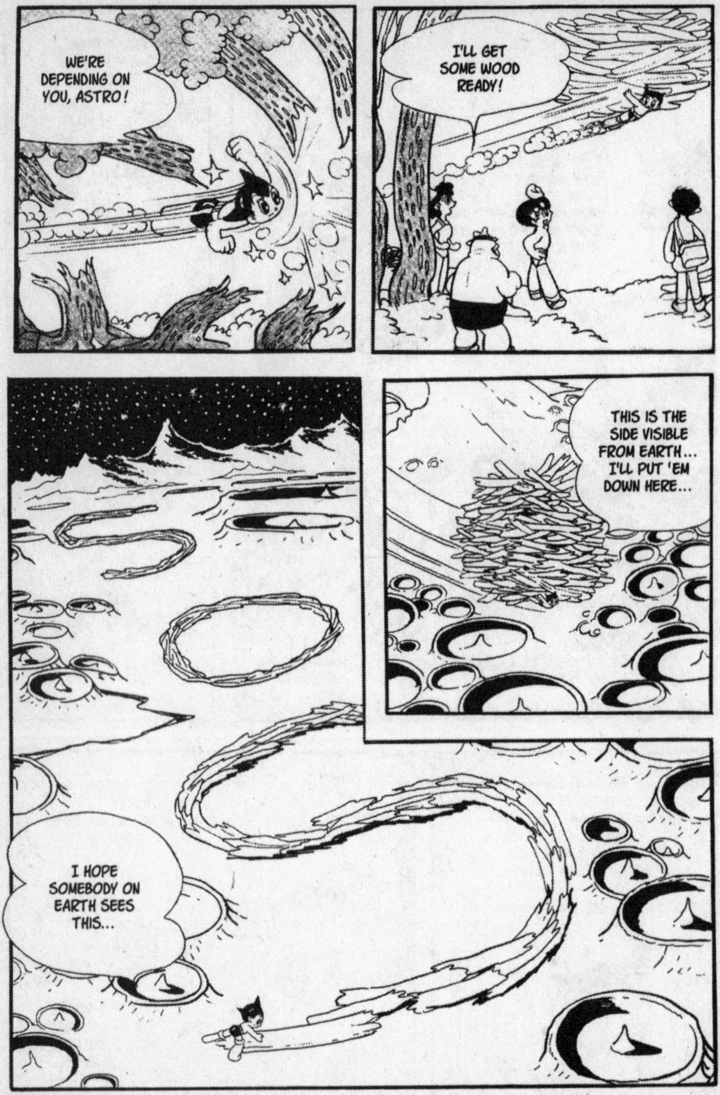
WE'RE DEPENDING ON YOU, ASTRO!
I'LL GET SOME WOOD READY!
THIS IS THE SIDE VISIBLE FROM EARTH... I'LL PUT 'EM DOWN HERE...
I HOPE SOMEBODY ON EARTH SEES THIS...

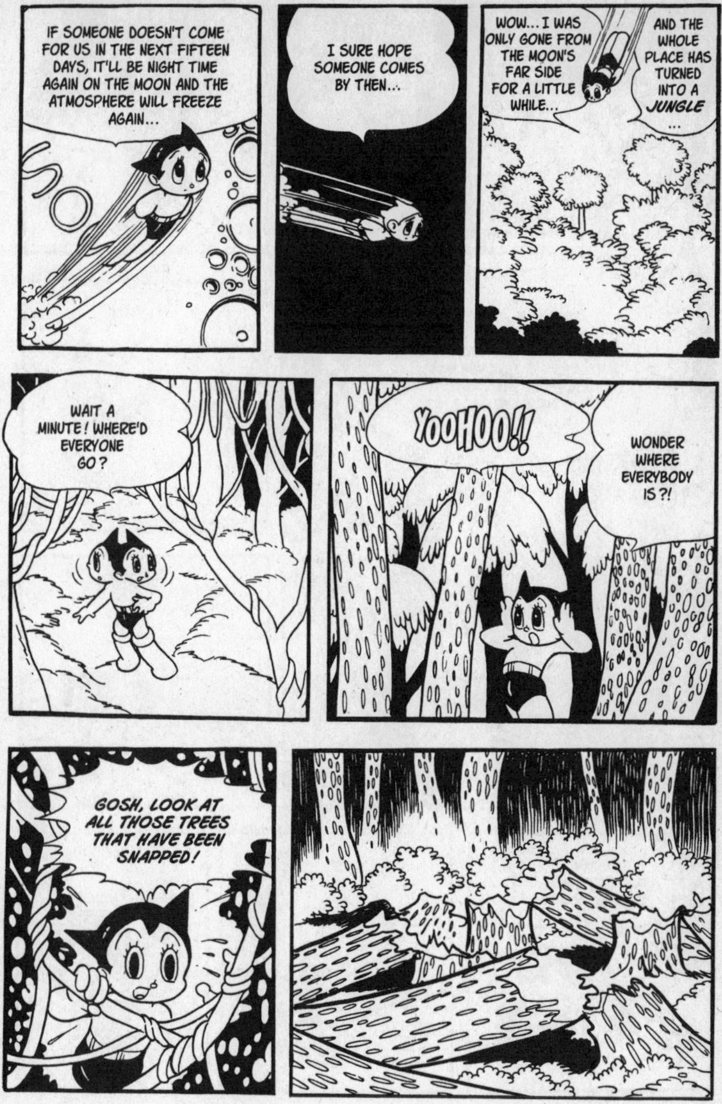
IF SOMEONE DOESN'T COME FOR US IN THE NEXT FIFTEEN DAYS, IT'LL BE NIGHT TIME AGAIN ON THE MOON AND THE ATMOSPHERE WILL FREEZE AGAIN...
I SURE HOPE SOMEONE COMES BY THEN...
WOW... I WAS ONLY GONE FROM THE MOON'S FAR SIDE FOR A LITTLE WHILE...
AND THE WHOLE PLACE HAS TURNED INTO A JUNGLE ...
WAIT A MINUTE! WHERE'D EVERYONE GO?
YOOHOO!!
WONDER WHERE EVERYBODY IS?!
GOSH, LOOK AT ALL THOSE TREES THAT HAVE BEEN SNAPPED!

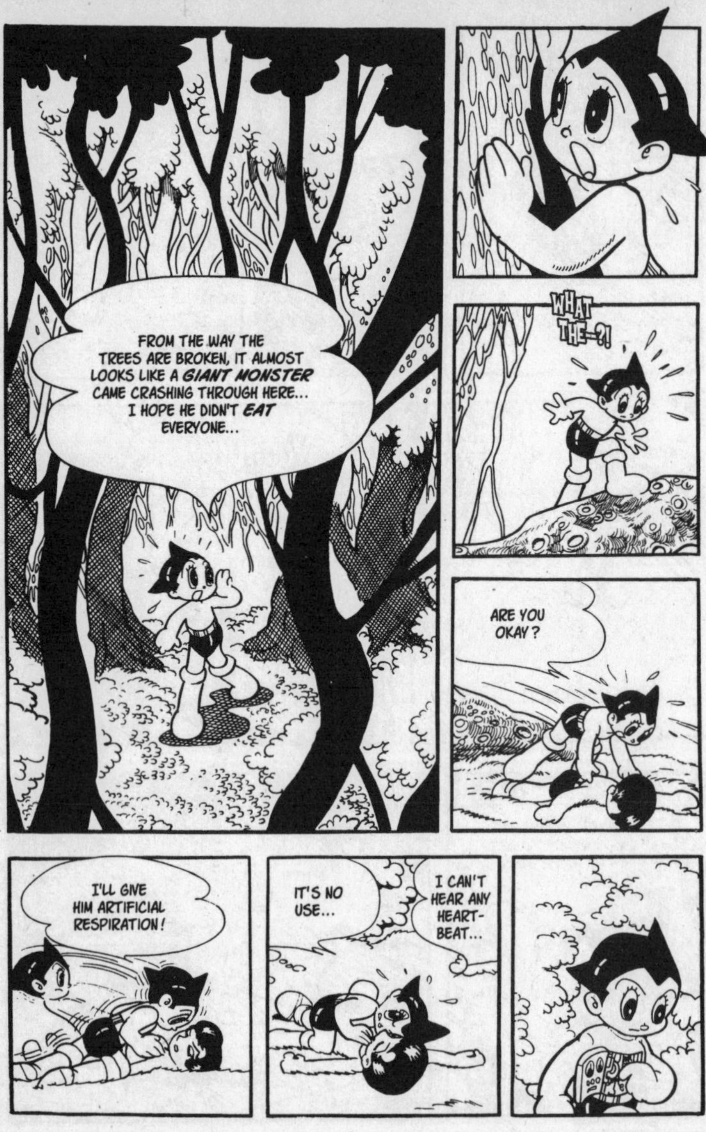
FROM THE WAY THE TREES ARE BROKEN, IT ALMOST LOOKS LIKE A *GIANT MONSTER* CAME CRASHING THROUGH HERE... I HOPE HE DIDN'T *EAT* EVERYONE...
WHAT THE--?!
ARE YOU OKAY?
I'LL GIVE HIM ARTIFICIAL RESPIRATION!
IT'S NO USE...
I CAN'T HEAR ANY HEART-BEAT...

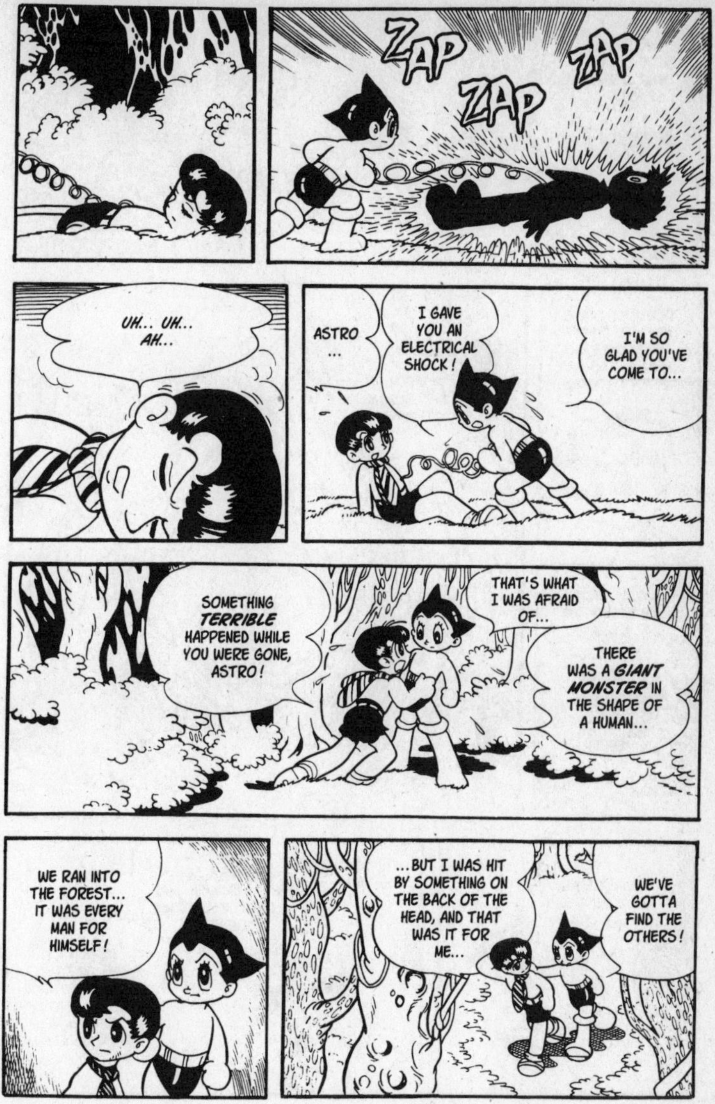
ZAP
ZAP
ZAP
UH... UH... AH...
ASTRO ...
I GAVE YOU AN ELECTRICAL SHOCK!
I'M SO GLAD YOU'VE COME TO...
SOMETHING TERRIBLE HAPPENED WHILE YOU WERE GONE, ASTRO!
THAT'S WHAT I WAS AFRAID OF...
THERE WAS A GIANT MONSTER IN THE SHAPE OF A HUMAN...
WE RAN INTO THE FOREST... IT WAS EVERY MAN FOR HIMSELF!
...BUT I WAS HIT BY SOMETHING ON THE BACK OF THE HEAD, AND THAT WAS IT FOR ME...
WE'VE GOTTA FIND THE OTHERS!

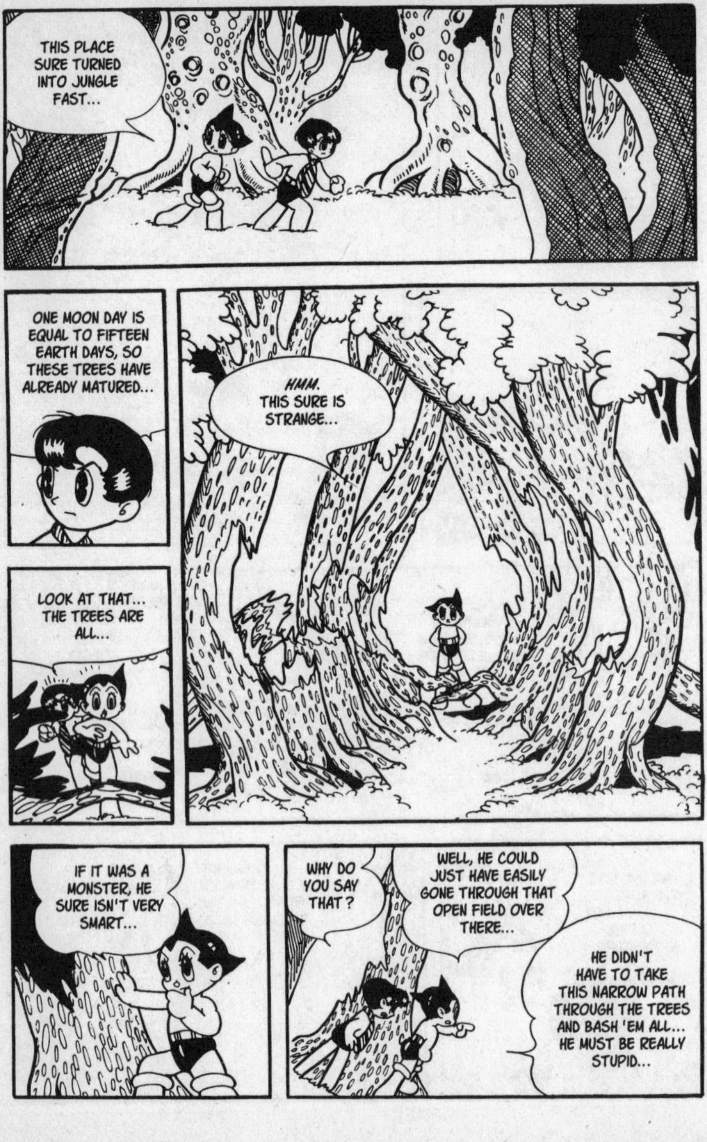
THIS PLACE SURE TURNED INTO JUNGLE FAST...
ONE MOON DAY IS EQUAL TO FIFTEEN EARTH DAYS, SO THESE TREES HAVE ALREADY MATURED...
LOOK AT THAT... THE TREES ARE ALL...
HMM. THIS SURE IS STRANGE...
IF IT WAS A MONSTER, HE SURE ISN'T VERY SMART...
WHY DO YOU SAY THAT?
WELL, HE COULD JUST HAVE EASILY GONE THROUGH THAT OPEN FIELD OVER THERE...
HE DIDN'T HAVE TO TAKE THIS NARROW PATH THROUGH THE TREES AND BASH 'EM ALL... HE MUST BE REALLY STUPID...

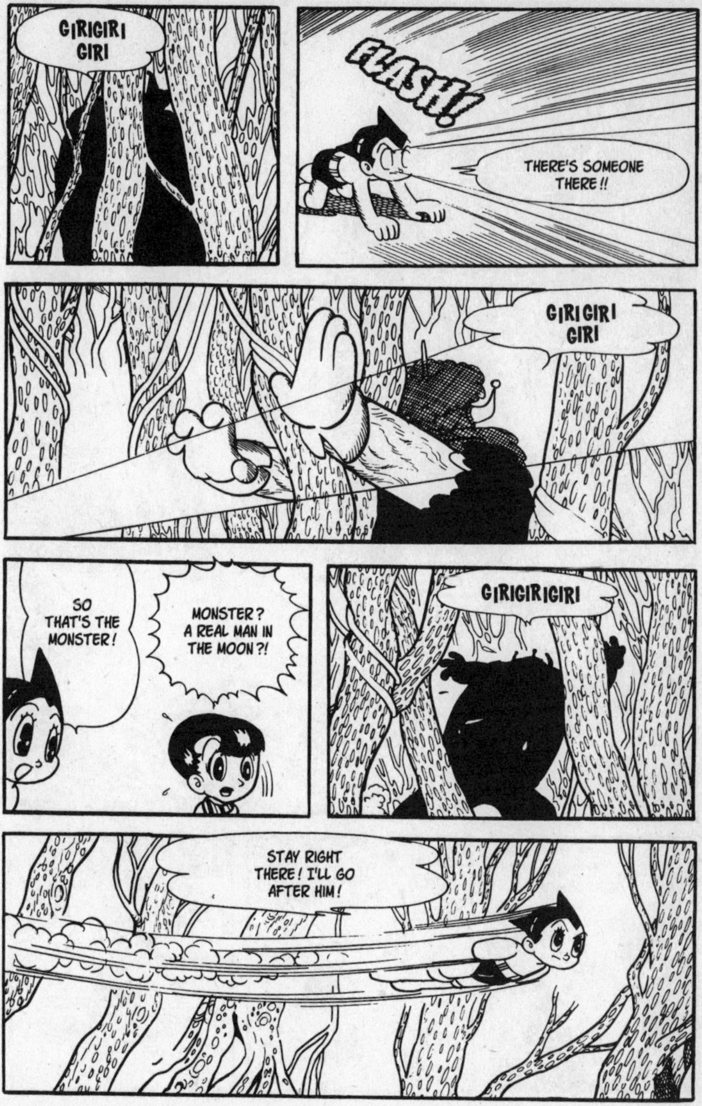
GIRIGIRI GIRI
FLASH!
THERE'S SOMEONE THERE!!
GIRIGIRI GIRI
SO THAT'S THE MONSTER!
MONSTER? A REAL MAN IN THE MOON?!
GIRIGIRIGIRI
STAY RIGHT THERE! I'LL GO AFTER HIM!

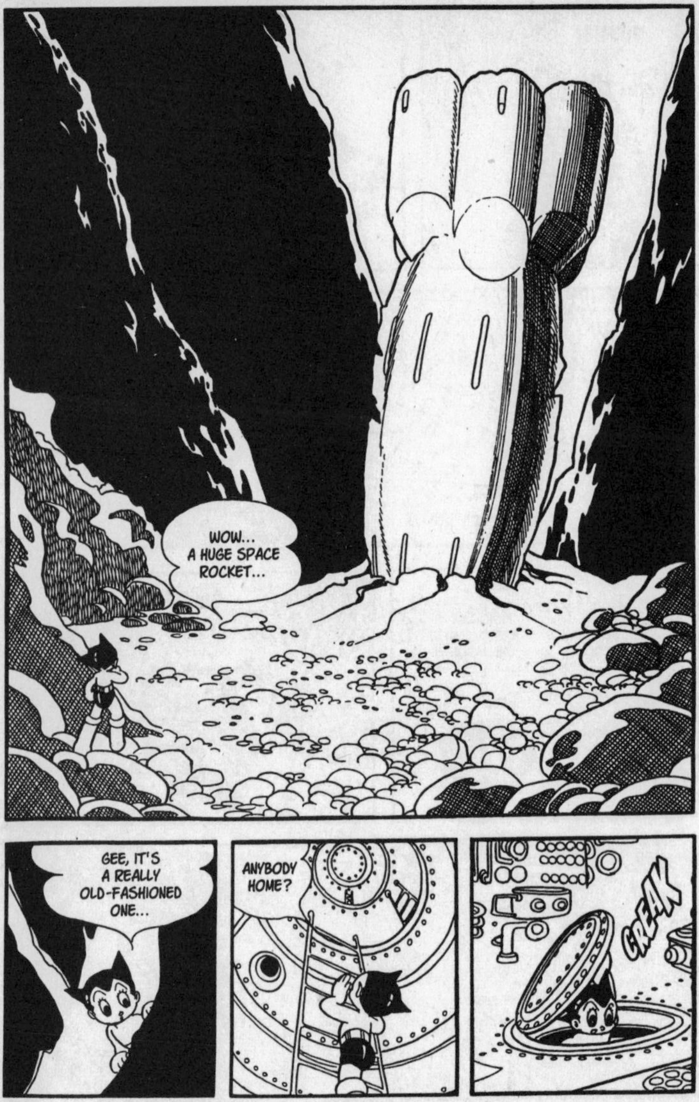
WOW... A HUGE SPACE ROCKET...
GEE, IT'S A REALLY OLD-FASHIONED ONE...
ANYBODY HOME?
CREAK

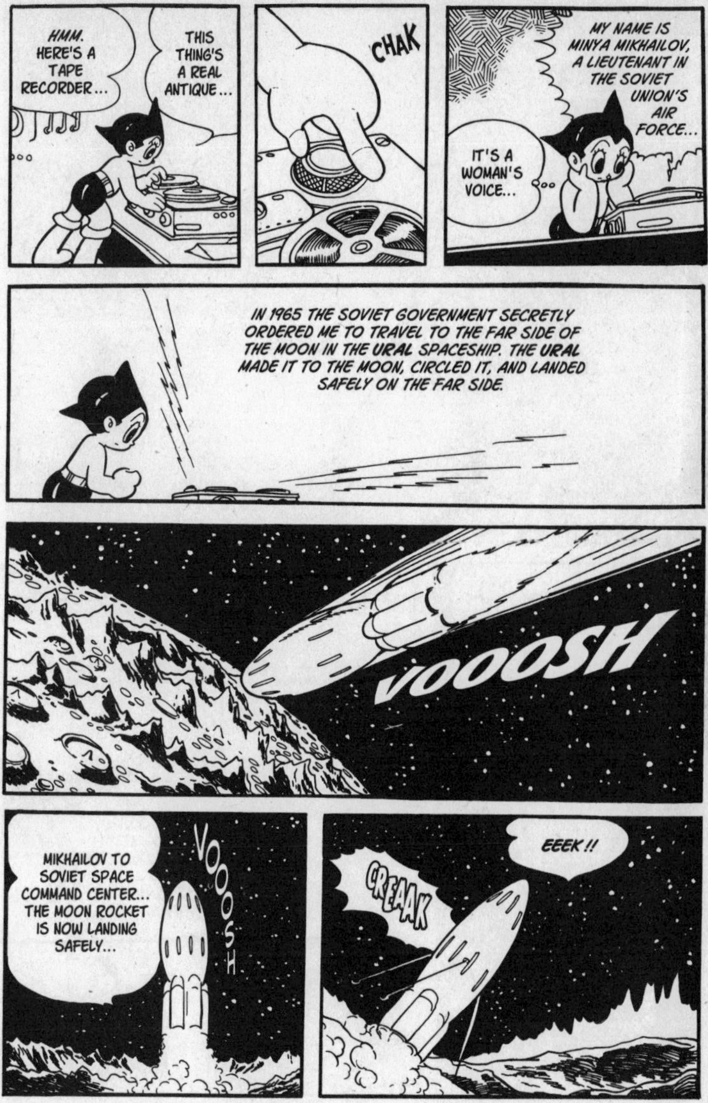
HMM. HERE'S A TAPE RECORDER...
THIS THING'S A REAL ANTIQUE...
CHAK
MY NAME IS MINYA MIKHAILOV, A LIEUTENANT IN THE SOVIET UNION'S AIR FORCE...
IT'S A WOMAN'S VOICE...
IN 1965 THE SOVIET GOVERNMENT SECRETLY ORDERED ME TO TRAVEL TO THE FAR SIDE OF THE MOON IN THE URAL SPACESHIP. THE URAL MADE IT TO THE MOON, CIRCLED IT, AND LANDED SAFELY ON THE FAR SIDE.
VOOOSH
MIKHAILOV TO SOVIET SPACE COMMAND CENTER... THE MOON ROCKET IS NOW LANDING SAFELY...
VOOOSH
EEEK!!
CREAAK

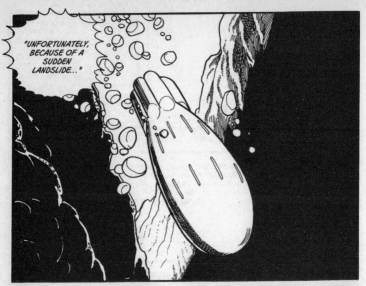

"UNFORTUNATELY, BECAUSE OF A SUDDEN LANDSLIDE..."

"...MY ROCKET FELL INTO A DEEP CREVASSE."

"I WAS UNHURT, BUT WHEN I CHECKED THE ROCKET I FOUND IT WAS BADLY DAMAGED."

"I KNEW I WOULD NEVER BE ABLE TO REPAIR IT. I TURNED PALE..."

"...AND I RAN OVER TO THE TRANSMITTER IN HOPES OF SENDING OUT AN SOS..."

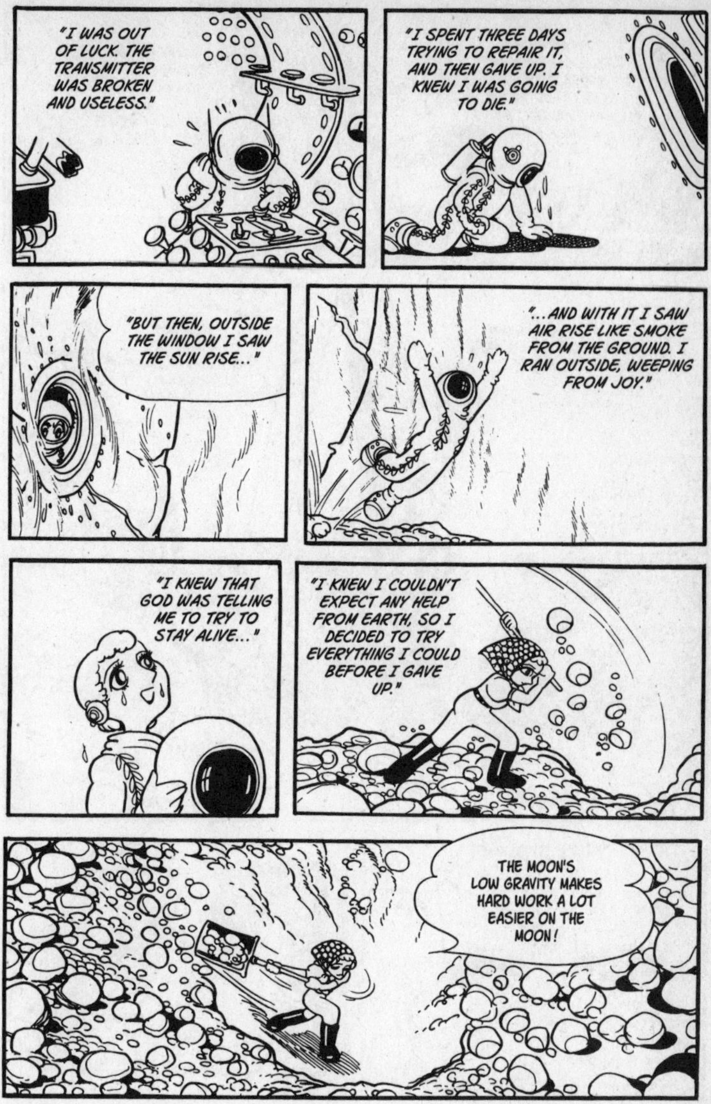
"I WAS OUT OF LUCK. THE TRANSMITTER WAS BROKEN AND USELESS."
"I SPENT THREE DAYS TRYING TO REPAIR IT, AND THEN GAVE UP. I KNEW I WAS GOING TO DIE."
"BUT THEN, OUTSIDE THE WINDOW I SAW THE SUN RISE..."
"...AND WITH IT I SAW AIR RISE LIKE SMOKE FROM THE GROUND. I RAN OUTSIDE, WEEPING FROM JOY."
"I KNEW THAT GOD WAS TELLING ME TO TRY TO STAY ALIVE..."
"I KNEW I COULDN'T EXPECT ANY HELP FROM EARTH, SO I DECIDED TO TRY EVERYTHING I COULD BEFORE I GAVE UP."
THE MOON'S LOW GRAVITY MAKES HARD WORK A LOT EASIER ON THE MOON!

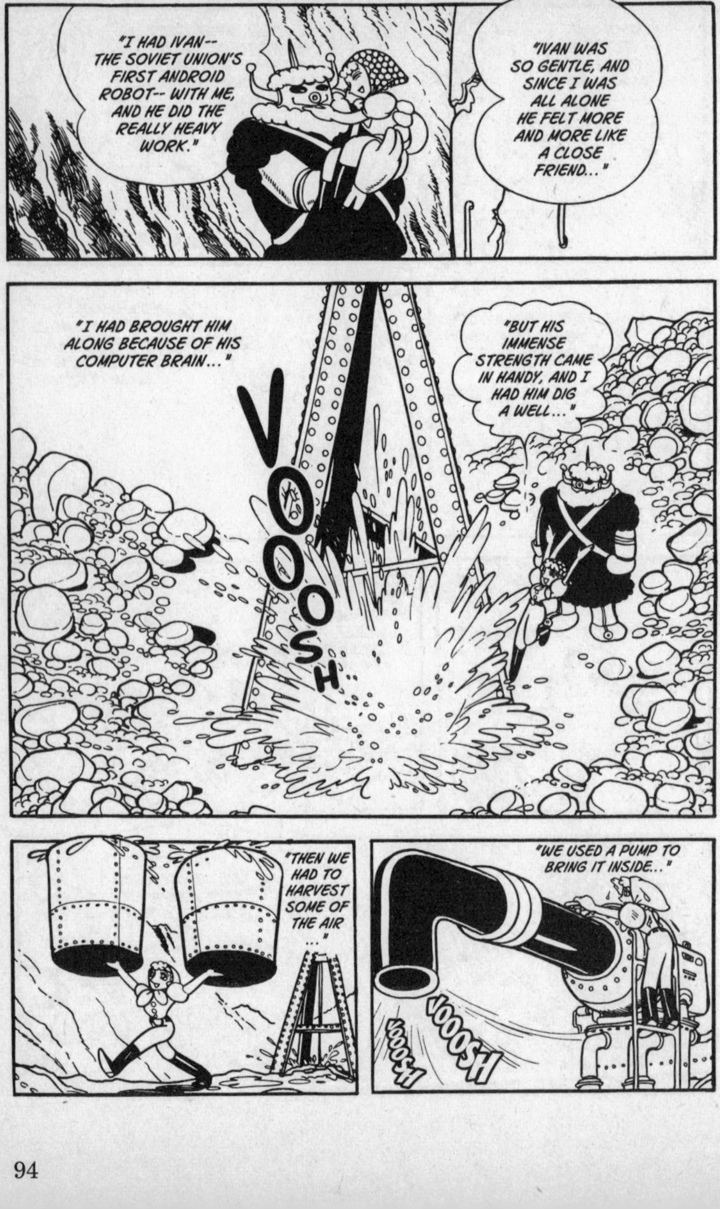
"I HAD IVAN-- THE SOVIET UNION'S FIRST ANDROID ROBOT-- WITH ME, AND HE DID THE REALLY HEAVY WORK."
"IVAN WAS SO GENTLE, AND SINCE I WAS ALL ALONE HE FELT MORE AND MORE LIKE A CLOSE FRIEND..."
"I HAD BROUGHT HIM ALONG BECAUSE OF HIS COMPUTER BRAIN..."
"BUT HIS IMMENSE STRENGTH CAME IN HANDY, AND I HAD HIM DIG A WELL..."
VOOOSH
"THEN WE HAD TO HARVEST SOME OF THE AIR ..."
"WE USED A PUMP TO BRING IT INSIDE..."
VOOOSH
VOOOSH

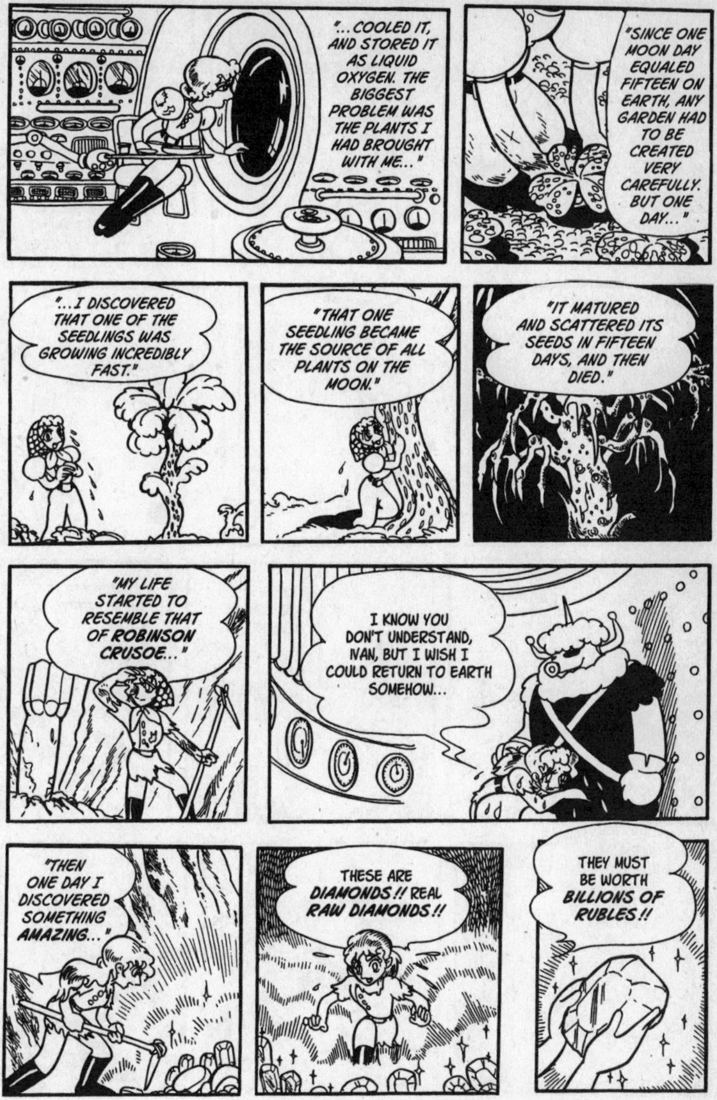
"...COOLED IT, AND STORED IT AS LIQUID OXYGEN. THE BIGGEST PROBLEM WAS THE PLANTS I HAD BROUGHT WITH ME..."
"SINCE ONE MOON DAY EQUALED FIFTEEN ON EARTH, ANY GARDEN HAD TO BE CREATED VERY CAREFULLY. BUT ONE DAY..."
"...I DISCOVERED THAT ONE OF THE SEEDLINGS WAS GROWING INCREDIBLY FAST."
"THAT ONE SEEDLING BECAME THE SOURCE OF ALL PLANTS ON THE MOON."
"IT MATURED AND SCATTERED ITS SEEDS IN FIFTEEN DAYS, AND THEN DIED."
"MY LIFE STARTED TO RESEMBLE THAT OF ROBINSON CRUSOE..."
I KNOW YOU DON'T UNDERSTAND, IVAN, BUT I WISH I COULD RETURN TO EARTH SOMEHOW...
"THEN ONE DAY I DISCOVERED SOMETHING AMAZING..."
THESE ARE DIAMONDS!! REAL RAW DIAMONDS!!
THEY MUST BE WORTH BILLIONS OF RUBLES!!

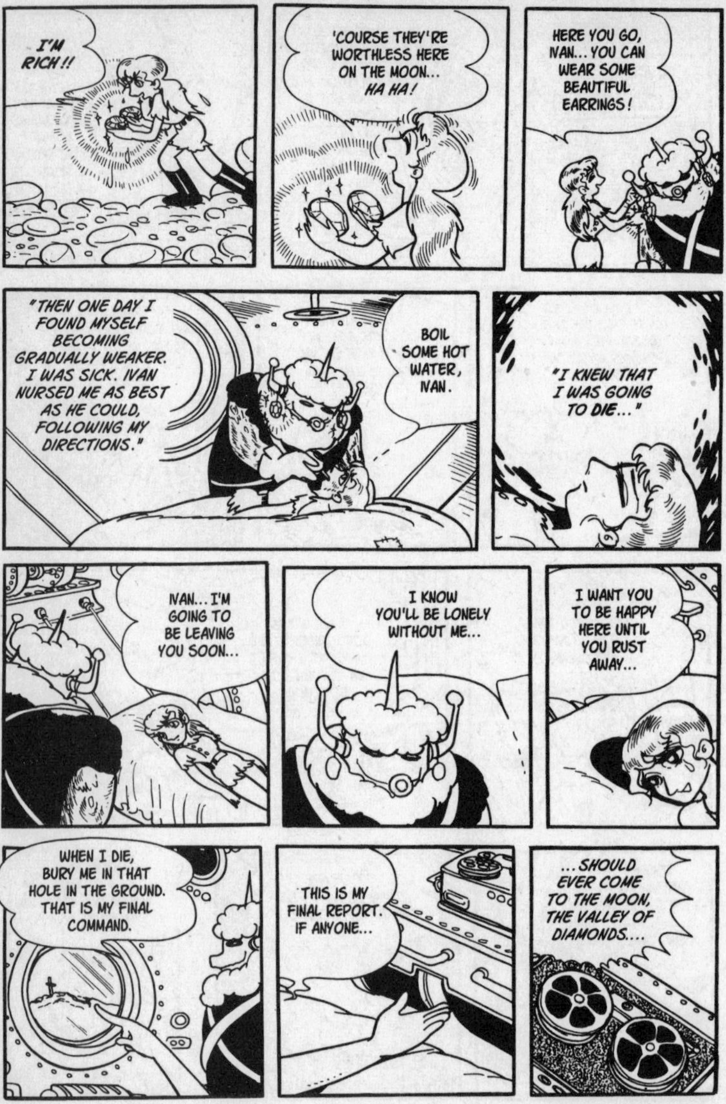
I'M RICH!!
'COURSE THEY'RE WORTHLESS HERE ON THE MOON... HA HA!
HERE YOU GO, IVAN... YOU CAN WEAR SOME BEAUTIFUL EARRINGS!
"THEN ONE DAY I FOUND MYSELF BECOMING GRADUALLY WEAKER. I WAS SICK. IVAN NURSED ME AS BEST AS HE COULD, FOLLOWING MY DIRECTIONS."
BOIL SOME HOT WATER, IVAN.
"I KNEW THAT I WAS GOING TO DIE..."
IVAN... I'M GOING TO BE LEAVING YOU SOON...
I KNOW YOU'LL BE LONELY WITHOUT ME...
I WANT YOU TO BE HAPPY HERE UNTIL YOU RUST AWAY...
WHEN I DIE, BURY ME IN THAT HOLE IN THE GROUND. THAT IS MY FINAL COMMAND.
THIS IS MY FINAL REPORT. IF ANYONE...
...SHOULD EVER COME TO THE MOON, THE VALLEY OF DIAMONDS....

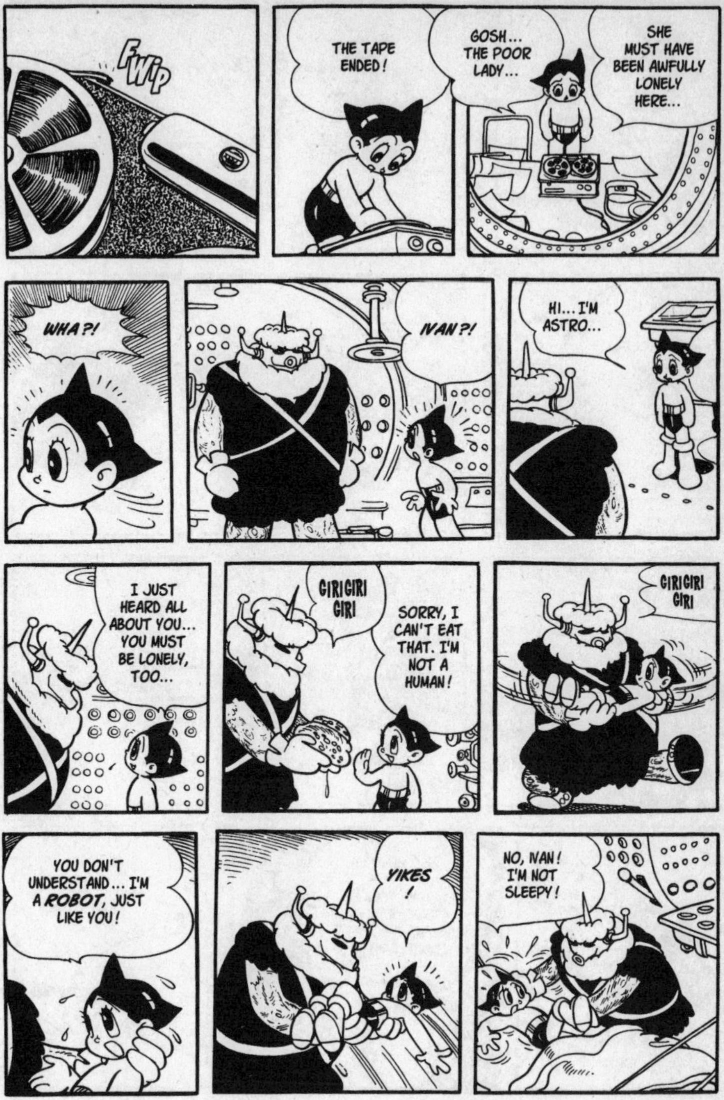
FWip
THE TAPE ENDED!
GOSH... THE POOR LADY...
SHE MUST HAVE BEEN AWFULLY LONELY HERE...
WHA?!
IVAN?!
HI... I'M ASTRO...
I JUST HEARD ALL ABOUT YOU... YOU MUST BE LONELY, TOO...
GIRIGIRI GIRI
SORRY, I CAN'T EAT THAT. I'M NOT A HUMAN!
GIRIGIRI GIRI
YOU DON'T UNDERSTAND... I'M A ROBOT, JUST LIKE YOU!
YIKES!
NO, IVAN! I'M NOT SLEEPY!

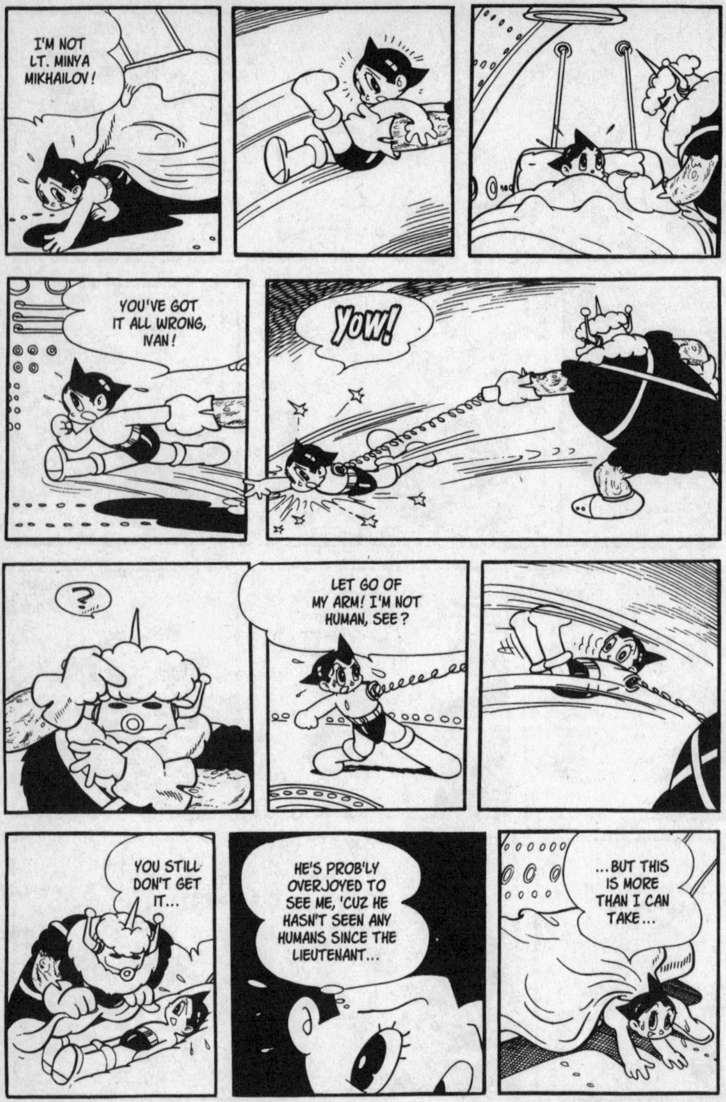

I'M NOT LT. MINYA MIKHAILOV!
YOU'VE GOT IT ALL WRONG, IVAN!
YOW!
?
LET GO OF MY ARM! I'M NOT HUMAN, SEE?
YOU STILL DON'T GET IT...
HE'S PROB'LY OVERJOYED TO SEE ME, 'CUZ HE HASN'T SEEN ANY HUMANS SINCE THE LIEUTENANT...
...BUT THIS IS MORE THAN I CAN TAKE...

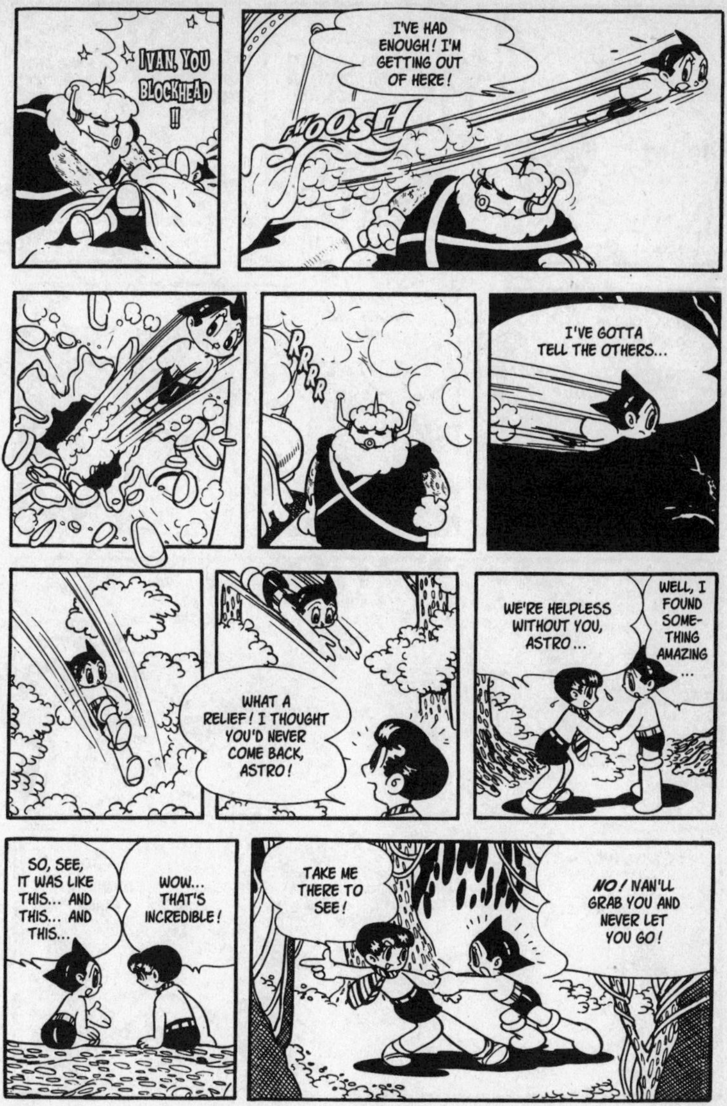
IVAN, YOU BLOCKHEAD !!
I'VE HAD ENOUGH! I'M GETTING OUT OF HERE!
FWOOSH
RRRR
I'VE GOTTA TELL THE OTHERS...
WHAT A RELIEF! I THOUGHT YOU'D NEVER COME BACK, ASTRO!
WE'RE HELPLESS WITHOUT YOU, ASTRO...
WELL, I FOUND SOME-THING AMAZING ...
SO, SEE, IT WAS LIKE THIS... AND THIS... AND THIS...
WOW... THAT'S INCREDIBLE!
TAKE ME THERE TO SEE!
NO! IVAN'LL GRAB YOU AND NEVER LET YOU GO!

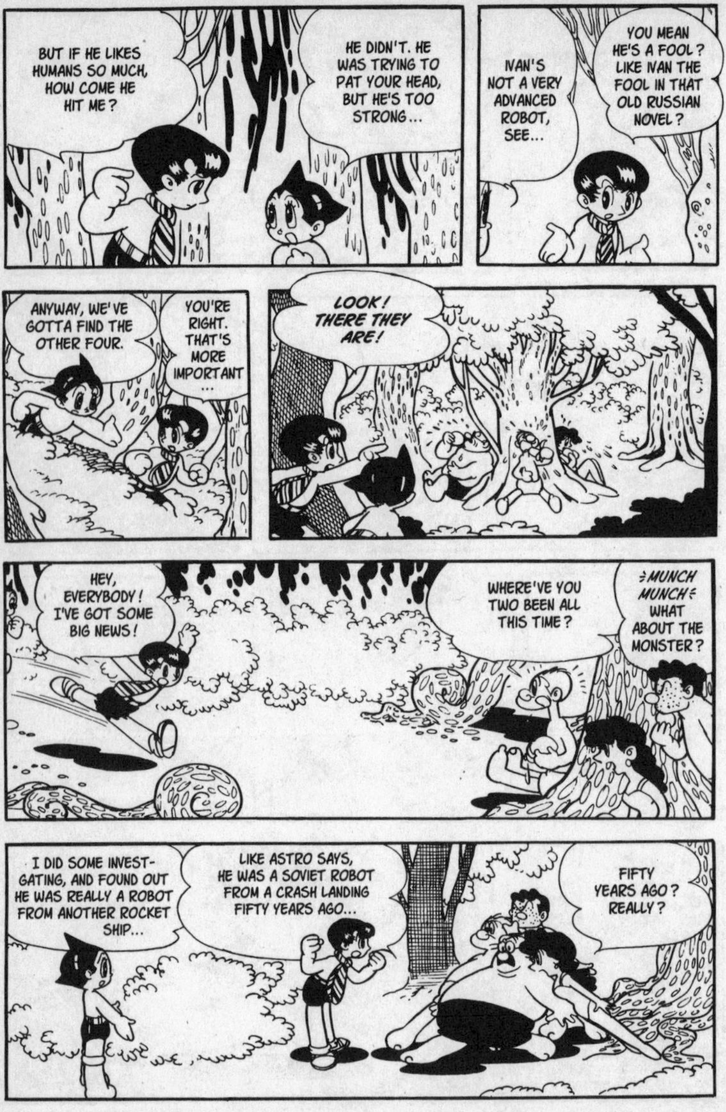
BUT IF HE LIKES HUMANS SO MUCH, HOW COME HE HIT ME?
HE DIDN'T. HE WAS TRYING TO PAT YOUR HEAD, BUT HE'S TOO STRONG...
IVAN'S NOT A VERY ADVANCED ROBOT, SEE...
YOU MEAN HE'S A FOOL? LIKE IVAN THE FOOL IN THAT OLD RUSSIAN NOVEL?
ANYWAY, WE'VE GOTTA FIND THE OTHER FOUR.
YOU'RE RIGHT. THAT'S MORE IMPORTANT ...
LOOK! THERE THEY ARE!
HEY, EVERYBODY! I'VE GOT SOME BIG NEWS!
WHERE'VE YOU TWO BEEN ALL THIS TIME?
MUNCH MUNCH WHAT ABOUT THE MONSTER?
I DID SOME INVESTIGATING, AND FOUND OUT HE WAS REALLY A ROBOT FROM ANOTHER ROCKET SHIP...
LIKE ASTRO SAYS, HE WAS A SOVIET ROBOT FROM A CRASH LANDING FIFTY YEARS AGO...
FIFTY YEARS AGO? REALLY?

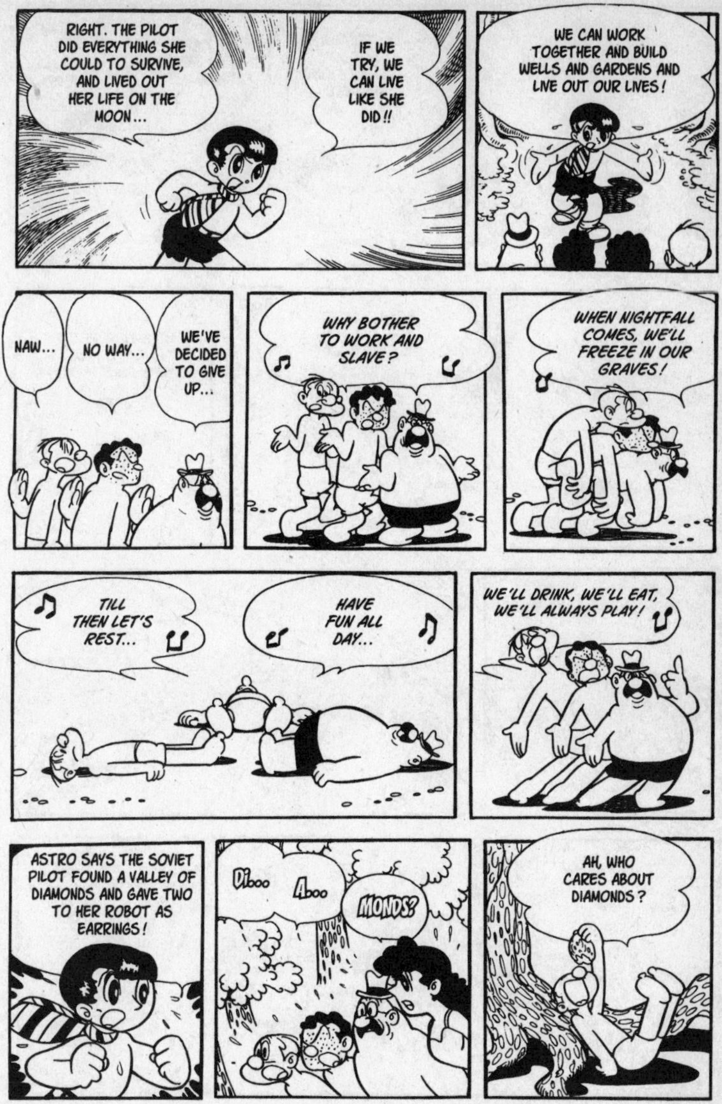
RIGHT. THE PILOT DID EVERYTHING SHE COULD TO SURVIVE, AND LIVED OUT HER LIFE ON THE MOON...
IF WE TRY, WE CAN LIVE LIKE SHE DID!!
WE CAN WORK TOGETHER AND BUILD WELLS AND GARDENS AND LIVE OUT OUR LIVES!
NAW...
NO WAY...
WE'VE DECIDED TO GIVE UP...
WHY BOTHER TO WORK AND SLAVE?
WHEN NIGHTFALL COMES, WE'LL FREEZE IN OUR GRAVES!
TILL THEN LET'S REST...
HAVE FUN ALL DAY...
WE'LL DRINK, WE'LL EAT, WE'LL ALWAYS PLAY!
ASTRO SAYS THE SOVIET PILOT FOUND A VALLEY OF DIAMONDS AND GAVE TWO TO HER ROBOT AS EARRINGS!
Di...
A...
MONDS?
AH, WHO CARES ABOUT DIAMONDS?

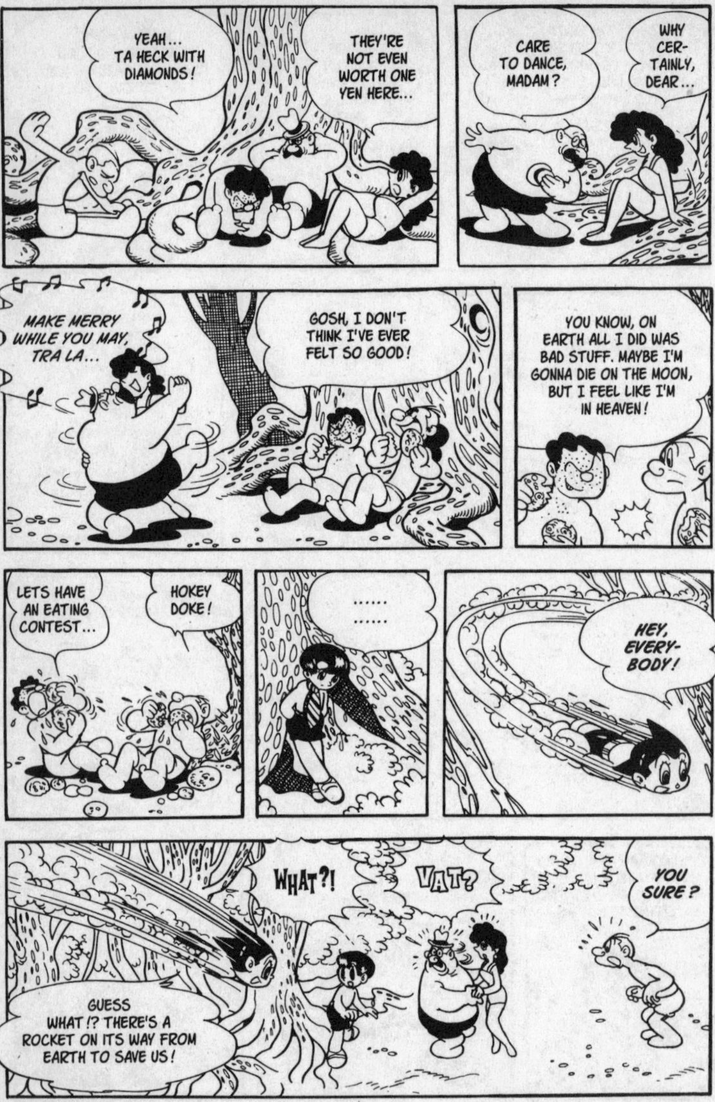
YEAH... TA HECK WITH DIAMONDS!
THEY'RE NOT EVEN WORTH ONE YEN HERE...
CARE TO DANCE, MADAM?
WHY CER-TAINLY, DEAR...
MAKE MERRY WHILE YOU MAY, TRA LA...
GOSH, I DON'T THINK I'VE EVER FELT SO GOOD!
YOU KNOW, ON EARTH ALL I DID WAS BAD STUFF. MAYBE I'M GONNA DIE ON THE MOON, BUT I FEEL LIKE I'M IN HEAVEN!
LETS HAVE AN EATING CONTEST...
HOKEY DOKE!
....
HEY, EVERY-BODY!
GUESS WHAT!? THERE'S A ROCKET ON ITS WAY FROM EARTH TO SAVE US!
WHAT?!
VAT?
YOU SURE?

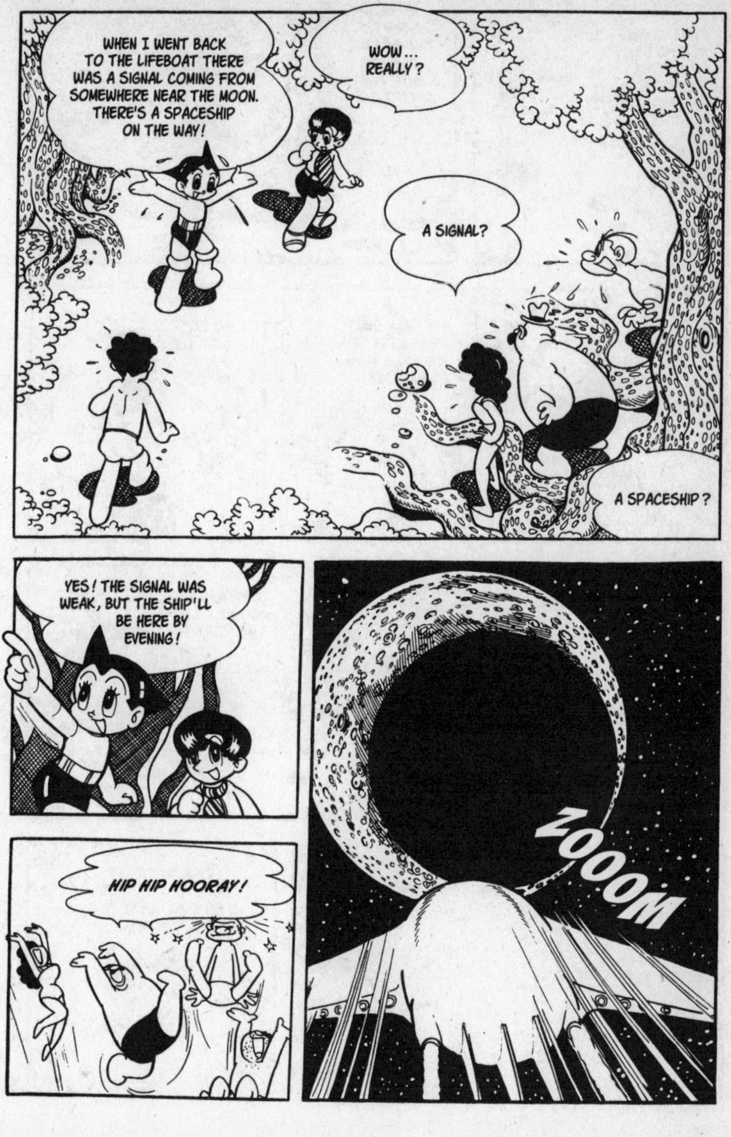
WHEN I WENT BACK TO THE LIFEBOAT THERE WAS A SIGNAL COMING FROM SOMEWHERE NEAR THE MOON. THERE'S A SPACESHIP ON THE WAY!
WOW... REALLY?
A SIGNAL?
A SPACESHIP?
YES! THE SIGNAL WAS WEAK, BUT THE SHIP'LL BE HERE BY EVENING!
HIP HIP HOORAY!
ZOOOM

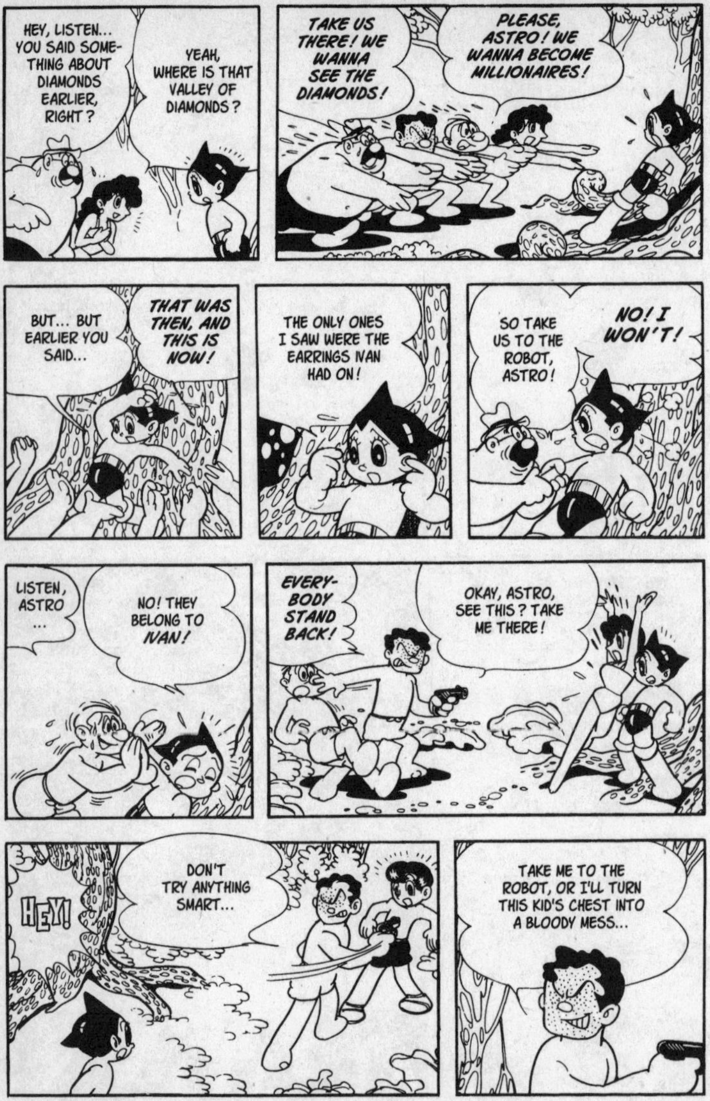
HEY, LISTEN... YOU SAID SOME-THING ABOUT DIAMONDS EARLIER, RIGHT?
YEAH, WHERE IS THAT VALLEY OF DIAMONDS?
TAKE US THERE! WE WANNA SEE THE DIAMONDS!
PLEASE, ASTRO! WE WANNA BECOME MILLIONAIRES!
BUT... BUT EARLIER YOU SAID...
THAT WAS THEN, AND THIS IS NOW!
THE ONLY ONES I SAW WERE THE EARRINGS IVAN HAD ON!
SO TAKE US TO THE ROBOT, ASTRO!
NO! I WON'T!
LISTEN, ASTRO ...
NO! THEY BELONG TO IVAN!
EVERY-BODY STAND BACK!
OKAY, ASTRO, SEE THIS? TAKE ME THERE!
HEY!
DON'T TRY ANYTHING SMART...
TAKE ME TO THE ROBOT, OR I'LL TURN THIS KID'S CHEST INTO A BLOODY MESS...

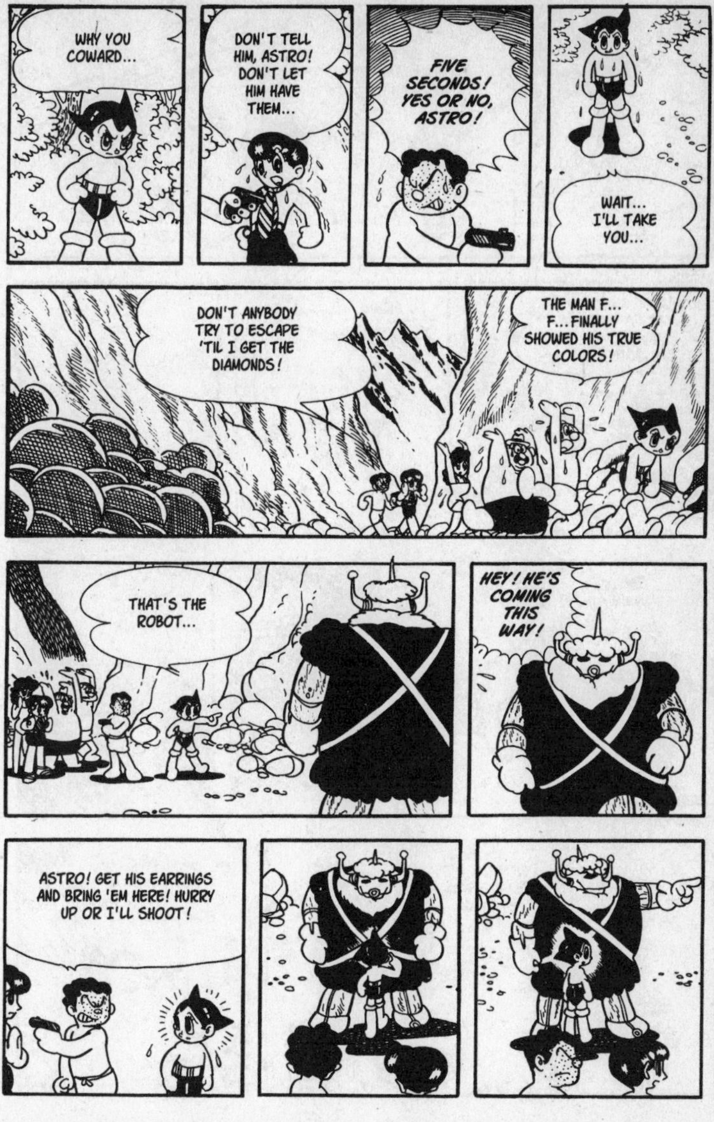
WHY YOU COWARD...
DON'T TELL HIM, ASTRO! DON'T LET HIM HAVE THEM...
FIVE SECONDS! YES OR NO, ASTRO!
WAIT... I'LL TAKE YOU...
DON'T ANYBODY TRY TO ESCAPE 'TIL I GET THE DIAMONDS!
THE MAN F... F...FINALLY SHOWED HIS TRUE COLORS!
THAT'S THE ROBOT...
HEY! HE'S COMING THIS WAY!
ASTRO! GET HIS EARRINGS AND BRING 'EM HERE! HURRY UP OR I'LL SHOOT!

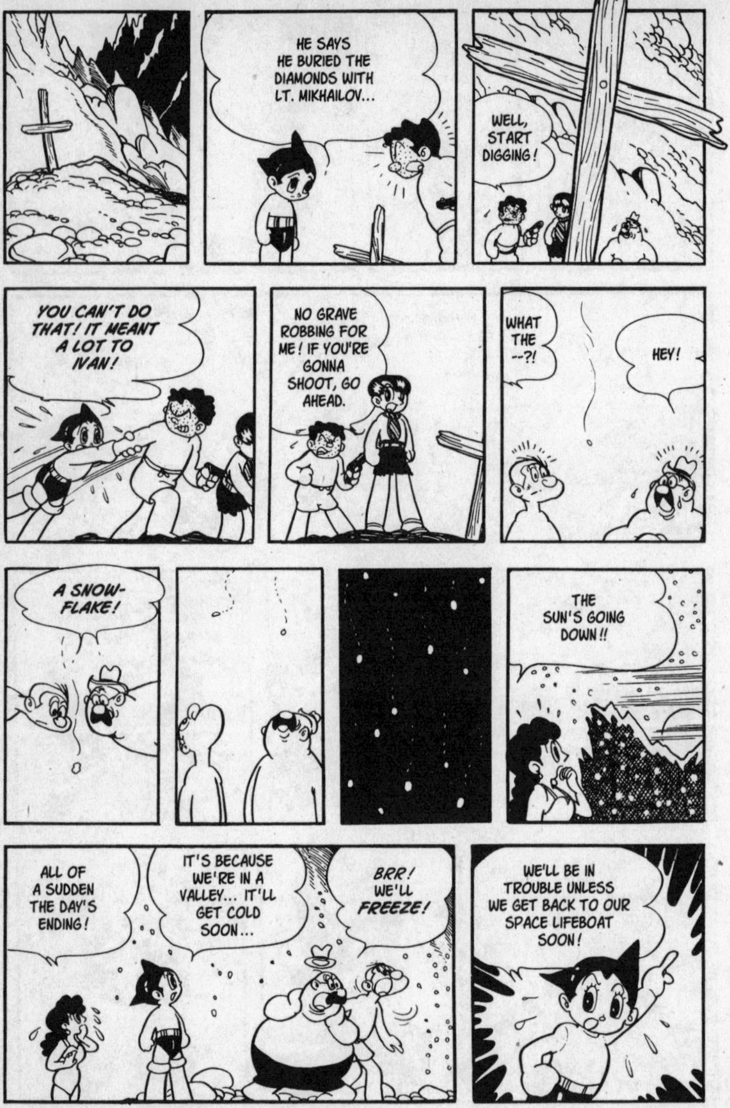

HE SAYS HE BURIED THE DIAMONDS WITH LT. MIKHAILOV...
WELL, START DIGGING!
YOU CAN'T DO THAT! IT MEANT A LOT TO IVAN!
NO GRAVE ROBBING FOR ME! IF YOU'RE GONNA SHOOT, GO AHEAD.
WHAT THE --?!
HEY!
A SNOW-FLAKE!
THE SUN'S GOING DOWN!!
ALL OF A SUDDEN THE DAY'S ENDING!
IT'S BECAUSE WE'RE IN A VALLEY... IT'LL GET COLD SOON...
BRR! WE'LL FREEZE!
WE'LL BE IN TROUBLE UNLESS WE GET BACK TO OUR SPACE LIFEBOAT SOON!

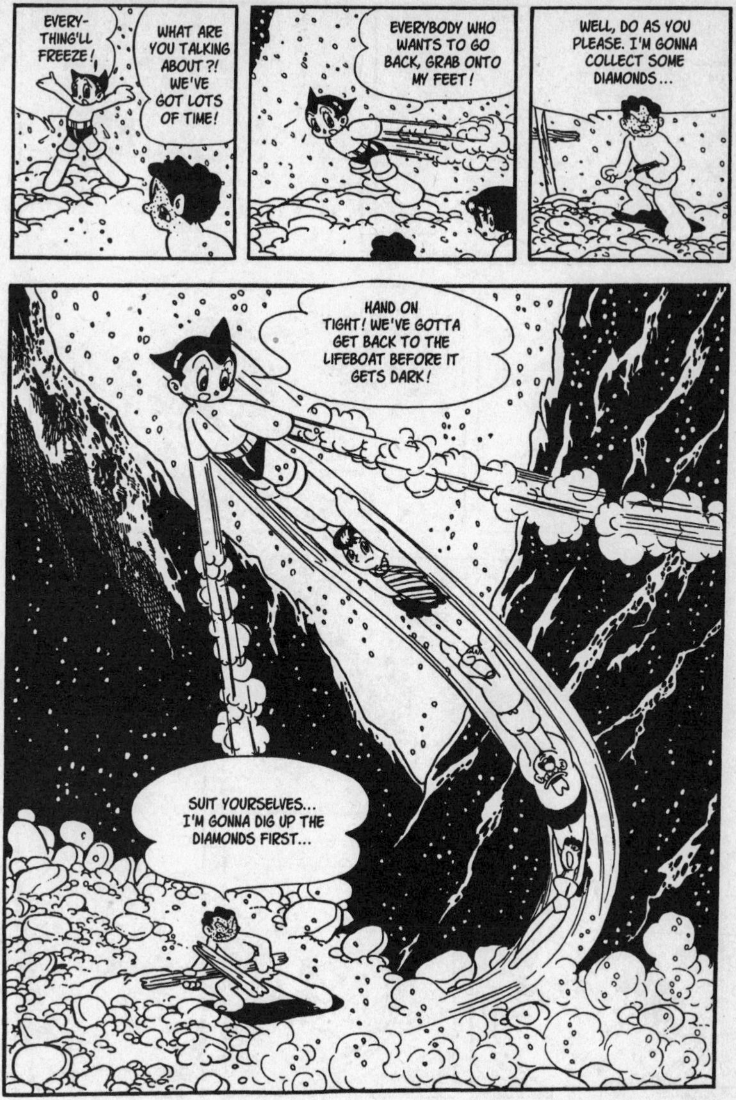
EVERY-THING'LL FREEZE!
WHAT ARE YOU TALKING ABOUT?! WE'VE GOT LOTS OF TIME!
EVERYBODY WHO WANTS TO GO BACK, GRAB ONTO MY FEET!
WELL, DO AS YOU PLEASE. I'M GONNA COLLECT SOME DIAMONDS...
HAND ON TIGHT! WE'VE GOTTA GET BACK TO THE LIFEBOAT BEFORE IT GETS DARK!
SUIT YOURSELVES... I'M GONNA DIG UP THE DIAMONDS FIRST...

HERE THEY ARE!!

THIS IS AMAZING! TWO DIAMONDS THE SIZE OF CHICKEN EGGS! I'LL BE THE RICHEST MAN ON EARTH!

ACK!!

GIRIGIRIGIRI

HEY! WHADDAYA THINK YOU'RE DOING!?

BUT I DON'T WANNA GO TO SLEEP NOW!

I CAN'T AFFORD TO STICK AROUND HERE!

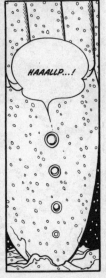

HAAALLP...!

THE SUN'S GOING DOWN!

HELP... I'M... GETTING... COLD!

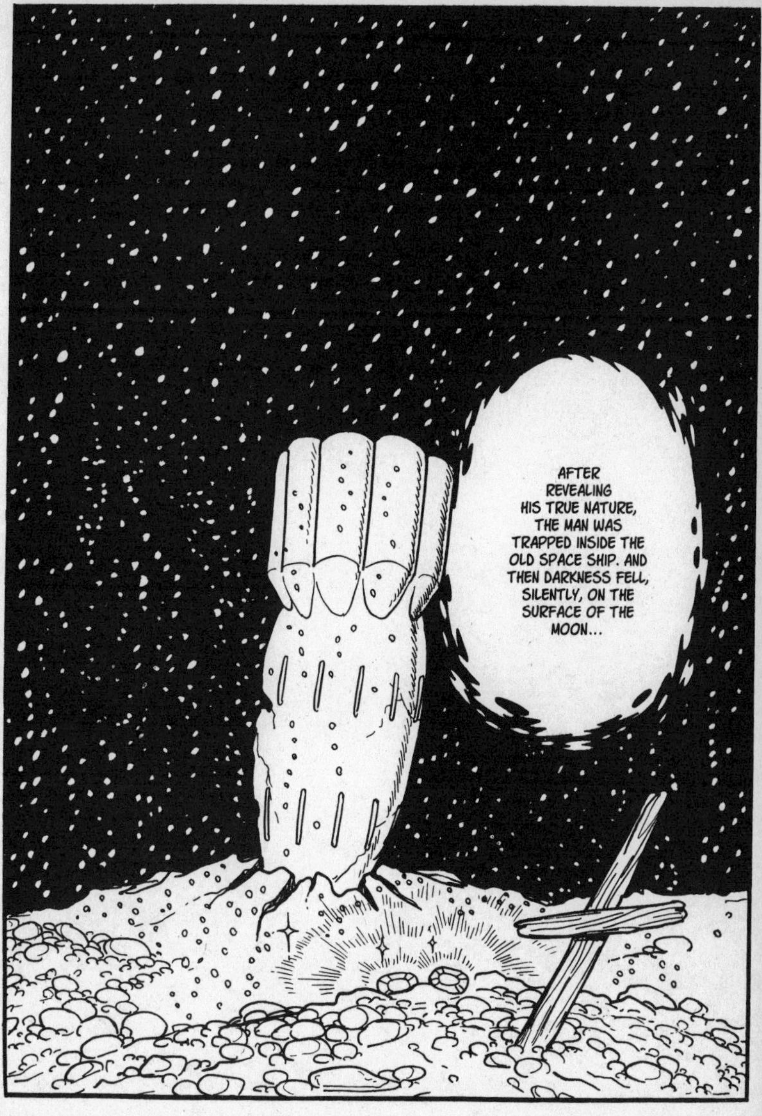
AFTER REVEALING HIS TRUE NATURE, THE MAN WAS TRAPPED INSIDE THE OLD SPACE SHIP. AND THEN DARKNESS FELL, SILENTLY, ON THE SURFACE OF THE MOON...

A DAY TO REMEMBER

First published in the special expanded 1960
summer edition of *Shonen* magazine.

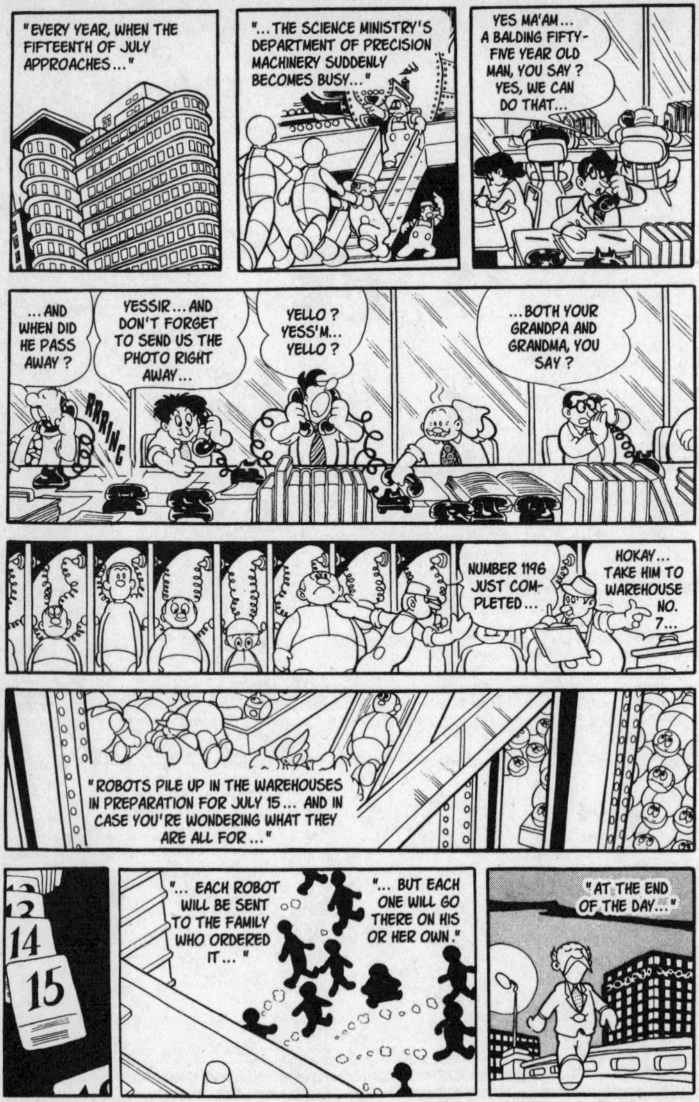
"EVERY YEAR, WHEN THE FIFTEENTH OF JULY APPROACHES..."
"...THE SCIENCE MINISTRY'S DEPARTMENT OF PRECISION MACHINERY SUDDENLY BECOMES BUSY..."
YES MA'AM... A BALDING FIFTY-FIVE YEAR OLD MAN, YOU SAY? YES, WE CAN DO THAT...
...AND WHEN DID HE PASS AWAY?
RRRING
YESSIR... AND DON'T FORGET TO SEND US THE PHOTO RIGHT AWAY...
YELLO? YESS'M... YELLO?
...BOTH YOUR GRANDPA AND GRANDMA, YOU SAY?
NUMBER 1196 JUST COMPLETED...
HOKAY... TAKE HIM TO WAREHOUSE NO. 7...
"ROBOTS PILE UP IN THE WAREHOUSES IN PREPARATION FOR JULY 15... AND IN CASE YOU'RE WONDERING WHAT THEY ARE ALL FOR..."
14
15
"... EACH ROBOT WILL BE SENT TO THE FAMILY WHO ORDERED IT..."
"... BUT EACH ONE WILL GO THERE ON HIS OR HER OWN."
"AT THE END OF THE DAY..."

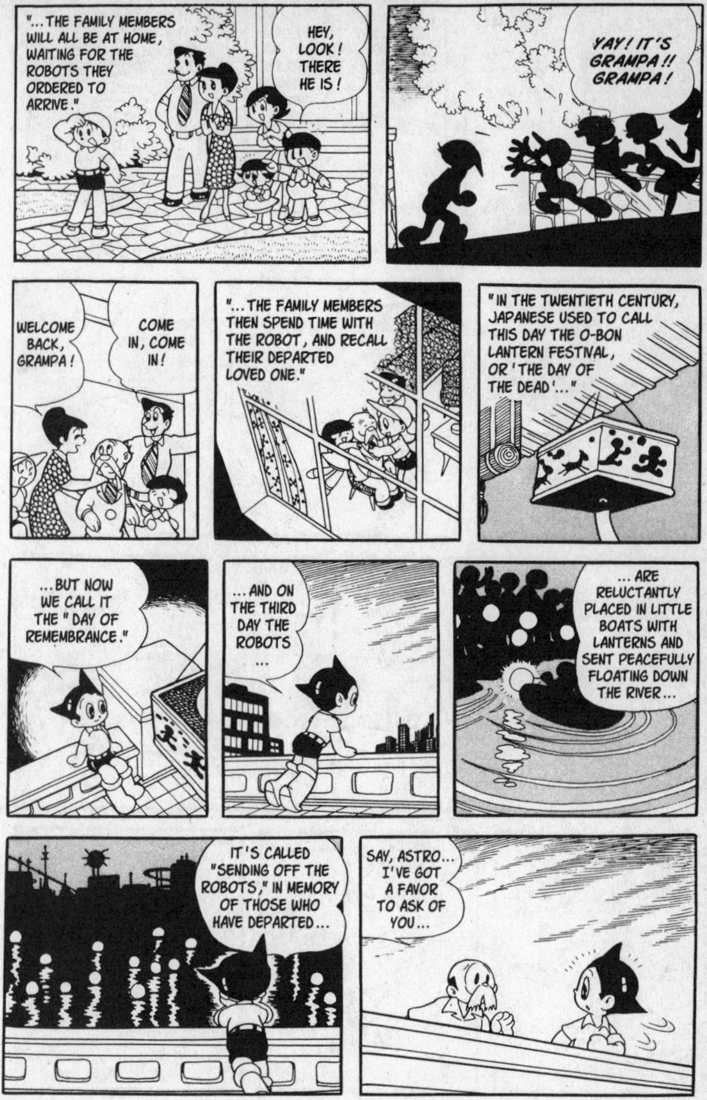
"... THE FAMILY MEMBERS WILL ALL BE AT HOME, WAITING FOR THE ROBOTS THEY ORDERED TO ARRIVE."
HEY, LOOK! THERE HE IS!
YAY! IT'S GRAMPA!! GRAMPA!
WELCOME BACK, GRAMPA!
COME IN, COME IN!
"... THE FAMILY MEMBERS THEN SPEND TIME WITH THE ROBOT, AND RECALL THEIR DEPARTED LOVED ONE."
"IN THE TWENTIETH CENTURY, JAPANESE USED TO CALL THIS DAY THE O-BON LANTERN FESTIVAL, OR 'THE DAY OF THE DEAD'..."
... BUT NOW WE CALL IT THE "DAY OF REMEMBRANCE."
... AND ON THE THIRD DAY THE ROBOTS ...
... ARE RELUCTANTLY PLACED IN LITTLE BOATS WITH LANTERNS AND SENT PEACEFULLY FLOATING DOWN THE RIVER...
IT'S CALLED "SENDING OFF THE ROBOTS," IN MEMORY OF THOSE WHO HAVE DEPARTED...
SAY, ASTRO... I'VE GOT A FAVOR TO ASK OF YOU...

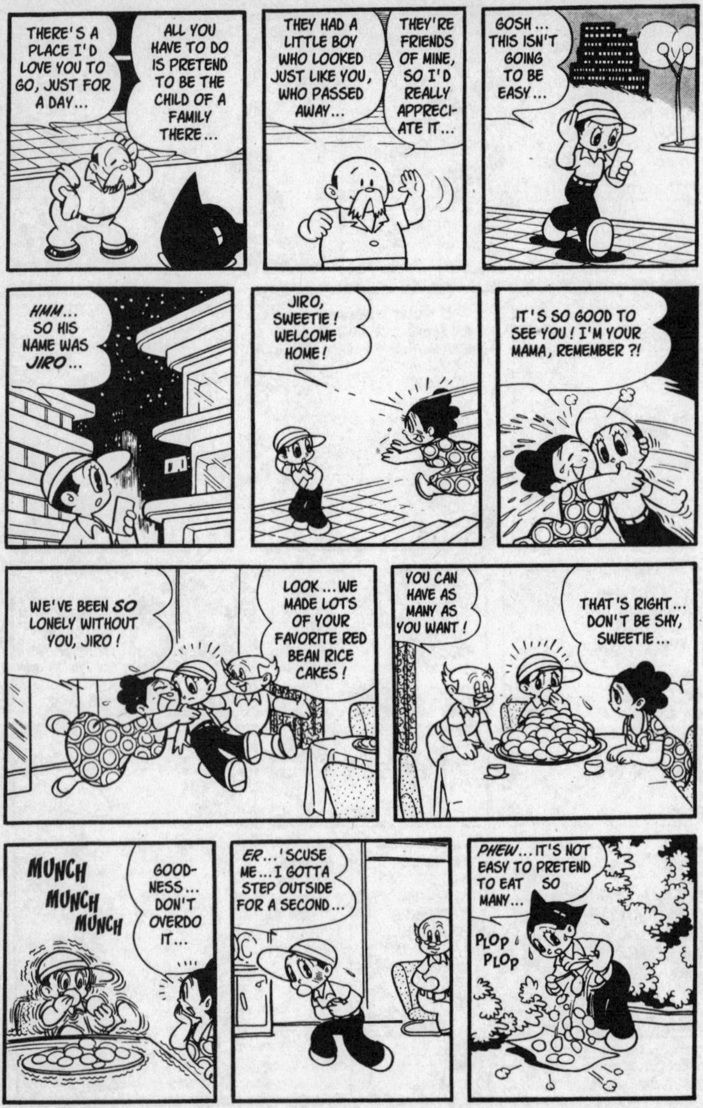
THERE'S A PLACE I'D LOVE YOU TO GO, JUST FOR A DAY...
ALL YOU HAVE TO DO IS PRETEND TO BE THE CHILD OF A FAMILY THERE...
THEY HAD A LITTLE BOY WHO LOOKED JUST LIKE YOU, WHO PASSED AWAY...
THEY'RE FRIENDS OF MINE, SO I'D REALLY APPRECI- ATE IT...
GOSH... THIS ISN'T GOING TO BE EASY...
HMM... SO HIS NAME WAS JIRO...
JIRO, SWEETIE! WELCOME HOME!
IT'S SO GOOD TO SEE YOU! I'M YOUR MAMA, REMEMBER?!
WE'VE BEEN SO LONELY WITHOUT YOU, JIRO!
LOOK... WE MADE LOTS OF YOUR FAVORITE RED BEAN RICE CAKES!
YOU CAN HAVE AS MANY AS YOU WANT!
THAT'S RIGHT... DON'T BE SHY, SWEETIE...
MUNCH MUNCH MUNCH
GOOD- NESS... DON'T OVERDO IT...
ER... 'SCUSE ME... I GOTTA STEP OUTSIDE FOR A SECOND...
PHEW... IT'S NOT EASY TO PRETEND TO EAT SO MANY...
PLOP PLOP

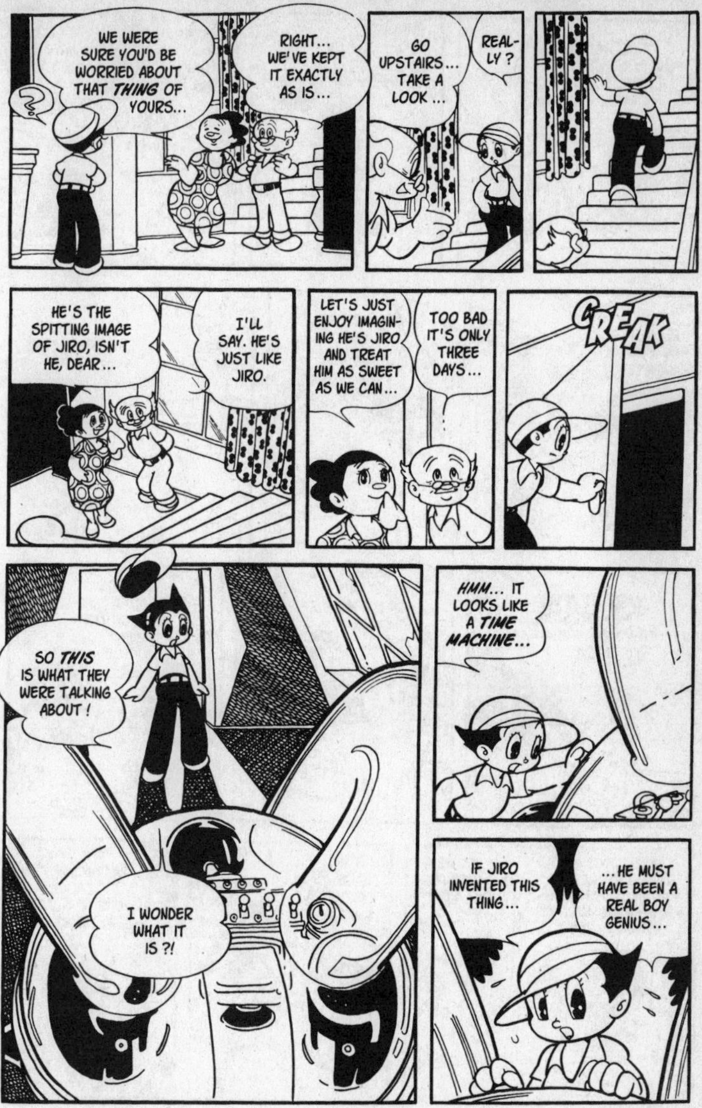
?
WE WERE SURE YOU'D BE WORRIED ABOUT THAT *THING* OF YOURS...
RIGHT... WE'VE KEPT IT EXACTLY AS IS...
GO UPSTAIRS... TAKE A LOOK...
REAL-LY ?
HE'S THE SPITTING IMAGE OF JIRO, ISN'T HE, DEAR...
I'LL SAY. HE'S JUST LIKE JIRO.
LET'S JUST ENJOY IMAGIN-ING HE'S JIRO AND TREAT HIM AS SWEET AS WE CAN...
TOO BAD IT'S ONLY THREE DAYS...
CREAK
SO *THIS* IS WHAT THEY WERE TALKING ABOUT !
I WONDER WHAT IT IS ?!
HMM... IT LOOKS LIKE A *TIME MACHINE...*
IF JIRO INVENTED THIS THING...
...HE MUST HAVE BEEN A REAL BOY GENIUS...

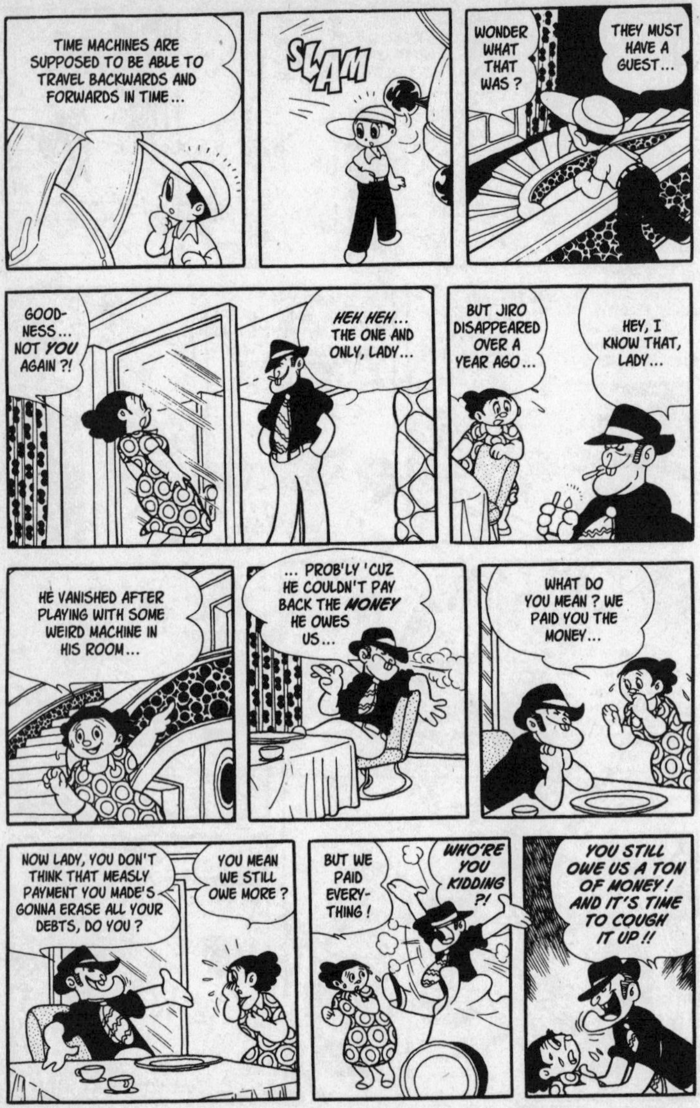
TIME MACHINES ARE SUPPOSED TO BE ABLE TO TRAVEL BACKWARDS AND FORWARDS IN TIME...
SLAM
WONDER WHAT THAT WAS ?
THEY MUST HAVE A GUEST...
GOOD-NESS... NOT YOU AGAIN ?!
HEH HEH... THE ONE AND ONLY, LADY...
BUT JIRO DISAPPEARED OVER A YEAR AGO...
HEY, I KNOW THAT, LADY...
HE VANISHED AFTER PLAYING WITH SOME WEIRD MACHINE IN HIS ROOM...
... PROB'LY 'CUZ HE COULDN'T PAY BACK THE MONEY HE OWES US...
WHAT DO YOU MEAN ? WE PAID YOU THE MONEY...
NOW LADY, YOU DON'T THINK THAT MEASLY PAYMENT YOU MADE'S GONNA ERASE ALL YOUR DEBTS, DO YOU ?
YOU MEAN WE STILL OWE MORE ?
BUT WE PAID EVERY-THING !
WHO'RE YOU KIDDING ?!
YOU STILL OWE US A TON OF MONEY ! AND IT'S TIME TO COUGH IT UP !!

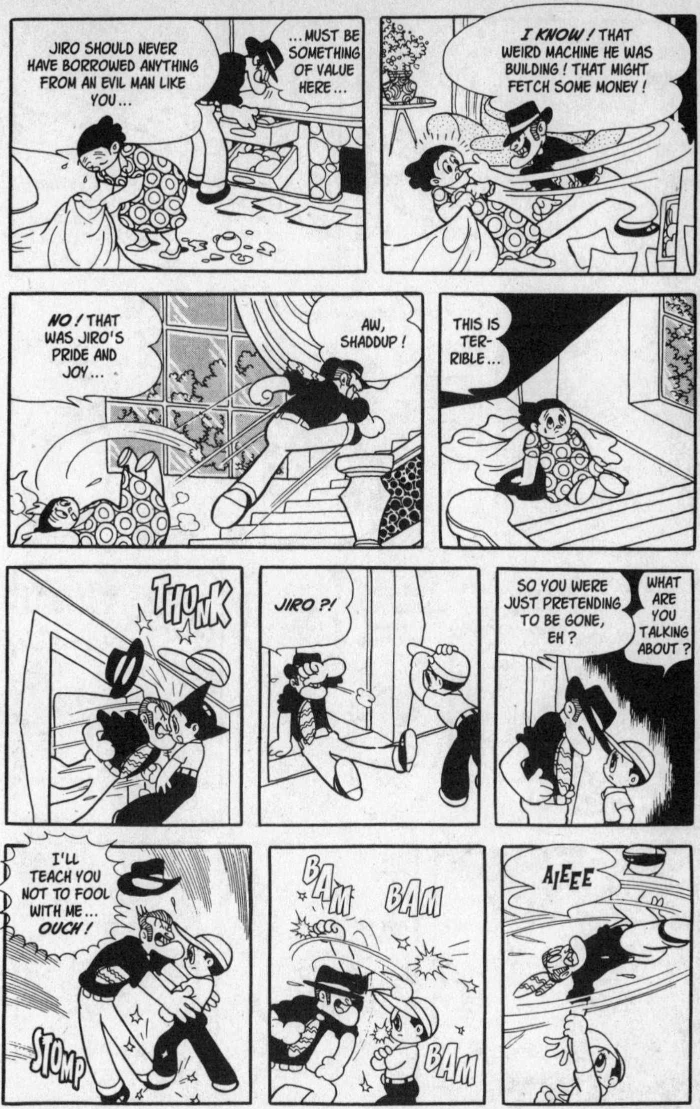
JIRO SHOULD NEVER HAVE BORROWED ANYTHING FROM AN EVIL MAN LIKE YOU...
...MUST BE SOMETHING OF VALUE HERE...
I KNOW! THAT WEIRD MACHINE HE WAS BUILDING! THAT MIGHT FETCH SOME MONEY!
NO! THAT WAS JIRO'S PRIDE AND JOY...
AW, SHADDUP!
THIS IS TER-RIBLE...
THUNK
JIRO?!
SO YOU WERE JUST PRETENDING TO BE GONE, EH?
WHAT ARE YOU TALKING ABOUT?
I'LL TEACH YOU NOT TO FOOL WITH ME... OUCH!
STOMP
BAM
BAM
BAM
AIEEE

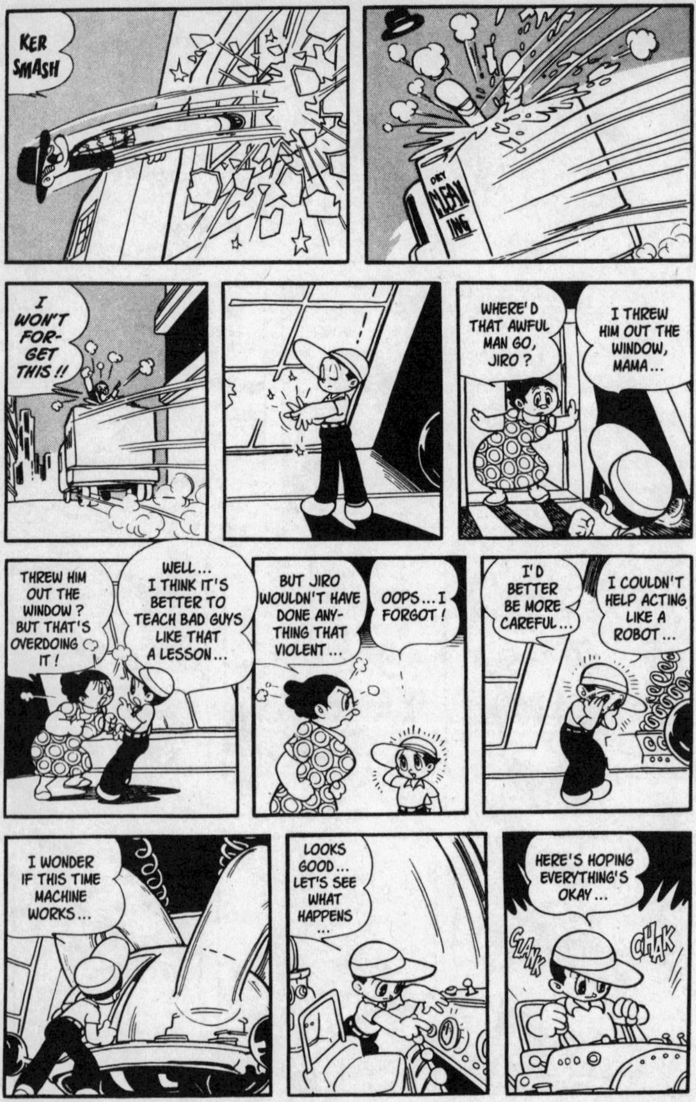
KER SMASH
DRY CLEAN ING
I WON'T FOR-GET THIS !!
WHERE'D THAT AWFUL MAN GO, JIRO ?
I THREW HIM OUT THE WINDOW, MAMA...
THREW HIM OUT THE WINDOW ? BUT THAT'S OVERDOING IT !
WELL... I THINK IT'S BETTER TO TEACH BAD GUYS LIKE THAT A LESSON...
BUT JIRO WOULDN'T HAVE DONE ANY-THING THAT VIOLENT...
OOPS... I FORGOT !
I'D BETTER BE MORE CAREFUL...
I COULDN'T HELP ACTING LIKE A ROBOT...
I WONDER IF THIS TIME MACHINE WORKS...
LOOKS GOOD... LET'S SEE WHAT HAPPENS...
HERE'S HOPING EVERYTHING'S OKAY...
CLANK
CHAK

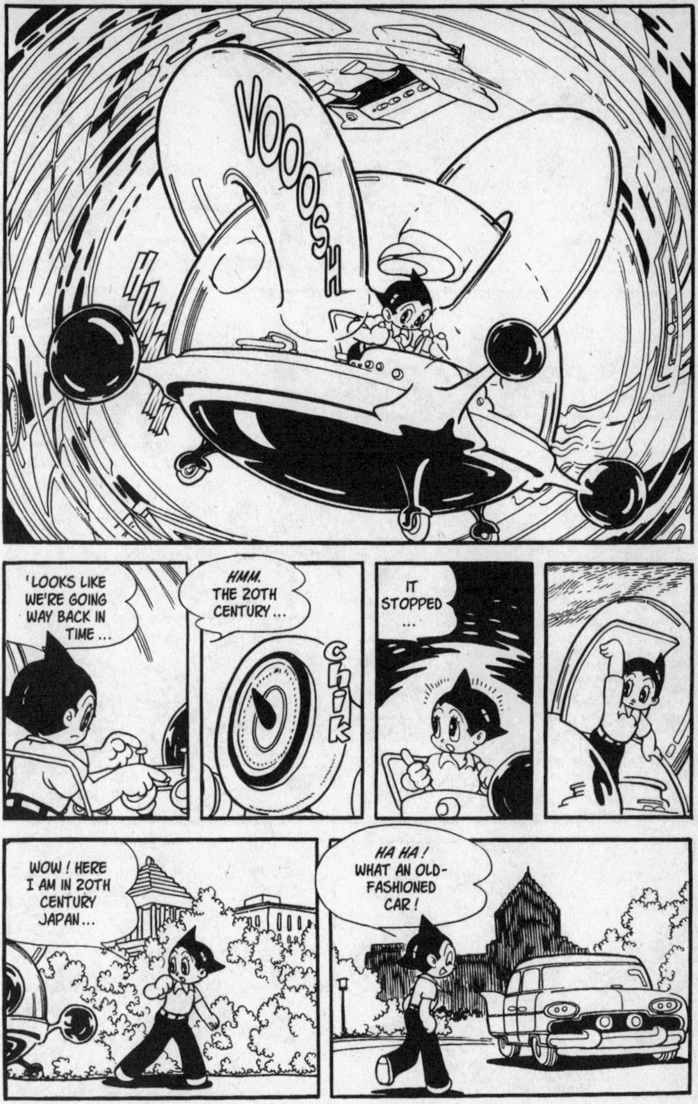

VOOOOSH
HUMMMM
'LOOKS LIKE WE'RE GOING WAY BACK IN TIME ...
HMM. THE 20TH CENTURY ...
Chik
IT STOPPED ...
WOW ! HERE I AM IN 20TH CENTURY JAPAN ...
HA HA ! WHAT AN OLD-FASHIONED CAR !

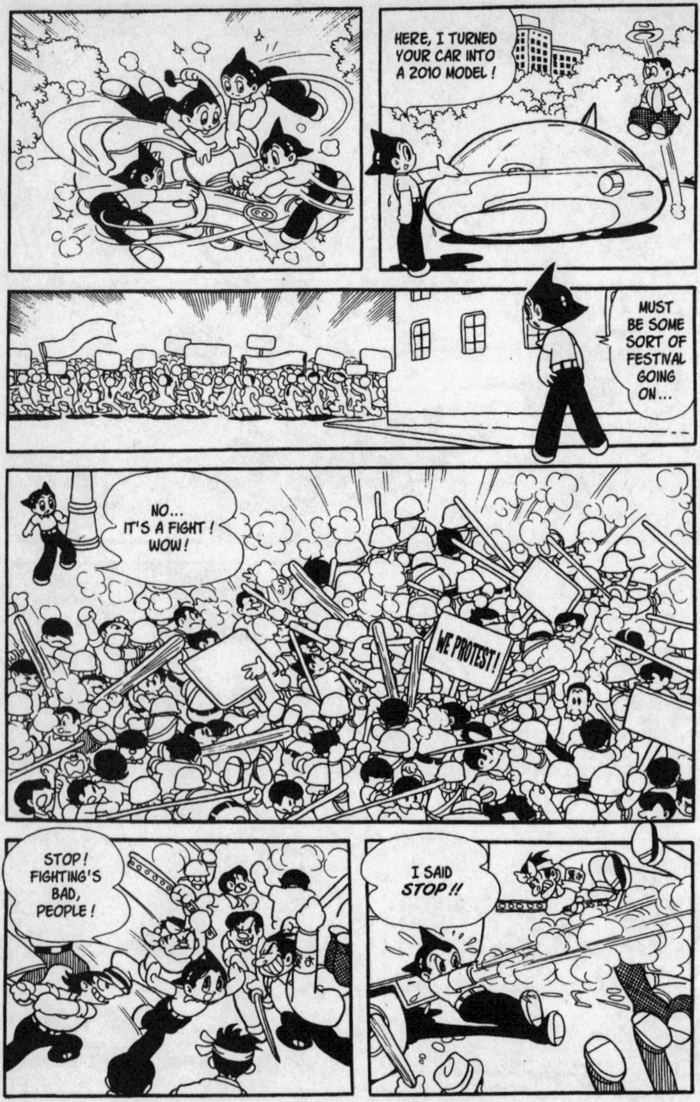

HERE, I TURNED YOUR CAR INTO A 2010 MODEL!
MUST BE SOME SORT OF FESTIVAL GOING ON...
NO... IT'S A FIGHT! WOW!
WE PROTEST!
STOP! FIGHTING'S BAD, PEOPLE!
I SAID STOP!!

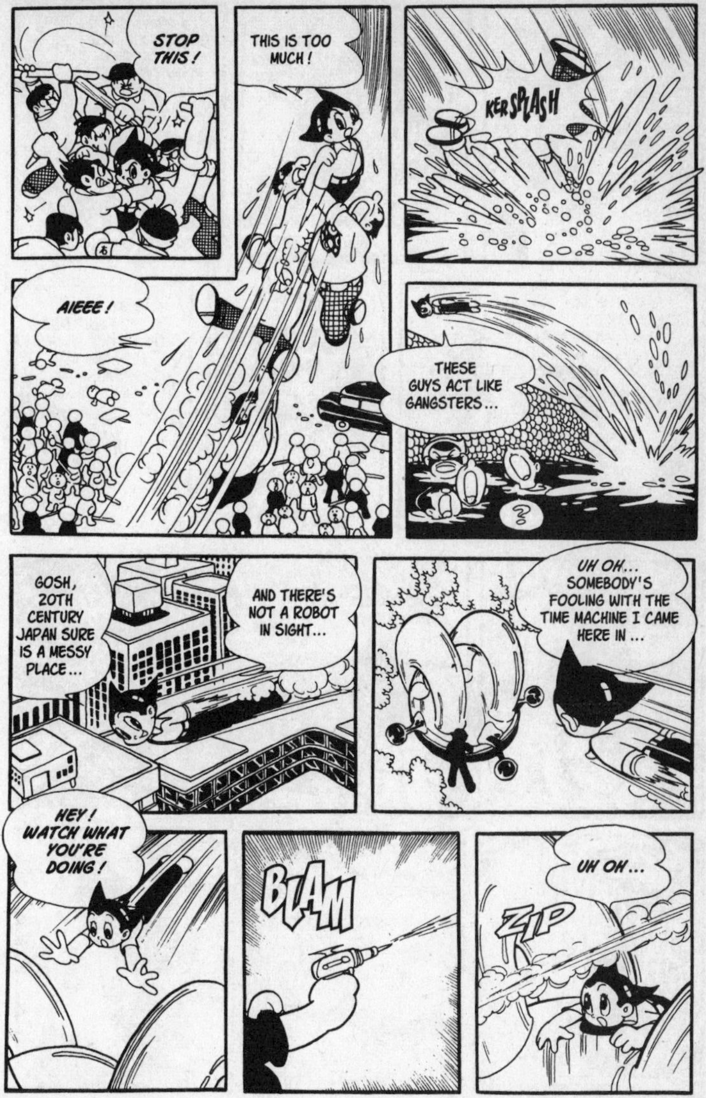
STOP THIS!
THIS IS TOO MUCH!
KERSPLASH
AIEEE!
THESE GUYS ACT LIKE GANGSTERS...
?
GOSH, 20TH CENTURY JAPAN SURE IS A MESSY PLACE...
AND THERE'S NOT A ROBOT IN SIGHT...
UH OH... SOMEBODY'S FOOLING WITH THE TIME MACHINE I CAME HERE IN ...
HEY! WATCH WHAT YOU'RE DOING!
BLAM
ZIP
UH OH...

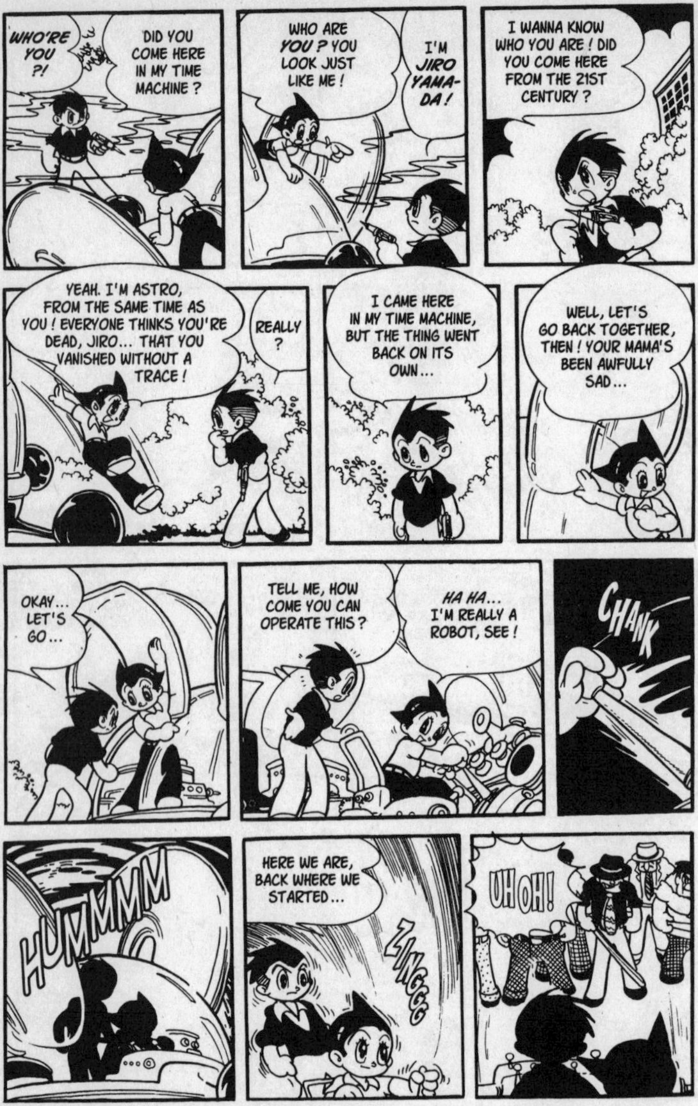
WHO'RE YOU ?!
DID YOU COME HERE IN MY TIME MACHINE ?
WHO ARE YOU ? YOU LOOK JUST LIKE ME !
I'M JIRO YAMA-DA !
I WANNA KNOW WHO YOU ARE ! DID YOU COME HERE FROM THE 21ST CENTURY ?
YEAH. I'M ASTRO, FROM THE SAME TIME AS YOU ! EVERYONE THINKS YOU'RE DEAD, JIRO... THAT YOU VANISHED WITHOUT A TRACE !
REALLY ?
I CAME HERE IN MY TIME MACHINE, BUT THE THING WENT BACK ON ITS OWN...
WELL, LET'S GO BACK TOGETHER, THEN ! YOUR MAMA'S BEEN AWFULLY SAD...
OKAY... LET'S GO...
TELL ME, HOW COME YOU CAN OPERATE THIS ?
HA HA... I'M REALLY A ROBOT, SEE !
CHANK
HUMMMM
HERE WE ARE, BACK WHERE WE STARTED...
ZINGGG
UH OH!

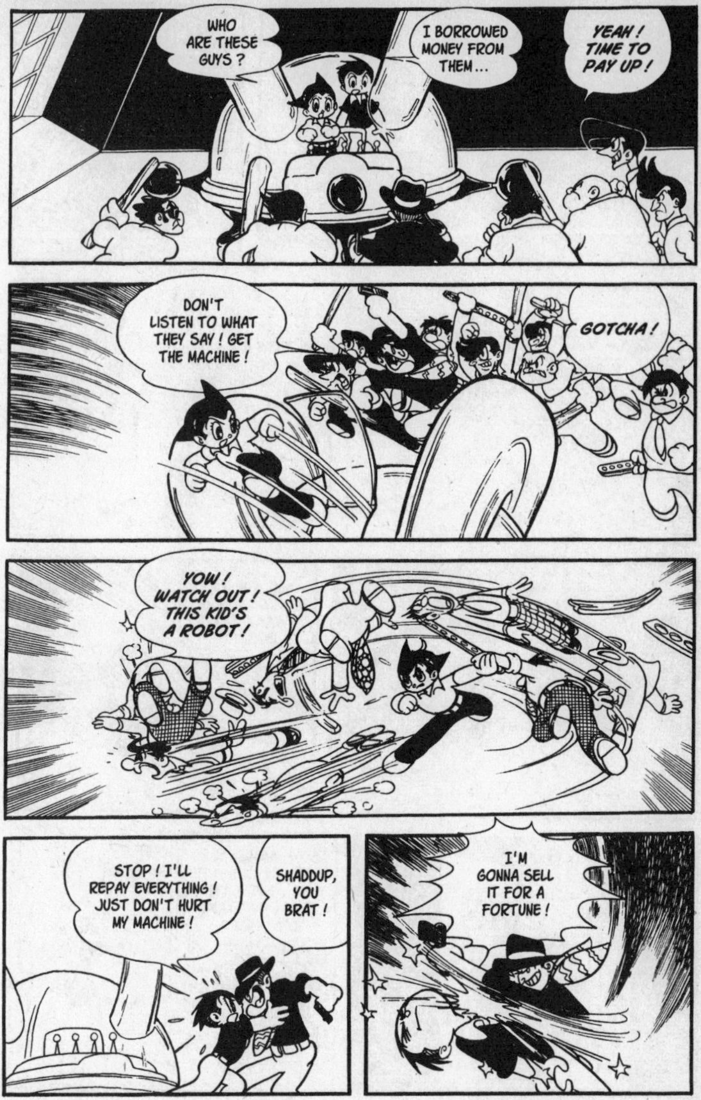
WHO ARE THESE GUYS ?
I BORROWED MONEY FROM THEM ...
YEAH ! TIME TO PAY UP !
DON'T LISTEN TO WHAT THEY SAY ! GET THE MACHINE !
GOTCHA !
YOW ! WATCH OUT ! THIS KID'S A ROBOT !
STOP ! I'LL REPAY EVERYTHING ! JUST DON'T HURT MY MACHINE !
SHADDUP, YOU BRAT !
I'M GONNA SELL IT FOR A FORTUNE !

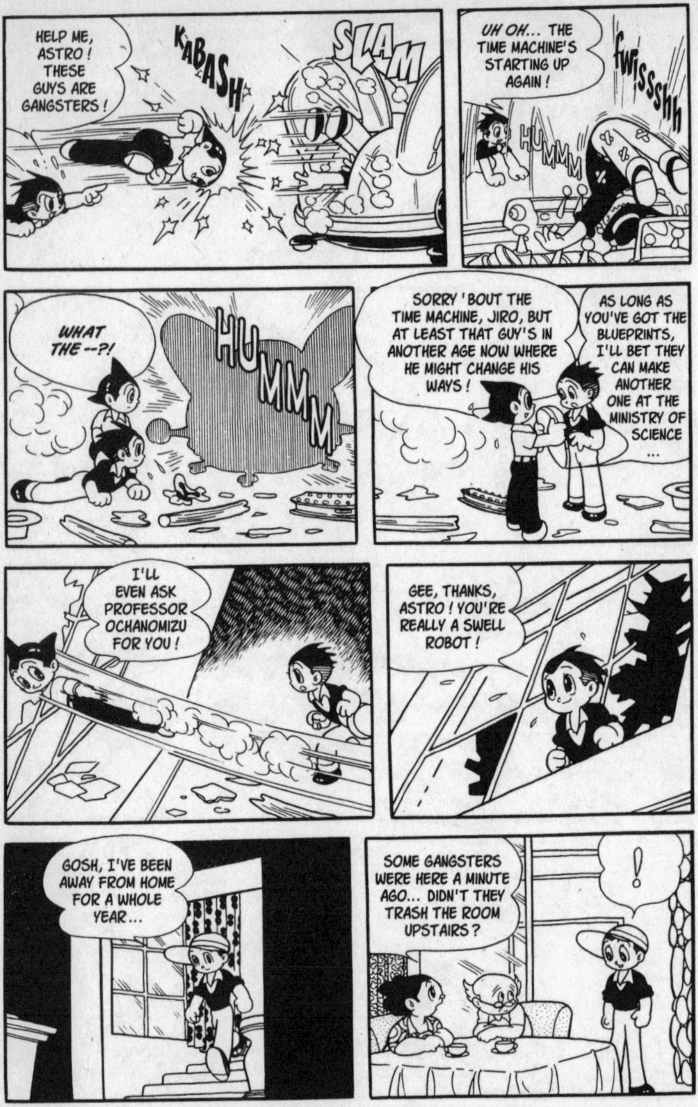
HELP ME, ASTRO! THESE GUYS ARE GANGSTERS!
KABASH
SLAM
UH OH... THE TIME MACHINE'S STARTING UP AGAIN!
HUMMM
fwissshh
WHAT THE --?!
HUMMMM
SORRY 'BOUT THE TIME MACHINE, JIRO, BUT AT LEAST THAT GUY'S IN ANOTHER AGE NOW WHERE HE MIGHT CHANGE HIS WAYS!
AS LONG AS YOU'VE GOT THE BLUEPRINTS, I'LL BET THEY CAN MAKE ANOTHER ONE AT THE MINISTRY OF SCIENCE ...
I'LL EVEN ASK PROFESSOR OCHANOMIZU FOR YOU!
GEE, THANKS, ASTRO! YOU'RE REALLY A SWELL ROBOT!
GOSH, I'VE BEEN AWAY FROM HOME FOR A WHOLE YEAR...
SOME GANGSTERS WERE HERE A MINUTE AGO... DIDN'T THEY TRASH THE ROOM UPSTAIRS?
!

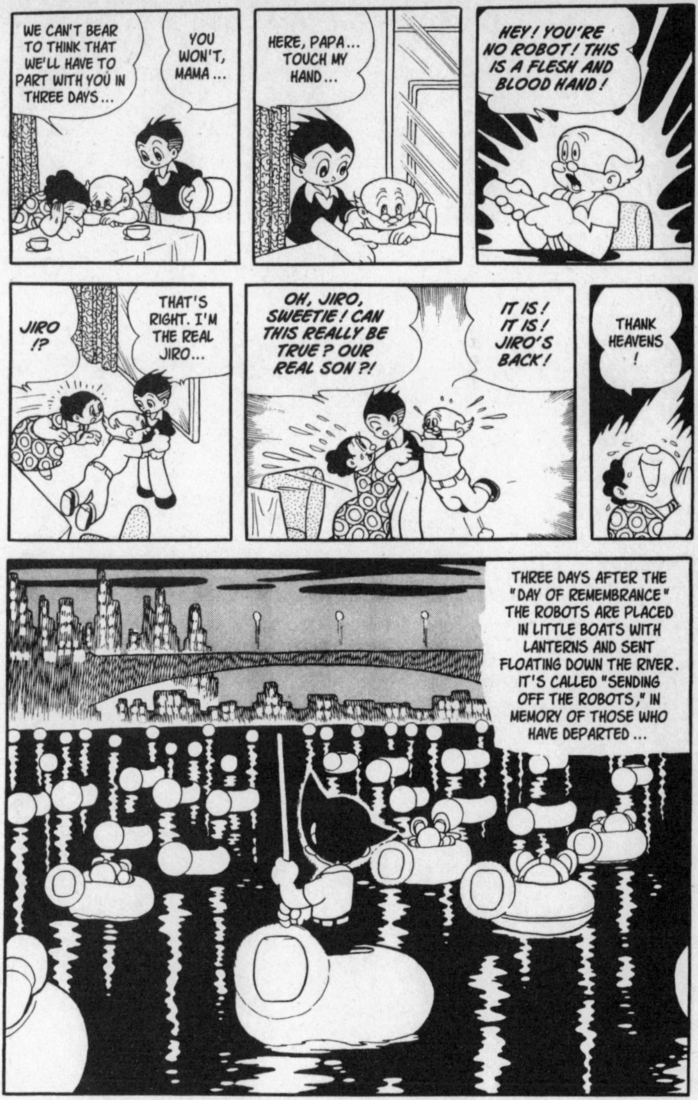
WE CAN'T BEAR TO THINK THAT WE'LL HAVE TO PART WITH YOU IN THREE DAYS...
YOU WON'T, MAMA ...
HERE, PAPA... TOUCH MY HAND...
HEY! YOU'RE NO ROBOT! THIS IS A FLESH AND BLOOD HAND!
JIRO !?
THAT'S RIGHT. I'M THE REAL JIRO...
OH, JIRO, SWEETIE! CAN THIS REALLY BE TRUE? OUR REAL SON?!
IT IS! IT IS! JIRO'S BACK!
THANK HEAVENS !
THREE DAYS AFTER THE "DAY OF REMEMBRANCE" THE ROBOTS ARE PLACED IN LITTLE BOATS WITH LANTERNS AND SENT FLOATING DOWN THE RIVER. IT'S CALLED "SENDING OFF THE ROBOTS," IN MEMORY OF THOSE WHO HAVE DEPARTED ...

GHOST MANUFACTURING MACHINE

First published in a 1957 supplement edition of *Shonen* magazine.

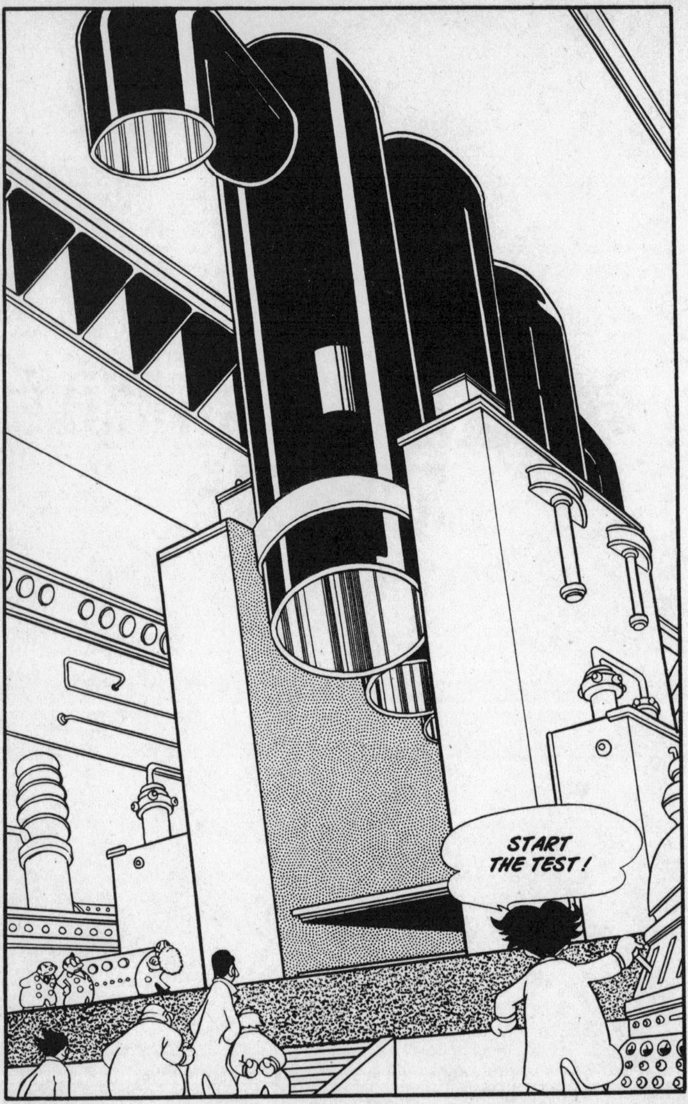
START THE TEST!

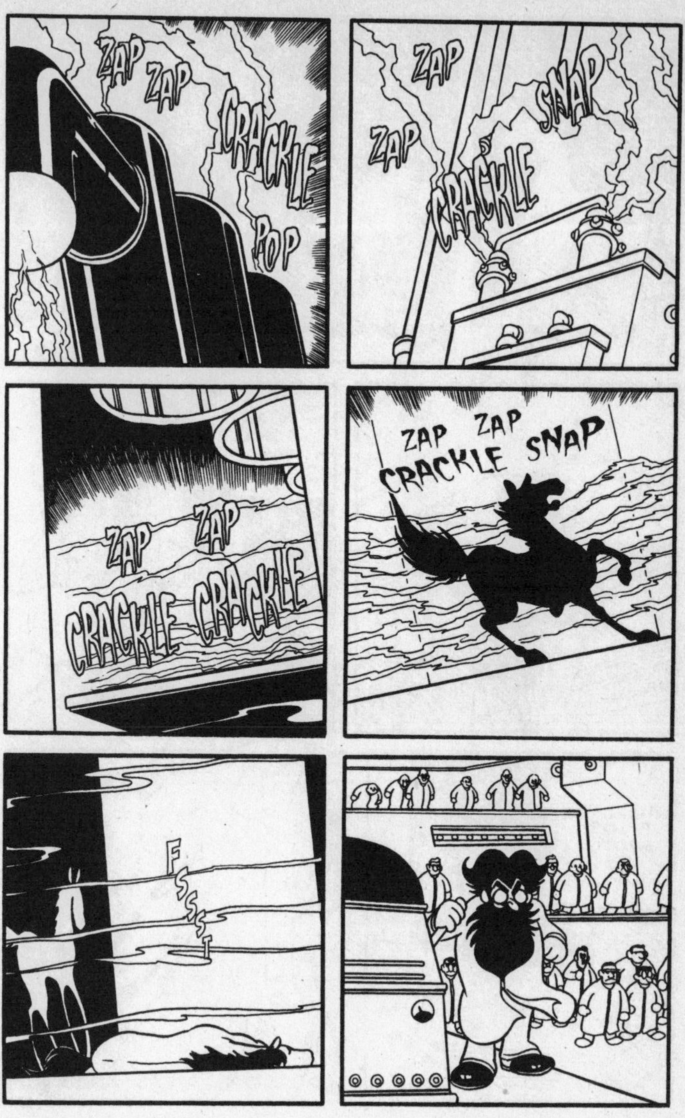
ZAP ZAP
CRACKLE
POP
ZAP
ZAP
CRACKLE
SNAP
ZAP ZAP
CRACKLE CRACKLE
ZAP ZAP
CRACKLE SNAP
FSSST

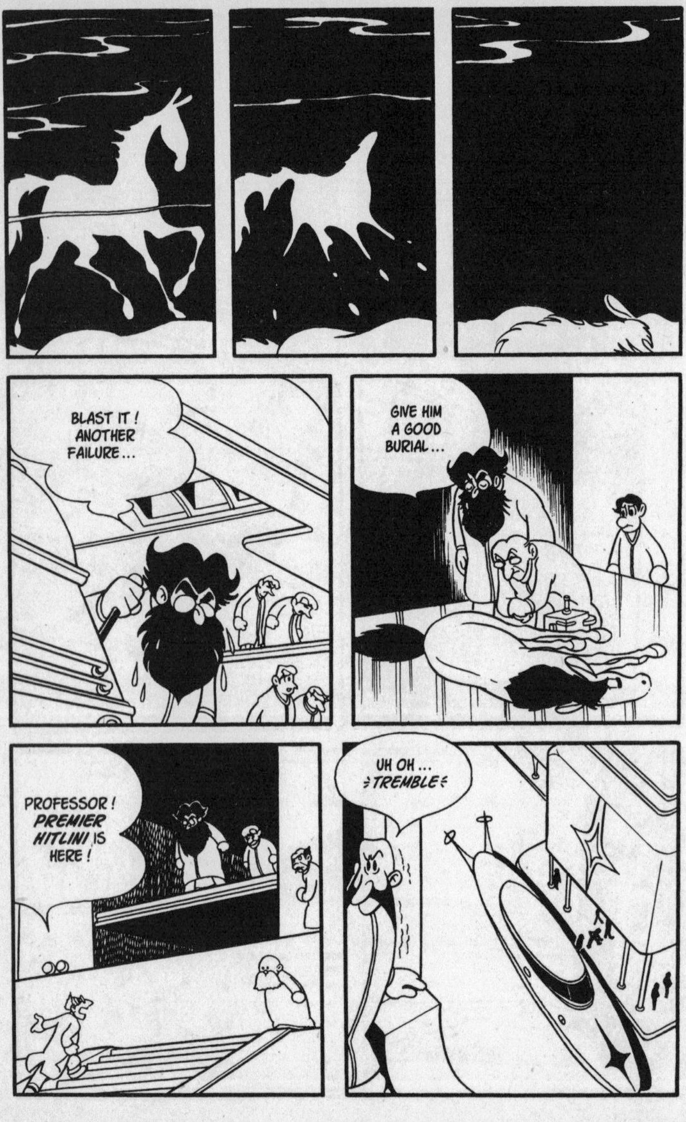
BLAST IT ! ANOTHER FAILURE ...
GIVE HIM A GOOD BURIAL ...
PROFESSOR ! PREMIER HITLINI IS HERE !
UH OH ... TREMBLE

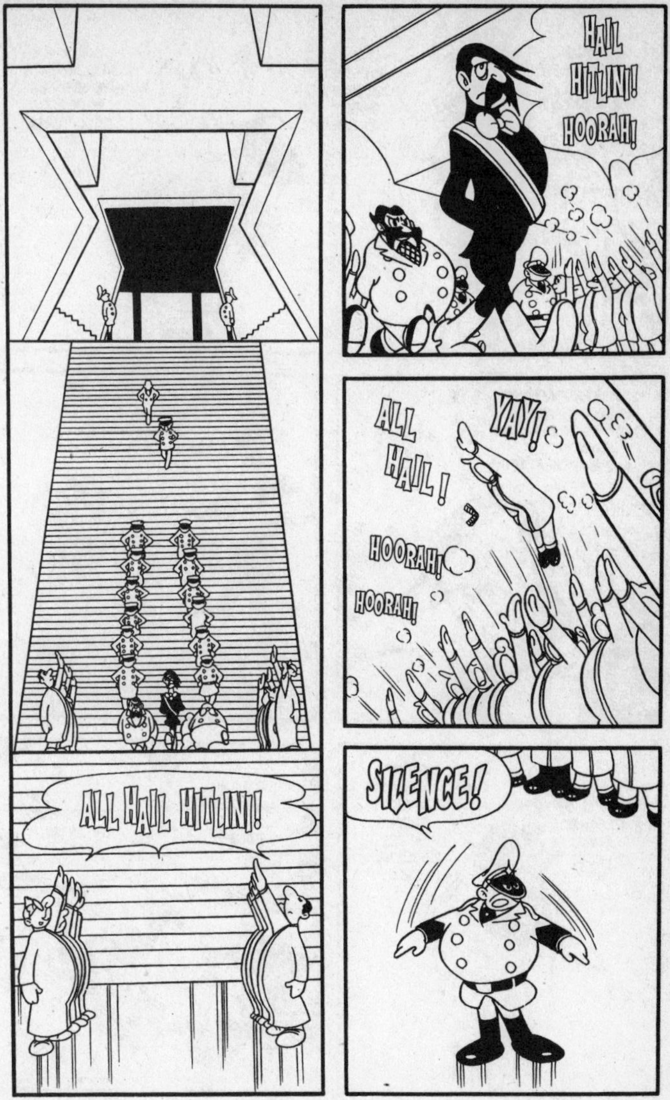
ALL HAIL HITLINI!
HAIL HITLINI! HOORAH!
ALL HAIL!
YAY!
HOORAH!
HOORAH!
SILENCE!

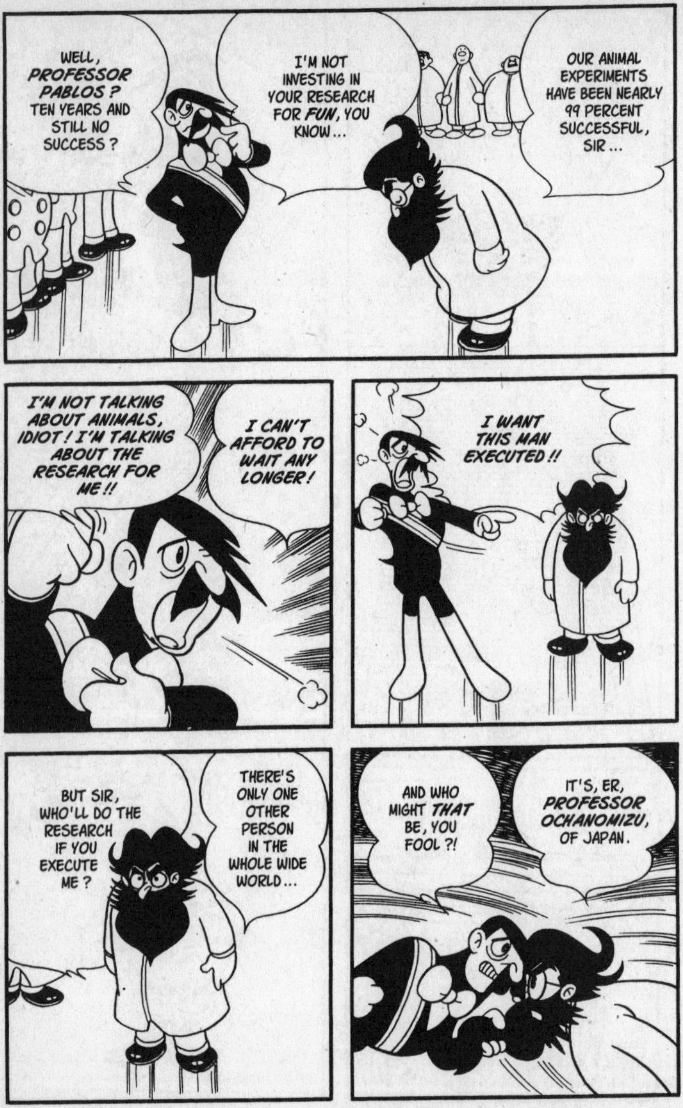
WELL, PROFESSOR PABLOS? TEN YEARS AND STILL NO SUCCESS?
I'M NOT INVESTING IN YOUR RESEARCH FOR FUN, YOU KNOW...
OUR ANIMAL EXPERIMENTS HAVE BEEN NEARLY 99 PERCENT SUCCESSFUL, SIR...
I'M NOT TALKING ABOUT ANIMALS, IDIOT! I'M TALKING ABOUT THE RESEARCH FOR ME!!
I CAN'T AFFORD TO WAIT ANY LONGER!
I WANT THIS MAN EXECUTED!!
BUT SIR, WHO'LL DO THE RESEARCH IF YOU EXECUTE ME?
THERE'S ONLY ONE OTHER PERSON IN THE WHOLE WIDE WORLD...
AND WHO MIGHT THAT BE, YOU FOOL?!
IT'S, ER, PROFESSOR OCHANOMIZU, OF JAPAN.

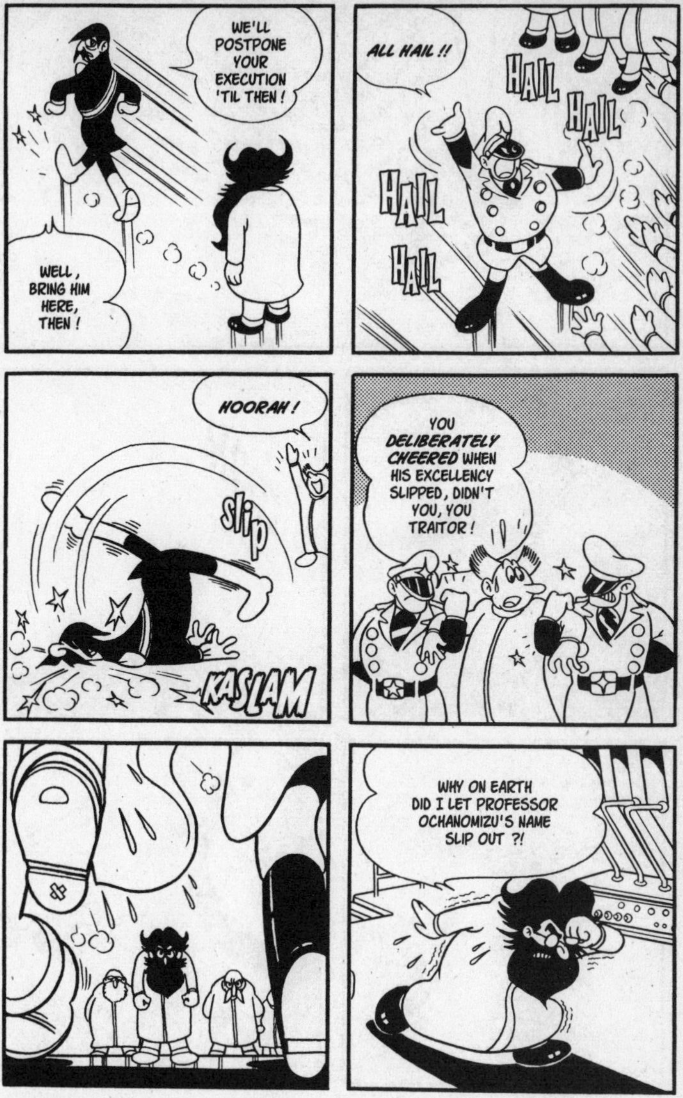
WE'LL POSTPONE YOUR EXECUTION 'TIL THEN !
WELL, BRING HIM HERE, THEN !
ALL HAIL !!
HAIL
HAIL
HAIL
HAIL
HOORAH !
slip
KASLAM
YOU DELIBERATELY CHEERED WHEN HIS EXCELLENCY SLIPPED, DIDN'T YOU, YOU TRAITOR !
WHY ON EARTH DID I LET PROFESSOR OCHANOMIZU'S NAME SLIP OUT ?!

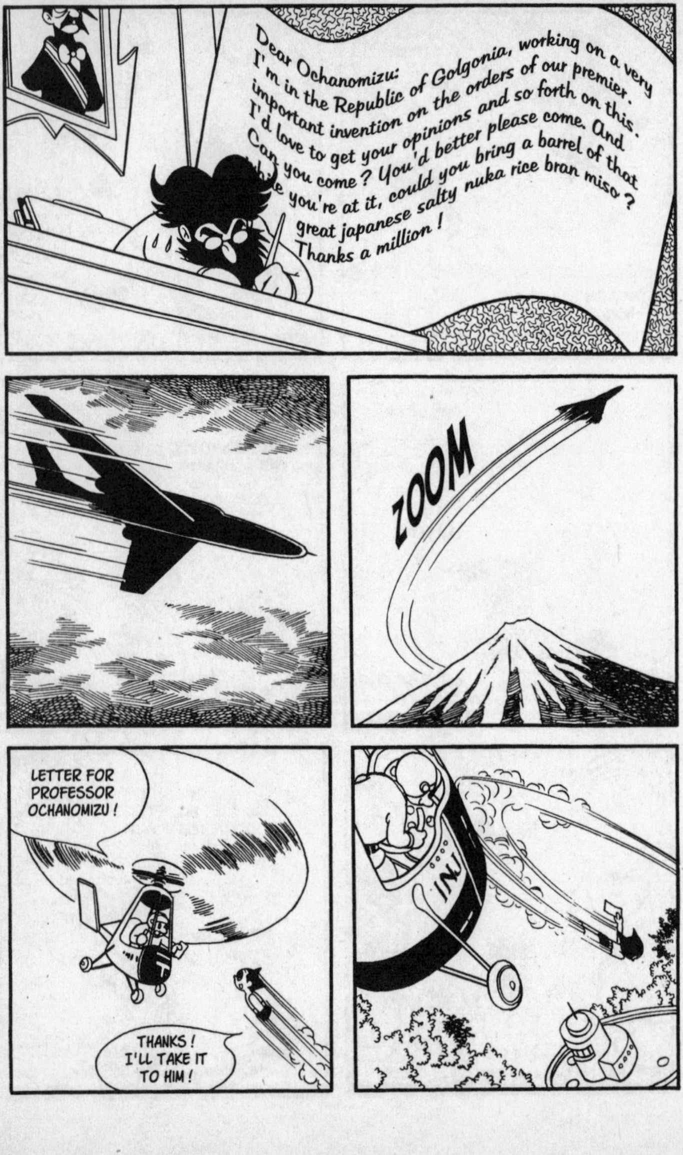
Dear Ochanomizu:
I'm in the Republic of Golgonia, working on a very important invention on the orders of our premier.
I'd love to get your opinions and so forth on this.
Can you come? You'd better please come. And while you're at it, could you bring a barrel of that great japanese salty nuka rice bran miso?
Thanks a million!
ZOOM
LETTER FOR PROFESSOR OCHANOMIZU!
THANKS! I'LL TAKE IT TO HIM!
INU

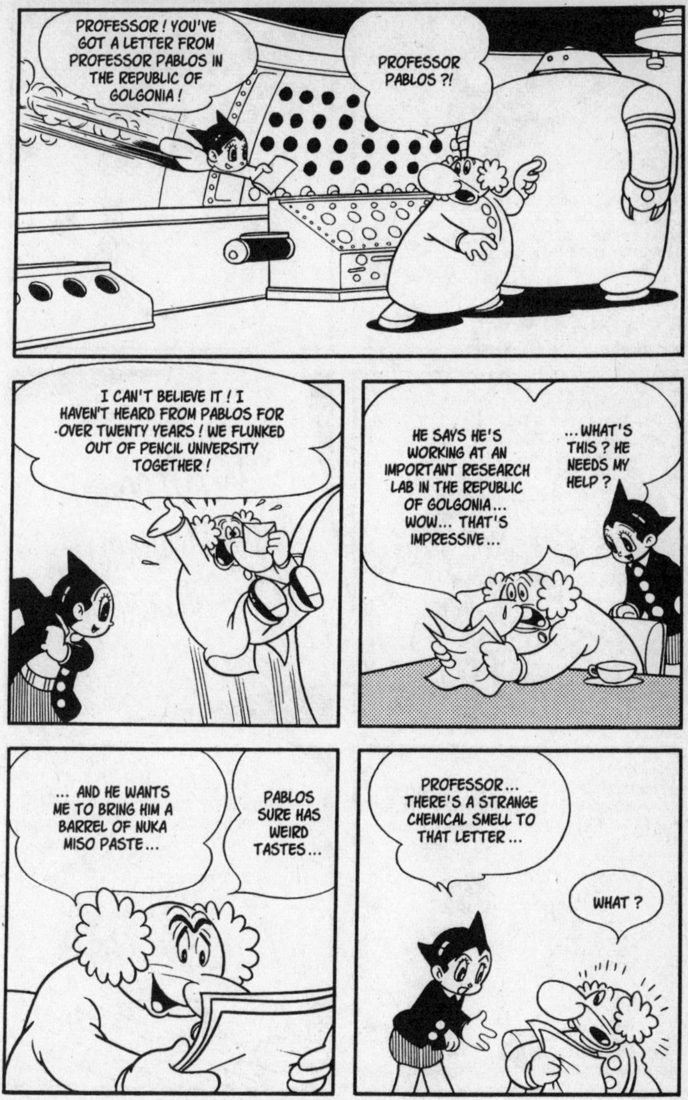
PROFESSOR! YOU'VE GOT A LETTER FROM PROFESSOR PABLOS IN THE REPUBLIC OF GOLGONIA!
PROFESSOR PABLOS?!
I CAN'T BELIEVE IT! I HAVEN'T HEARD FROM PABLOS FOR OVER TWENTY YEARS! WE FLUNKED OUT OF PENCIL UNIVERSITY TOGETHER!
HE SAYS HE'S WORKING AT AN IMPORTANT RESEARCH LAB IN THE REPUBLIC OF GOLGONIA... WOW... THAT'S IMPRESSIVE...
...WHAT'S THIS? HE NEEDS MY HELP?
... AND HE WANTS ME TO BRING HIM A BARREL OF NUKA MISO PASTE...
PABLOS SURE HAS WEIRD TASTES...
PROFESSOR... THERE'S A STRANGE CHEMICAL SMELL TO THAT LETTER...
WHAT?

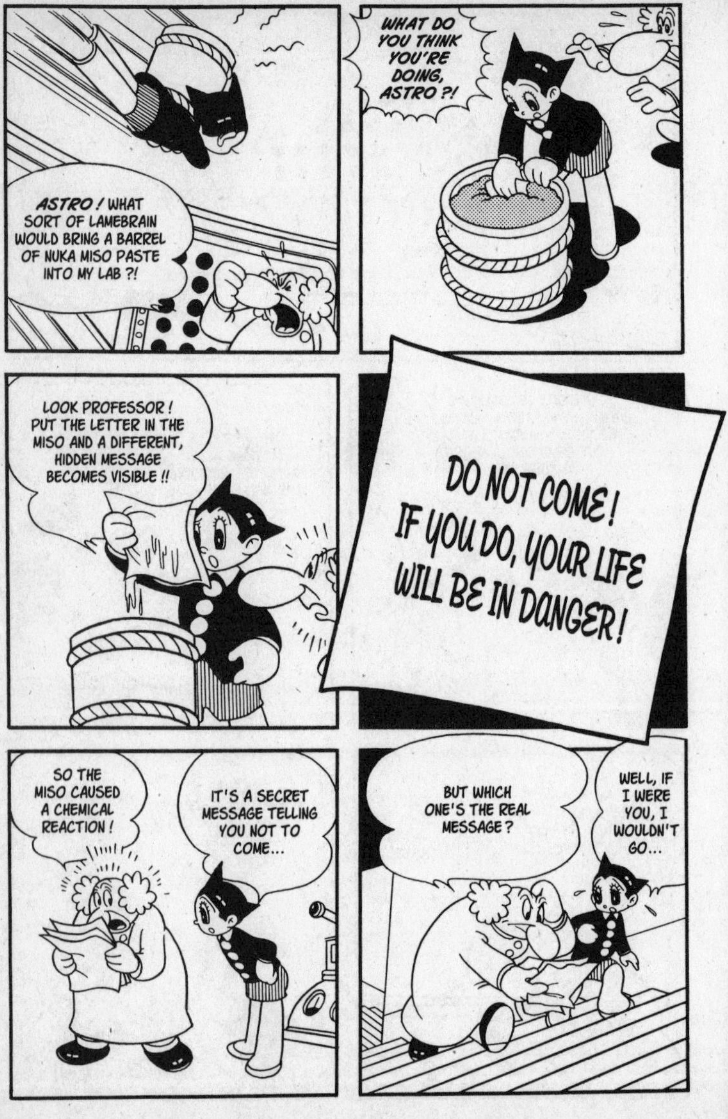
ASTRO ! WHAT SORT OF LAMEBRAIN WOULD BRING A BARREL OF NUKA MISO PASTE INTO MY LAB ?!
WHAT DO YOU THINK YOU'RE DOING, ASTRO ?!
LOOK PROFESSOR ! PUT THE LETTER IN THE MISO AND A DIFFERENT, HIDDEN MESSAGE BECOMES VISIBLE !!
DO NOT COME ! IF YOU DO, YOUR LIFE WILL BE IN DANGER !
SO THE MISO CAUSED A CHEMICAL REACTION !
IT'S A SECRET MESSAGE TELLING YOU NOT TO COME...
BUT WHICH ONE'S THE REAL MESSAGE ?
WELL, IF I WERE YOU, I WOULDN'T GO...

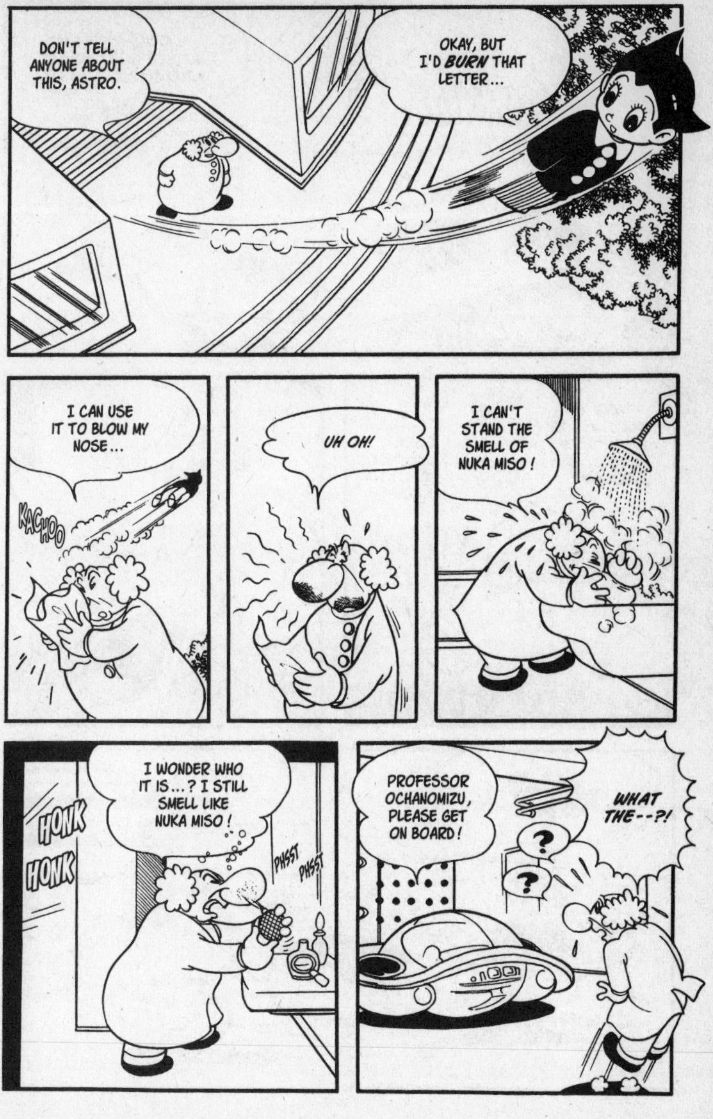
DON'T TELL ANYONE ABOUT THIS, ASTRO.
OKAY, BUT I'D BURN THAT LETTER...
I CAN USE IT TO BLOW MY NOSE...
KACHOO
UH OH!
I CAN'T STAND THE SMELL OF NUKA MISO!
HONK
HONK
I WONDER WHO IT IS...? I STILL SMELL LIKE NUKA MISO!
PHSST
PHSST
PROFESSOR OCHANOMIZU, PLEASE GET ON BOARD!
?
?
WHAT THE--?!

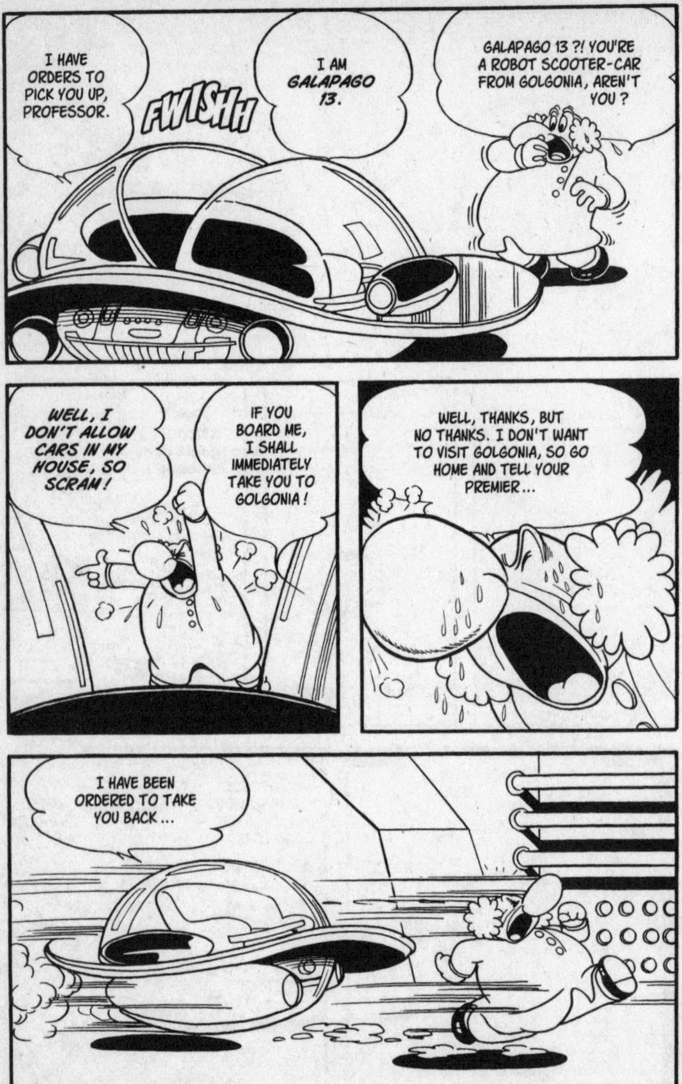
I HAVE ORDERS TO PICK YOU UP, PROFESSOR.
FWISHH
I AM GALAPAGO 13.
GALAPAGO 13 ?! YOU'RE A ROBOT SCOOTER-CAR FROM GOLGONIA, AREN'T YOU ?
WELL, I DON'T ALLOW CARS IN MY HOUSE, SO SCRAM !
IF YOU BOARD ME, I SHALL IMMEDIATELY TAKE YOU TO GOLGONIA !
WELL, THANKS, BUT NO THANKS. I DON'T WANT TO VISIT GOLGONIA, SO GO HOME AND TELL YOUR PREMIER...
I HAVE BEEN ORDERED TO TAKE YOU BACK...

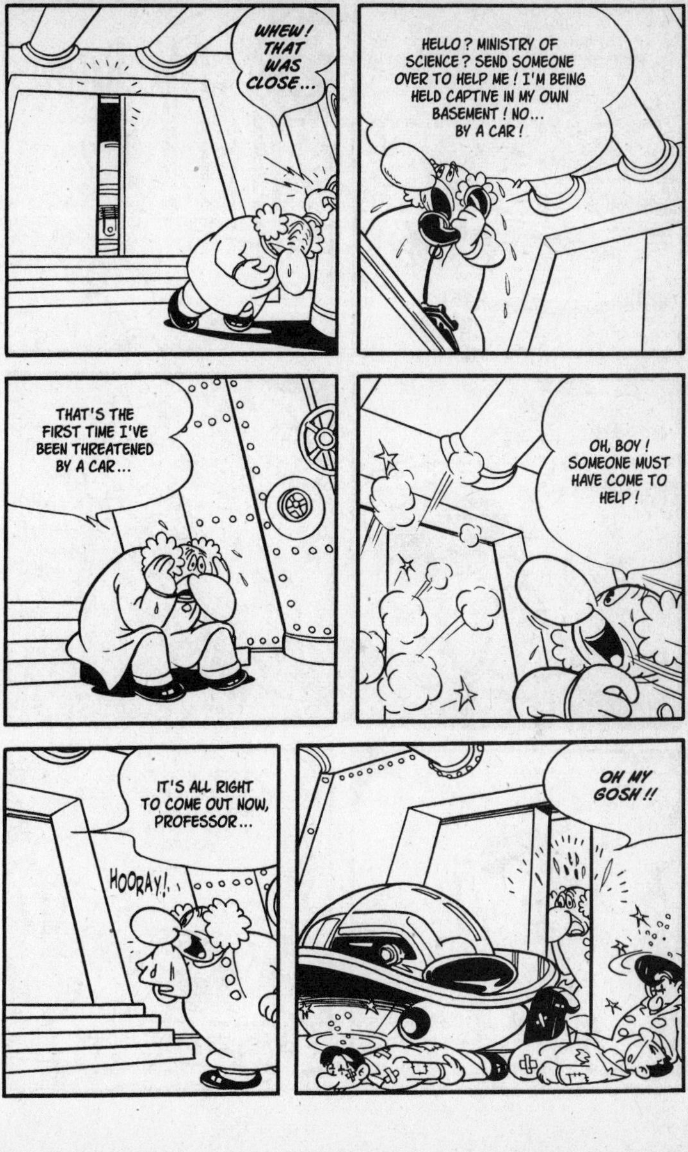
WHEW! THAT WAS CLOSE...
HELLO? MINISTRY OF SCIENCE? SEND SOMEONE OVER TO HELP ME! I'M BEING HELD CAPTIVE IN MY OWN BASEMENT! NO... BY A CAR!
THAT'S THE FIRST TIME I'VE BEEN THREATENED BY A CAR...
OH, BOY! SOMEONE MUST HAVE COME TO HELP!
IT'S ALL RIGHT TO COME OUT NOW, PROFESSOR...
HOORAY!
OH MY GOSH!!

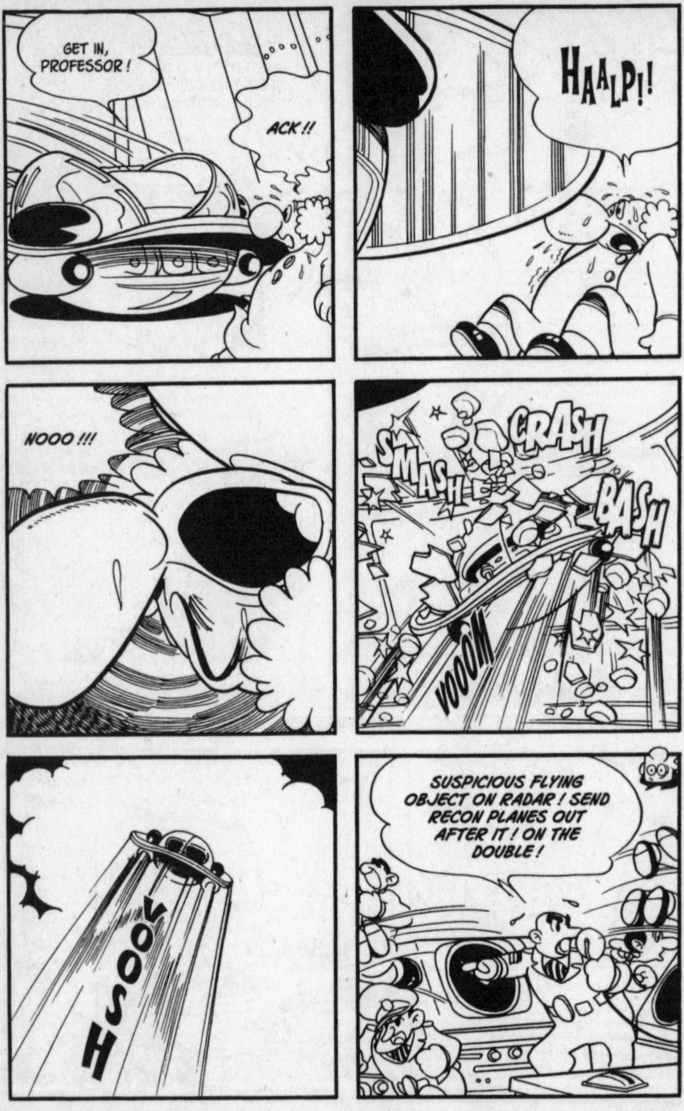
GET IN, PROFESSOR!
ACK!!
HAALP!!
NOOO!!!
SMASH
CRASH
BASH
VOOOM
VOOSH
SUSPICIOUS FLYING OBJECT ON RADAR! SEND RECON PLANES OUT AFTER IT! ON THE DOUBLE!

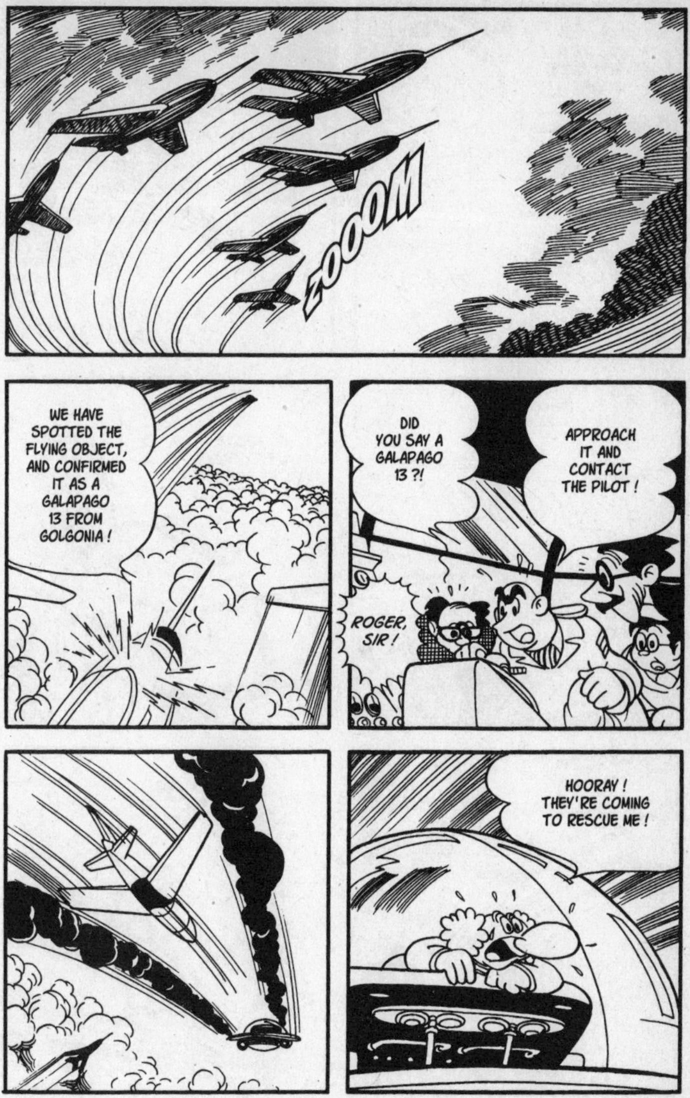
ZOOOM
WE HAVE SPOTTED THE FLYING OBJECT, AND CONFIRMED IT AS A GALAPAGO 13 FROM GOLGONIA !
DID YOU SAY A GALAPAGO 13 ?!
APPROACH IT AND CONTACT THE PILOT !
ROGER, SIR !
HOORAY ! THEY'RE COMING TO RESCUE ME !

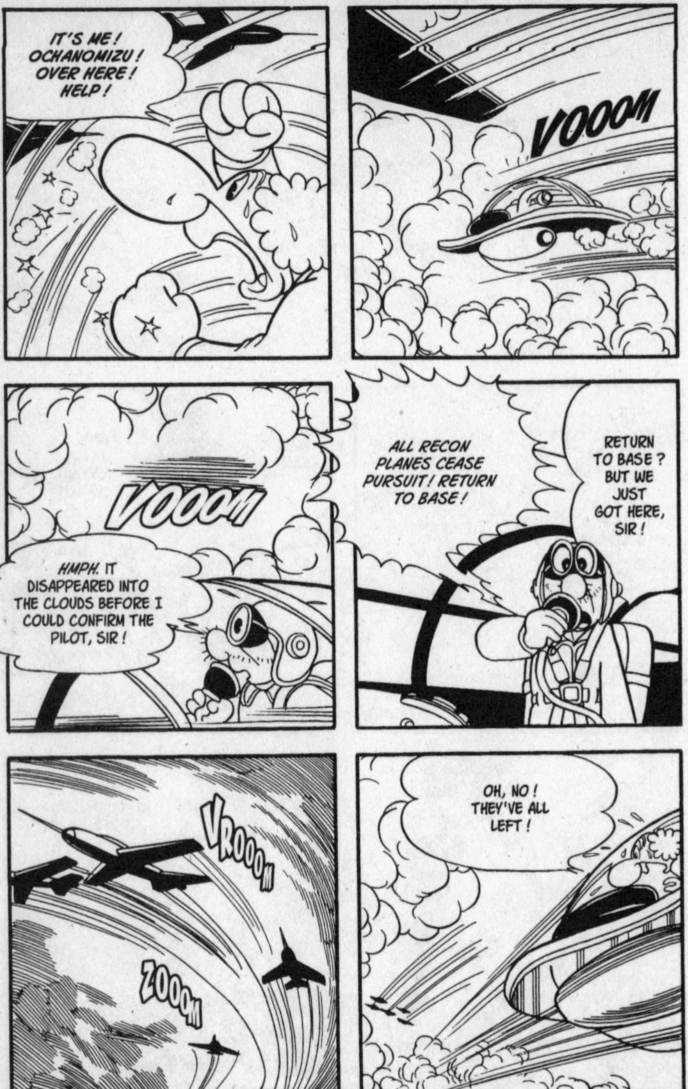
IT'S ME! OCHANOMIZU! OVER HERE! HELP!
VOOOM
VOOOM
HMPH. IT DISAPPEARED INTO THE CLOUDS BEFORE I COULD CONFIRM THE PILOT, SIR!
ALL RECON PLANES CEASE PURSUIT! RETURN TO BASE!
RETURN TO BASE? BUT WE JUST GOT HERE, SIR!
VROOOM
ZOOOM
OH, NO! THEY'VE ALL LEFT!

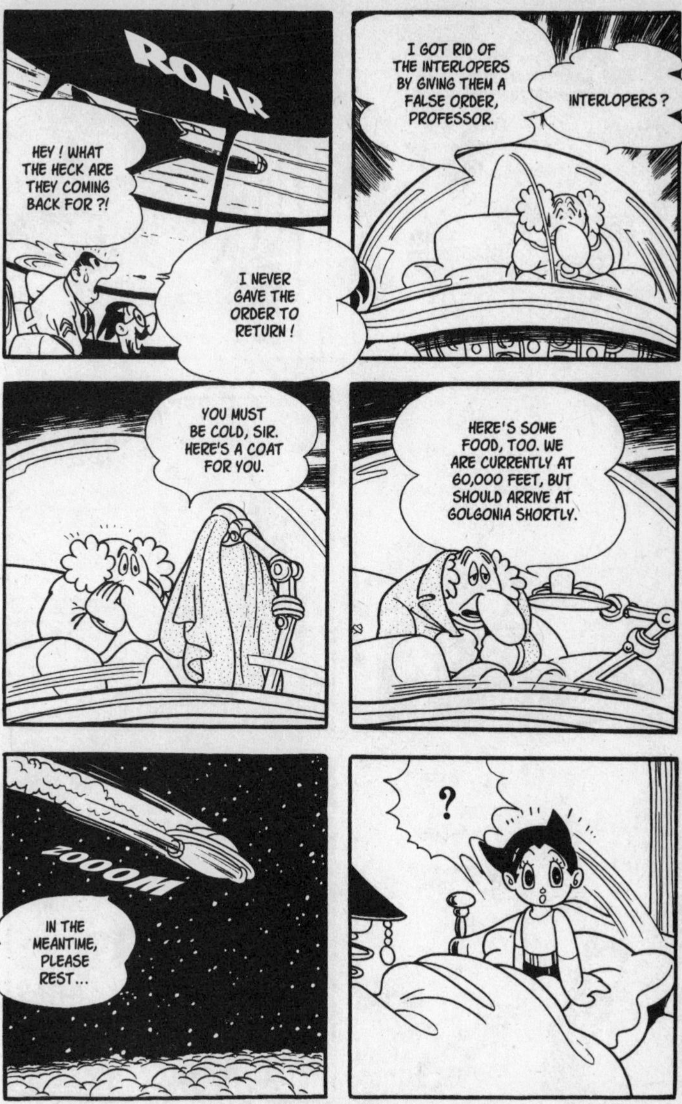
ROAR
HEY ! WHAT THE HECK ARE THEY COMING BACK FOR ?!
I NEVER GAVE THE ORDER TO RETURN !
I GOT RID OF THE INTERLOPERS BY GIVING THEM A FALSE ORDER, PROFESSOR.
INTERLOPERS ?
YOU MUST BE COLD, SIR. HERE'S A COAT FOR YOU.
HERE'S SOME FOOD, TOO. WE ARE CURRENTLY AT 60,000 FEET, BUT SHOULD ARRIVE AT GOLGONIA SHORTLY.
ZOOOM
IN THE MEANTIME, PLEASE REST...
?

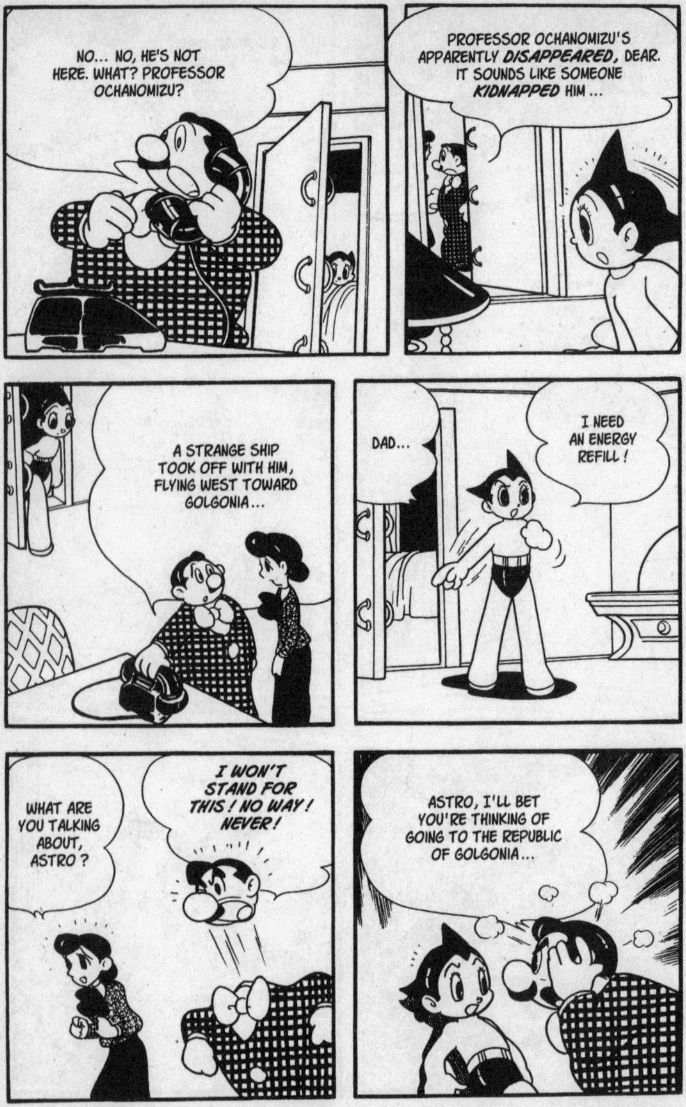
NO... NO, HE'S NOT HERE. WHAT? PROFESSOR OCHANOMIZU?
PROFESSOR OCHANOMIZU'S APPARENTLY DISAPPEARED, DEAR. IT SOUNDS LIKE SOMEONE KIDNAPPED HIM ...
A STRANGE SHIP TOOK OFF WITH HIM, FLYING WEST TOWARD GOLGONIA...
DAD...
I NEED AN ENERGY REFILL!
WHAT ARE YOU TALKING ABOUT, ASTRO?
I WON'T STAND FOR THIS! NO WAY! NEVER!
ASTRO, I'LL BET YOU'RE THINKING OF GOING TO THE REPUBLIC OF GOLGONIA...

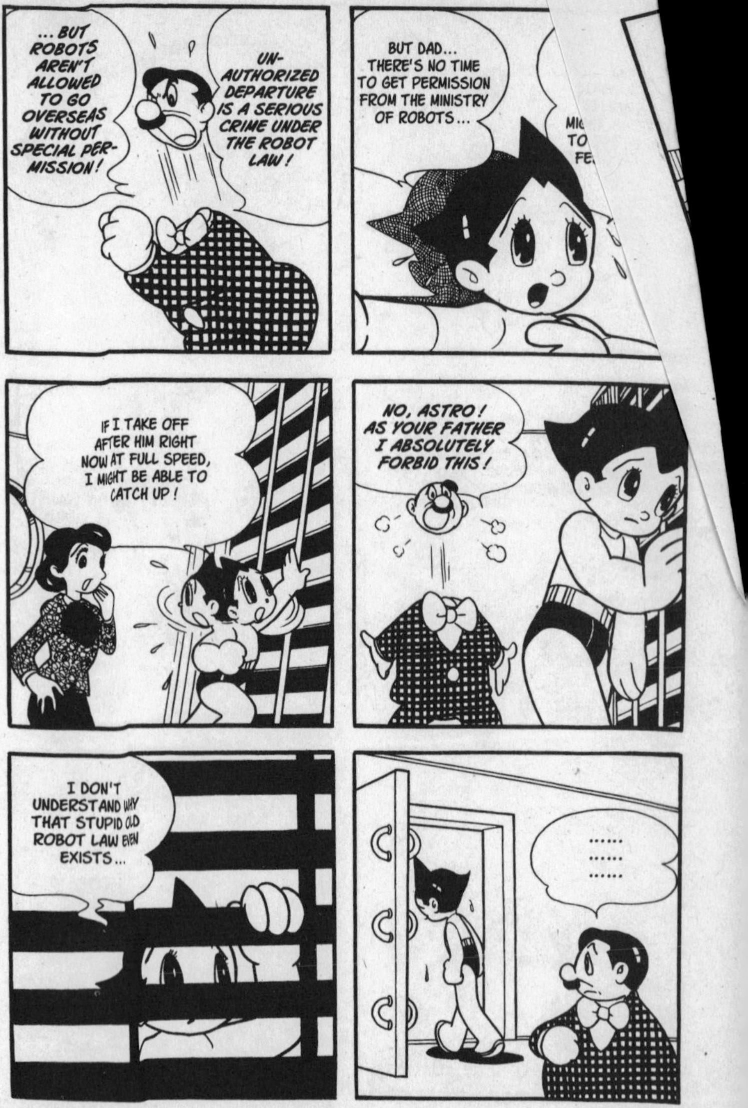
... BUT ROBOTS AREN'T ALLOWED TO GO OVERSEAS WITHOUT SPECIAL PERMISSION!
UN-AUTHORIZED DEPARTURE IS A SERIOUS CRIME UNDER THE ROBOT LAW!
BUT DAD... THERE'S NO TIME TO GET PERMISSION FROM THE MINISTRY OF ROBOTS...
IF I TAKE OFF AFTER HIM RIGHT NOW AT FULL SPEED, I MIGHT BE ABLE TO CATCH UP!
NO, ASTRO! AS YOUR FATHER I ABSOLUTELY FORBID THIS!
I DON'T UNDERSTAND WHY THAT STUPID OLD ROBOT LAW EVEN EXISTS...
......
......
......

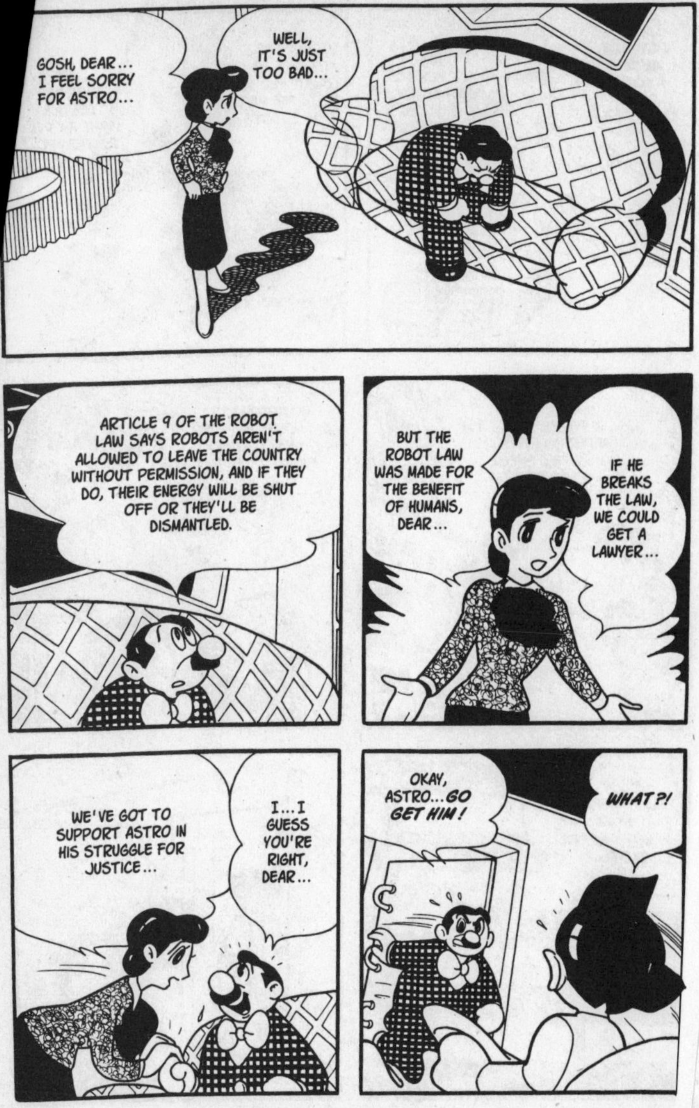
GOSH, DEAR... I FEEL SORRY FOR ASTRO...
WELL, IT'S JUST TOO BAD...
ARTICLE 9 OF THE ROBOT LAW SAYS ROBOTS AREN'T ALLOWED TO LEAVE THE COUNTRY WITHOUT PERMISSION, AND IF THEY DO, THEIR ENERGY WILL BE SHUT OFF OR THEY'LL BE DISMANTLED.
BUT THE ROBOT LAW WAS MADE FOR THE BENEFIT OF HUMANS, DEAR...
IF HE BREAKS THE LAW, WE COULD GET A LAWYER...
WE'VE GOT TO SUPPORT ASTRO IN HIS STRUGGLE FOR JUSTICE...
I...I GUESS YOU'RE RIGHT, DEAR...
OKAY, ASTRO...GO GET HIM!
WHAT?!

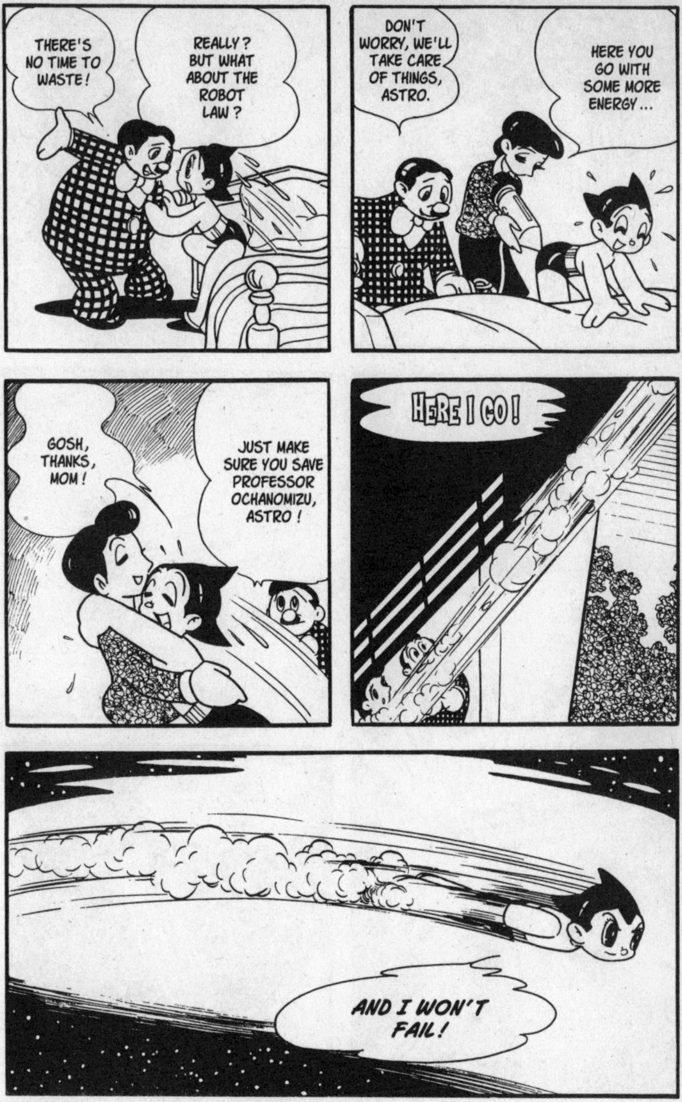
THERE'S NO TIME TO WASTE!
REALLY? BUT WHAT ABOUT THE ROBOT LAW?
DON'T WORRY, WE'LL TAKE CARE OF THINGS, ASTRO.
HERE YOU GO WITH SOME MORE ENERGY...
GOSH, THANKS, MOM!
JUST MAKE SURE YOU SAVE PROFESSOR OCHANOMIZU, ASTRO!
HERE I GO!
AND I WON'T FAIL!

ZOOOM

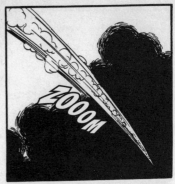

ZOOOM

CRACK

RUMBLE

RUMBLE

POW

THESE THUNDERHEADS CAN'T STOP ME!

NEXT IT'S ICE CLOUDS...

THEN I COME OUT ABOVE THE CLOUDS...

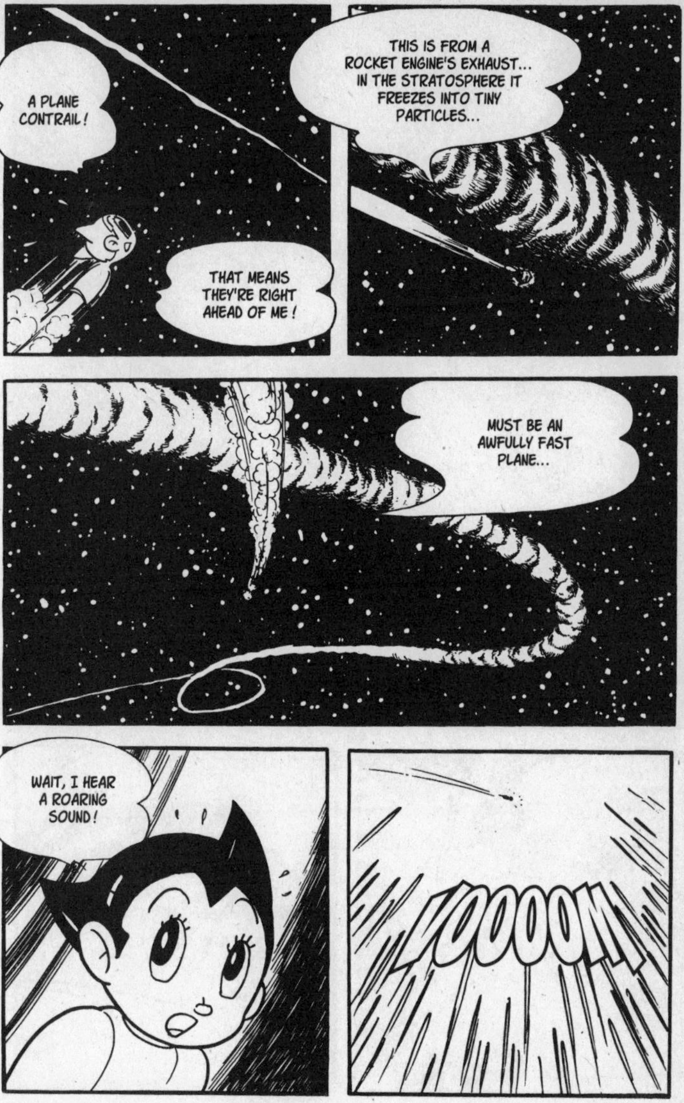

A PLANE CONTRAIL!
THAT MEANS THEY'RE RIGHT AHEAD OF ME!
THIS IS FROM A ROCKET ENGINE'S EXHAUST... IN THE STRATOSPHERE IT FREEZES INTO TINY PARTICLES...
MUST BE AN AWFULLY FAST PLANE...
WAIT, I HEAR A ROARING SOUND!
VOOOOM

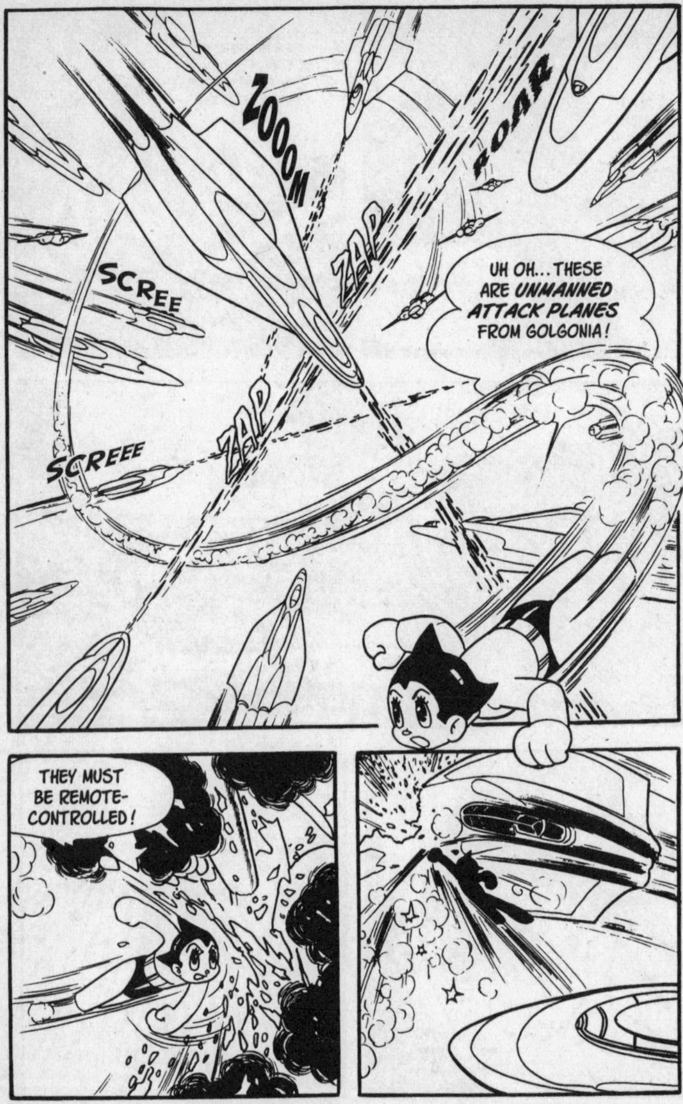
ZOOOM
ROAR
ZAP
SCREE
UH OH... THESE ARE UNMANNED ATTACK PLANES FROM GOLGONIA!
ZAP
SCREEE
THEY MUST BE REMOTE-CONTROLLED!

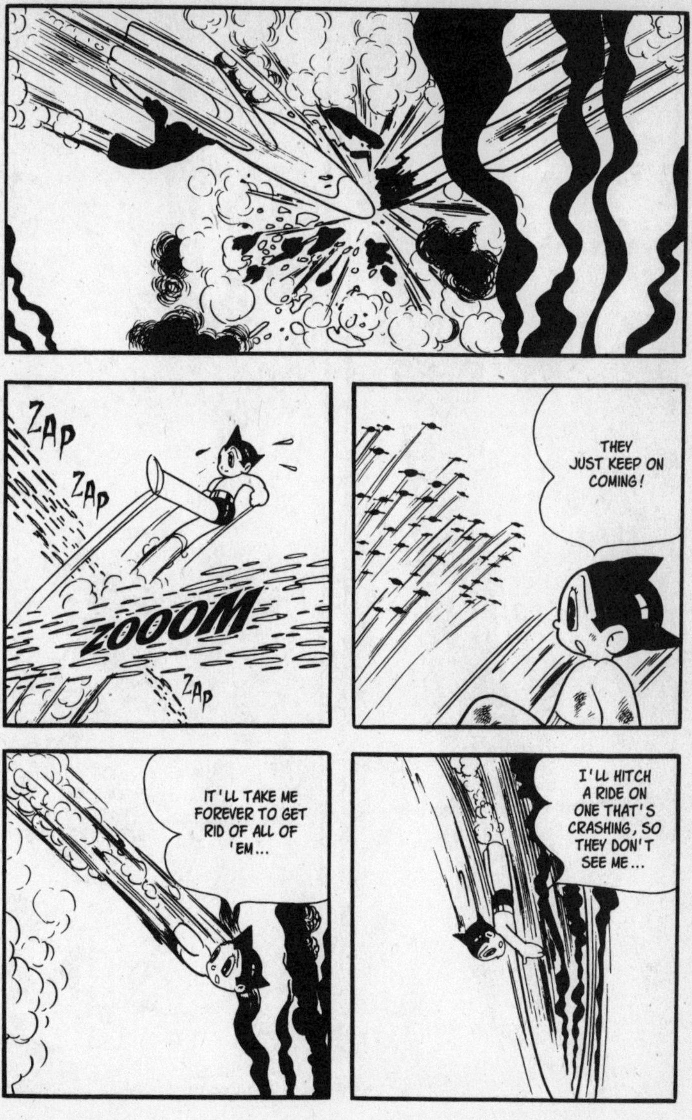
ZAP
ZAP
ZOOOM
ZAP
THEY JUST KEEP ON COMING!
IT'LL TAKE ME FOREVER TO GET RID OF ALL OF 'EM...
I'LL HITCH A RIDE ON ONE THAT'S CRASHING, SO THEY DON'T SEE ME...

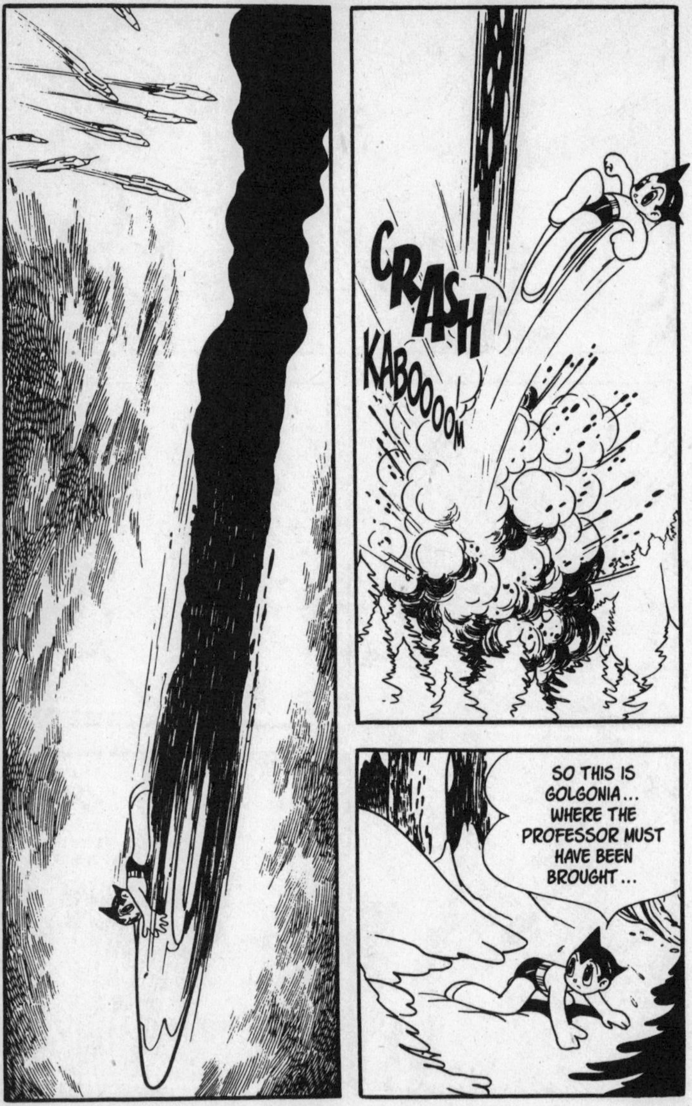
CRASH
KABOOOOOM
SO THIS IS GOLGONIA... WHERE THE PROFESSOR MUST HAVE BEEN BROUGHT...

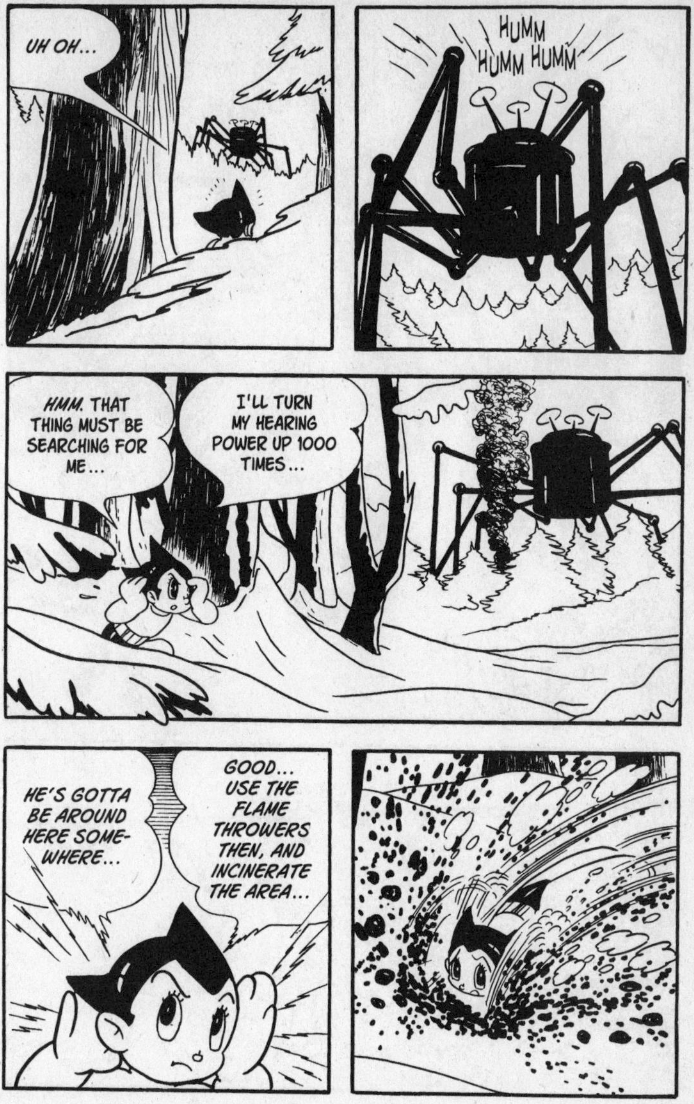
UH OH...
HUMM
HUMM HUMM
HMM. THAT THING MUST BE SEARCHING FOR ME...
I'LL TURN MY HEARING POWER UP 1000 TIMES...
HE'S GOTTA BE AROUND HERE SOME-WHERE...
GOOD... USE THE FLAME THROWERS THEN, AND INCINERATE THE AREA...

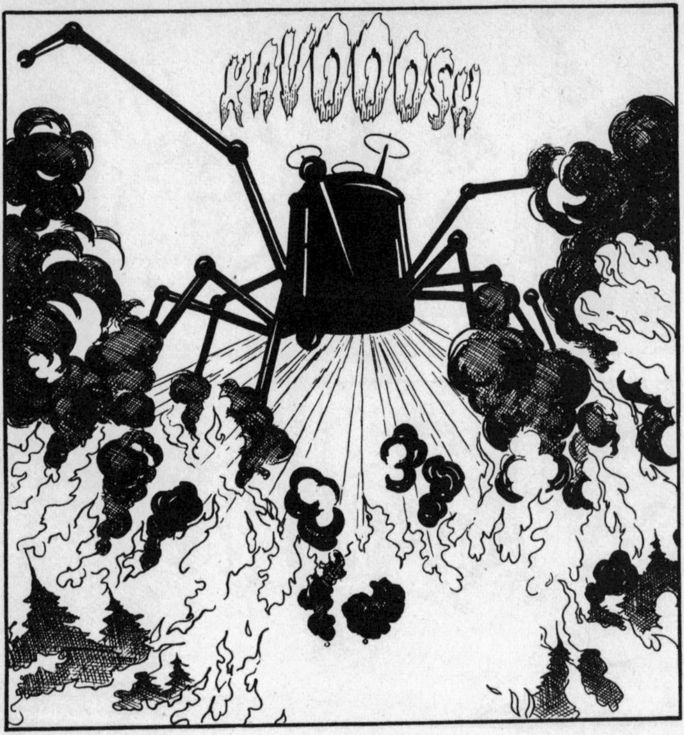
KAVOOOSH

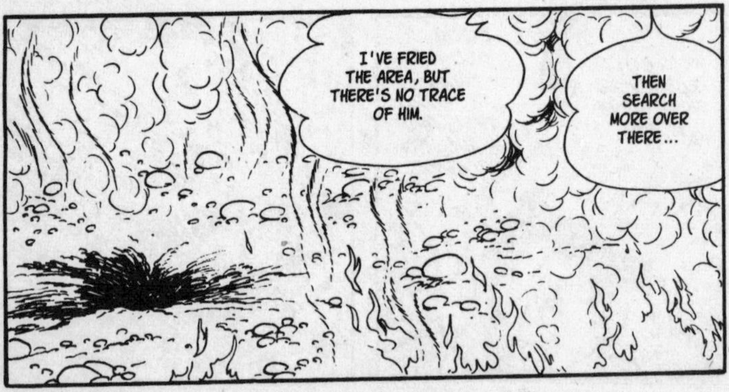
I'VE FRIED THE AREA, BUT THERE'S NO TRACE OF HIM.
THEN SEARCH MORE OVER THERE...

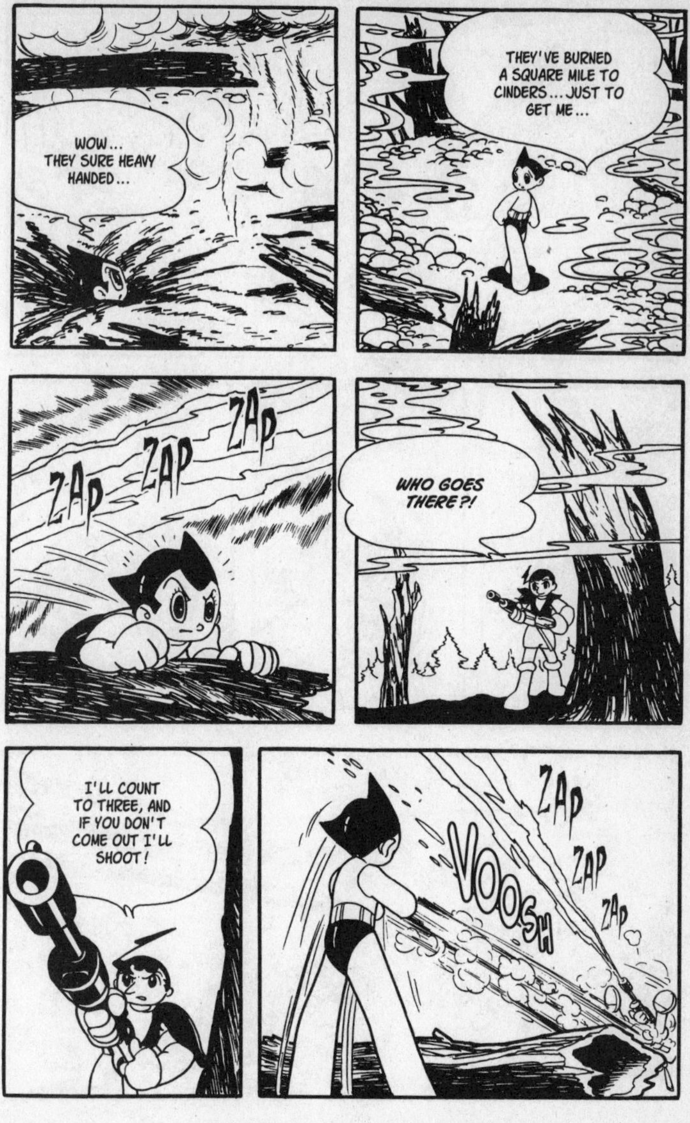
WOW... THEY SURE HEAVY HANDED...
THEY'VE BURNED A SQUARE MILE TO CINDERS... JUST TO GET ME...
ZAP
ZAP
ZAP
WHO GOES THERE?!
I'LL COUNT TO THREE, AND IF YOU DON'T COME OUT I'LL SHOOT!
VOOSH
ZAP
ZAP
ZAP

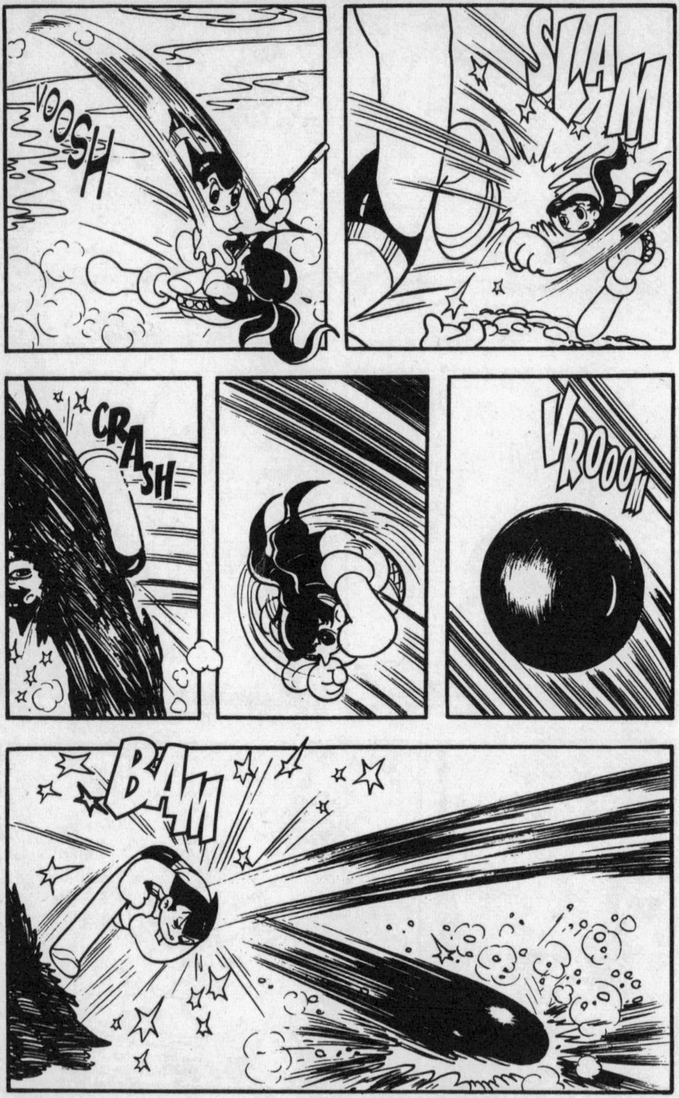
VOOSH
SLAM
CRASH
VROOOM
BAM

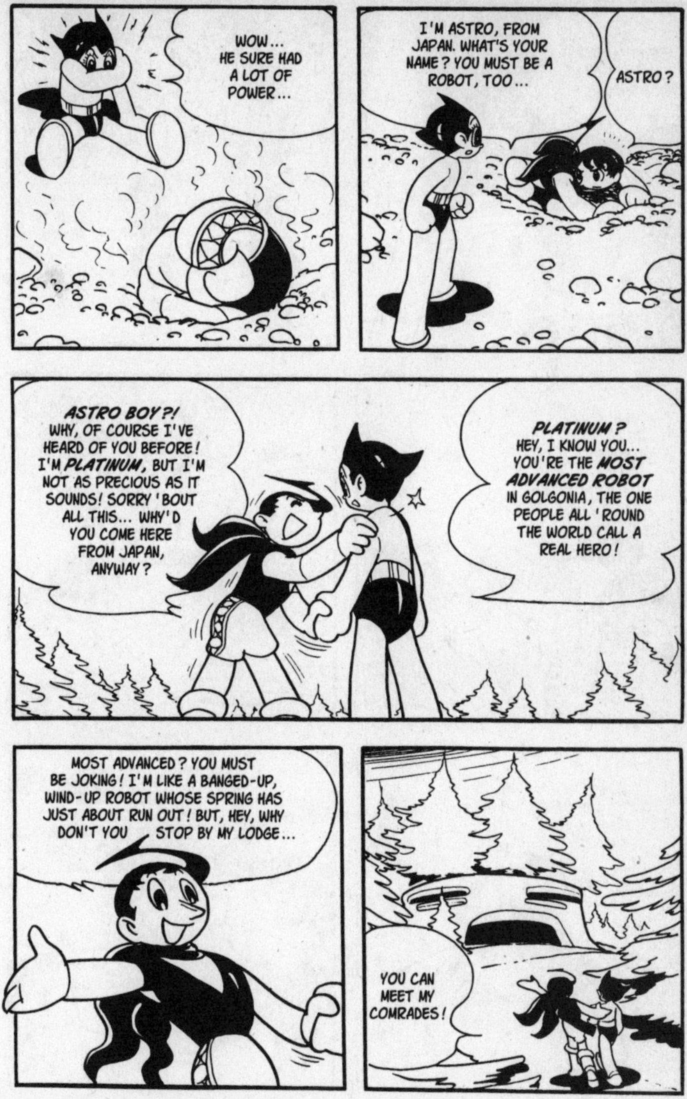

WOW... HE SURE HAD A LOT OF POWER...
I'M ASTRO, FROM JAPAN. WHAT'S YOUR NAME? YOU MUST BE A ROBOT, TOO...
ASTRO?
ASTRO BOY?! WHY, OF COURSE I'VE HEARD OF YOU BEFORE! I'M PLATINUM, BUT I'M NOT AS PRECIOUS AS IT SOUNDS! SORRY 'BOUT ALL THIS... WHY'D YOU COME HERE FROM JAPAN, ANYWAY?
PLATINUM? HEY, I KNOW YOU... YOU'RE THE MOST ADVANCED ROBOT IN GOLGONIA, THE ONE PEOPLE ALL 'ROUND THE WORLD CALL A REAL HERO!
MOST ADVANCED? YOU MUST BE JOKING! I'M LIKE A BANGED-UP, WIND-UP ROBOT WHOSE SPRING HAS JUST ABOUT RUN OUT! BUT, HEY, WHY DON'T YOU STOP BY MY LODGE...
YOU CAN MEET MY COMRADES!

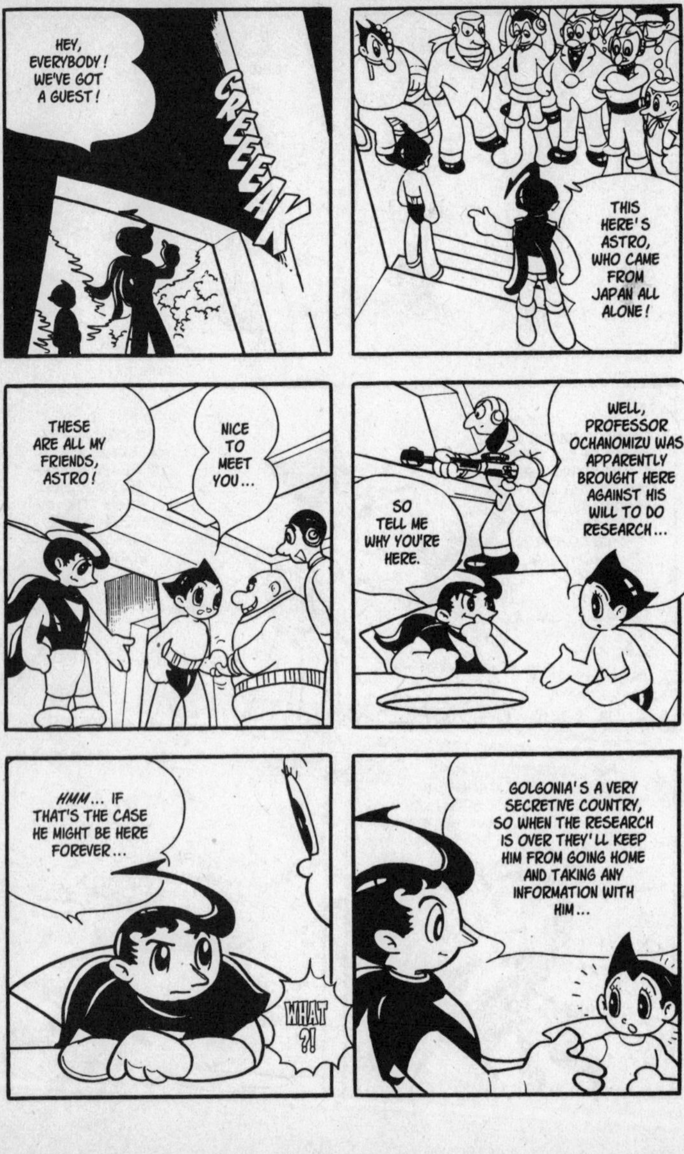
HEY, EVERYBODY! WE'VE GOT A GUEST!
CREEEAK
THIS HERE'S ASTRO, WHO CAME FROM JAPAN ALL ALONE!
THESE ARE ALL MY FRIENDS, ASTRO!
NICE TO MEET YOU...
SO TELL ME WHY YOU'RE HERE.
WELL, PROFESSOR OCHANOMIZU WAS APPARENTLY BROUGHT HERE AGAINST HIS WILL TO DO RESEARCH...
HMM... IF THAT'S THE CASE HE MIGHT BE HERE FOREVER...
WHAT?!
GOLGONIA'S A VERY SECRETIVE COUNTRY, SO WHEN THE RESEARCH IS OVER THEY'LL KEEP HIM FROM GOING HOME AND TAKING ANY INFORMATION WITH HIM...

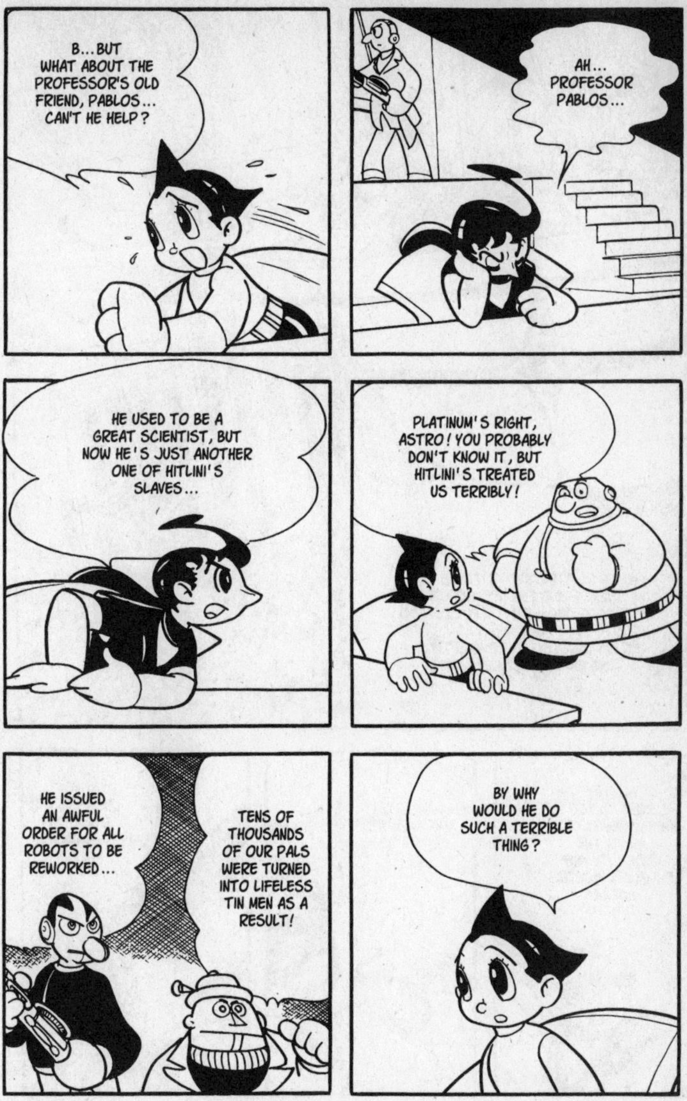
B... BUT WHAT ABOUT THE PROFESSOR'S OLD FRIEND, PABLOS... CAN'T HE HELP?
AH... PROFESSOR PABLOS...
HE USED TO BE A GREAT SCIENTIST, BUT NOW HE'S JUST ANOTHER ONE OF HITLINI'S SLAVES...
PLATINUM'S RIGHT, ASTRO! YOU PROBABLY DON'T KNOW IT, BUT HITLINI'S TREATED US TERRIBLY!
HE ISSUED AN AWFUL ORDER FOR ALL ROBOTS TO BE REWORKED...
TENS OF THOUSANDS OF OUR PALS WERE TURNED INTO LIFELESS TIN MEN AS A RESULT!
BY WHY WOULD HE DO SUCH A TERRIBLE THING?

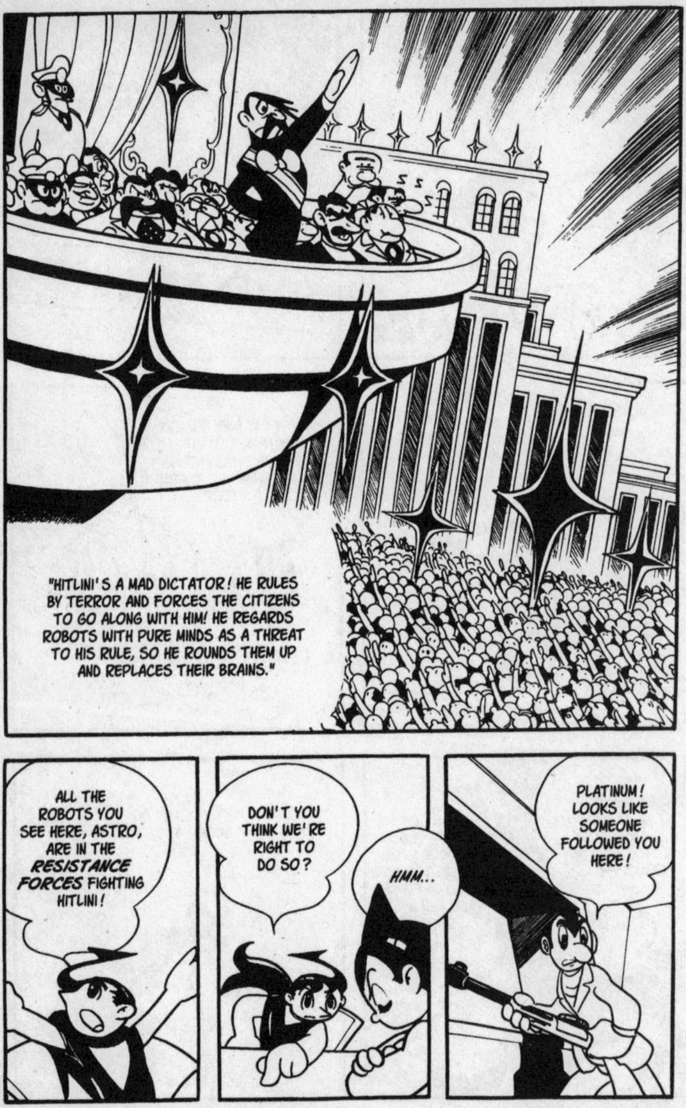
"HITLINI'S A MAD DICTATOR! HE RULES BY TERROR AND FORCES THE CITIZENS TO GO ALONG WITH HIM! HE REGARDS ROBOTS WITH PURE MINDS AS A THREAT TO HIS RULE, SO HE ROUNDS THEM UP AND REPLACES THEIR BRAINS."
ALL THE ROBOTS YOU SEE HERE, ASTRO, ARE IN THE *RESISTANCE FORCES* FIGHTING HITLINI!
DON'T YOU THINK WE'RE RIGHT TO DO SO?
HMM...
PLATINUM! LOOKS LIKE SOMEONE FOLLOWED YOU HERE!

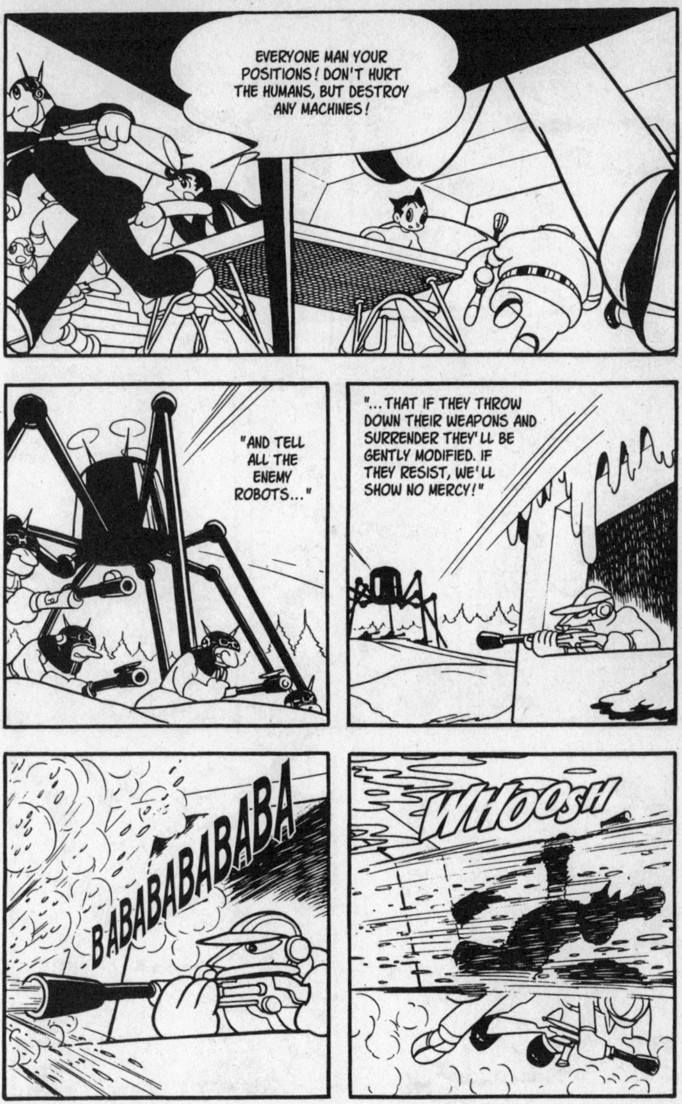
EVERYONE MAN YOUR POSITIONS! DON'T HURT THE HUMANS, BUT DESTROY ANY MACHINES!
"AND TELL ALL THE ENEMY ROBOTS..."
"...THAT IF THEY THROW DOWN THEIR WEAPONS AND SURRENDER THEY'LL BE GENTLY MODIFIED. IF THEY RESIST, WE'LL SHOW NO MERCY!"
BABABABABABA
WHOOSH

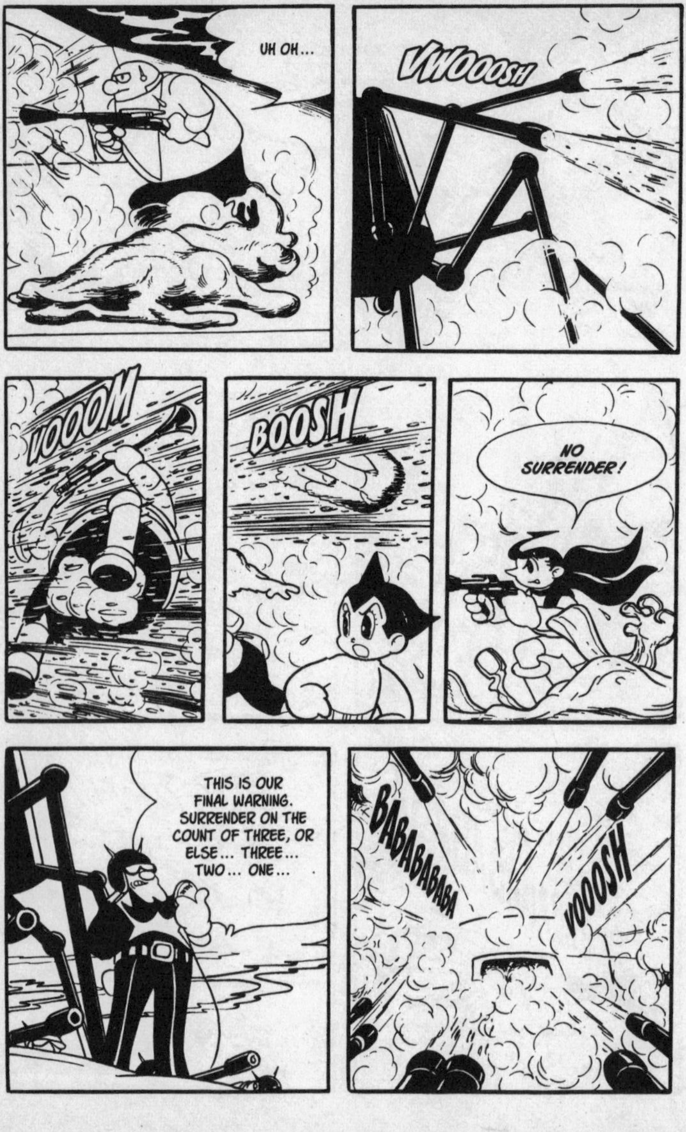
UH OH...
VWOOOSH
VOOOM
BOOSH
NO SURRENDER!
THIS IS OUR FINAL WARNING. SURRENDER ON THE COUNT OF THREE, OR ELSE... THREE... TWO... ONE...
BABABABABA
VOOOSH

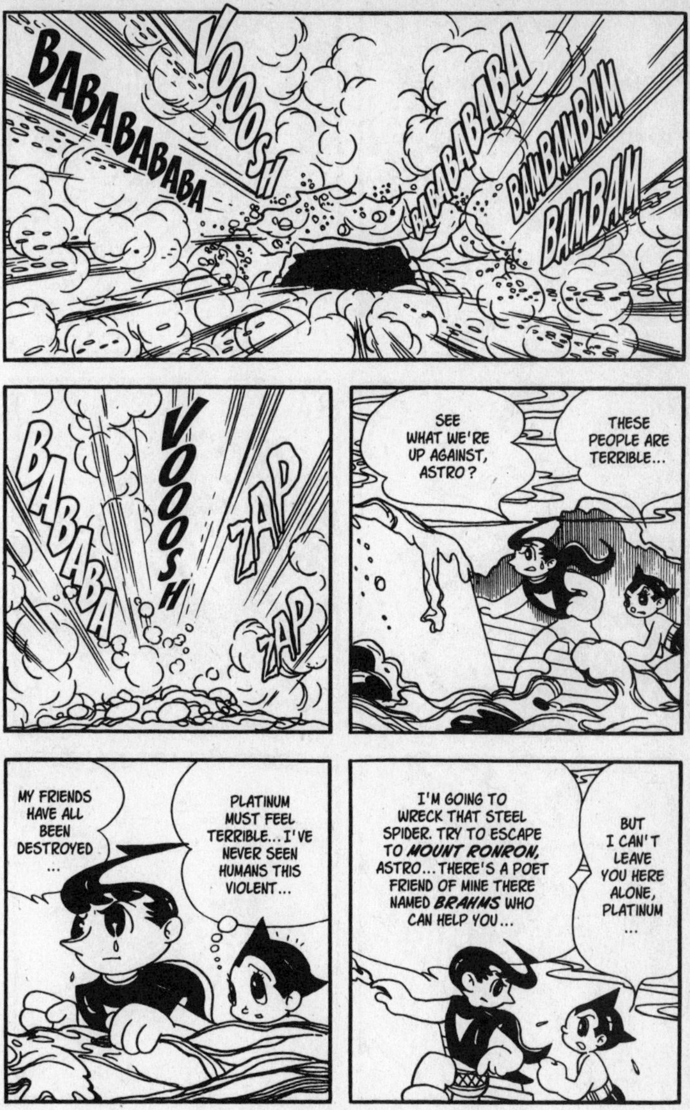
BABABABABABA
VOOOSH
BABABABABA
BAMBAMBAM
BAMBAM
BABABABA
VOOOOSH
ZAP
ZAP
SEE WHAT WE'RE UP AGAINST, ASTRO?
THESE PEOPLE ARE TERRIBLE...
MY FRIENDS HAVE ALL BEEN DESTROYED ...
PLATINUM MUST FEEL TERRIBLE... I'VE NEVER SEEN HUMANS THIS VIOLENT...
I'M GOING TO WRECK THAT STEEL SPIDER. TRY TO ESCAPE TO MOUNT RONRON, ASTRO... THERE'S A POET FRIEND OF MINE THERE NAMED BRAHMS WHO CAN HELP YOU...
BUT I CAN'T LEAVE YOU HERE ALONE, PLATINUM ...

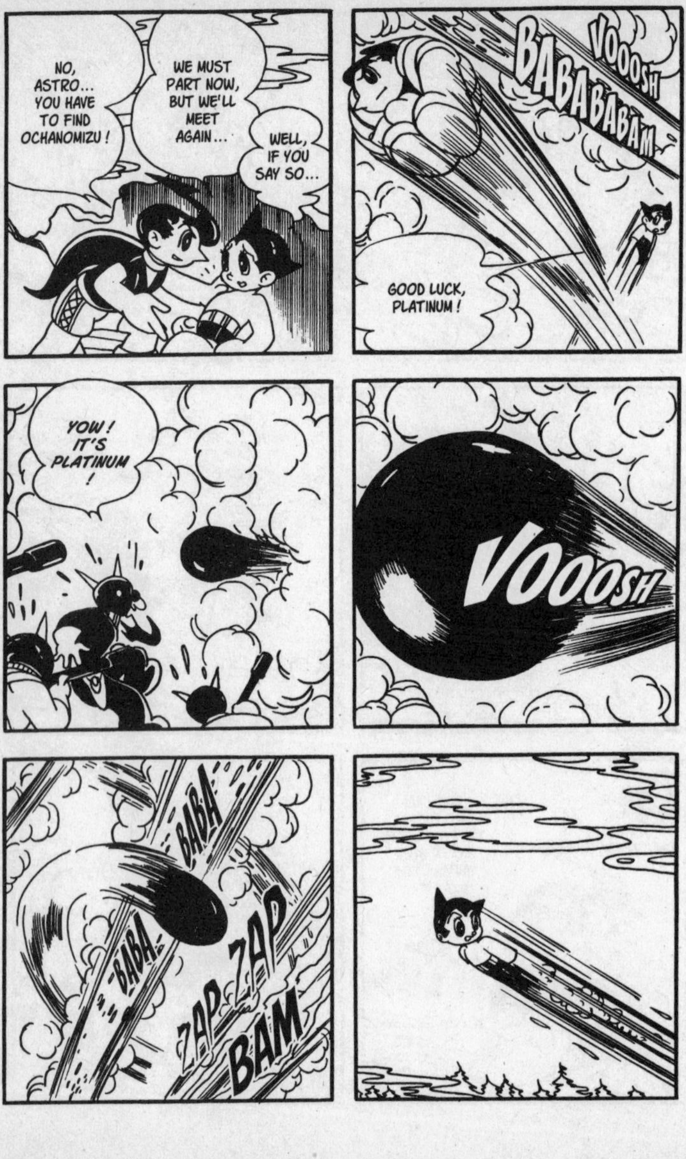
NO, ASTRO... YOU HAVE TO FIND OCHANOMIZU !
WE MUST PART NOW, BUT WE'LL MEET AGAIN...
WELL, IF YOU SAY SO...
VOOOSH
BABABABABAM
GOOD LUCK, PLATINUM !
YOW ! IT'S PLATINUM !
VOOOSH
BABA
BABA
ZAP ZAP ZAP
BAM

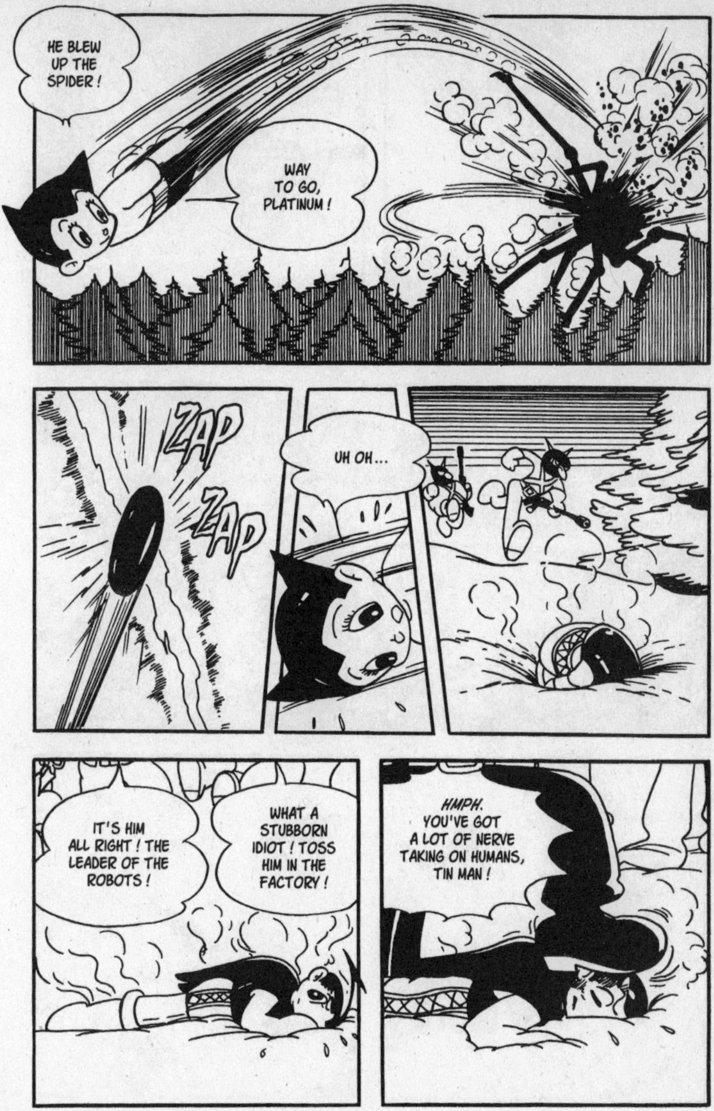
HE BLEW UP THE SPIDER !
WAY TO GO, PLATINUM !
ZAP
ZAP
UH OH...
IT'S HIM ALL RIGHT ! THE LEADER OF THE ROBOTS !
WHAT A STUBBORN IDIOT ! TOSS HIM IN THE FACTORY !
HMPH. YOU'VE GOT A LOT OF NERVE TAKING ON HUMANS, TIN MAN !

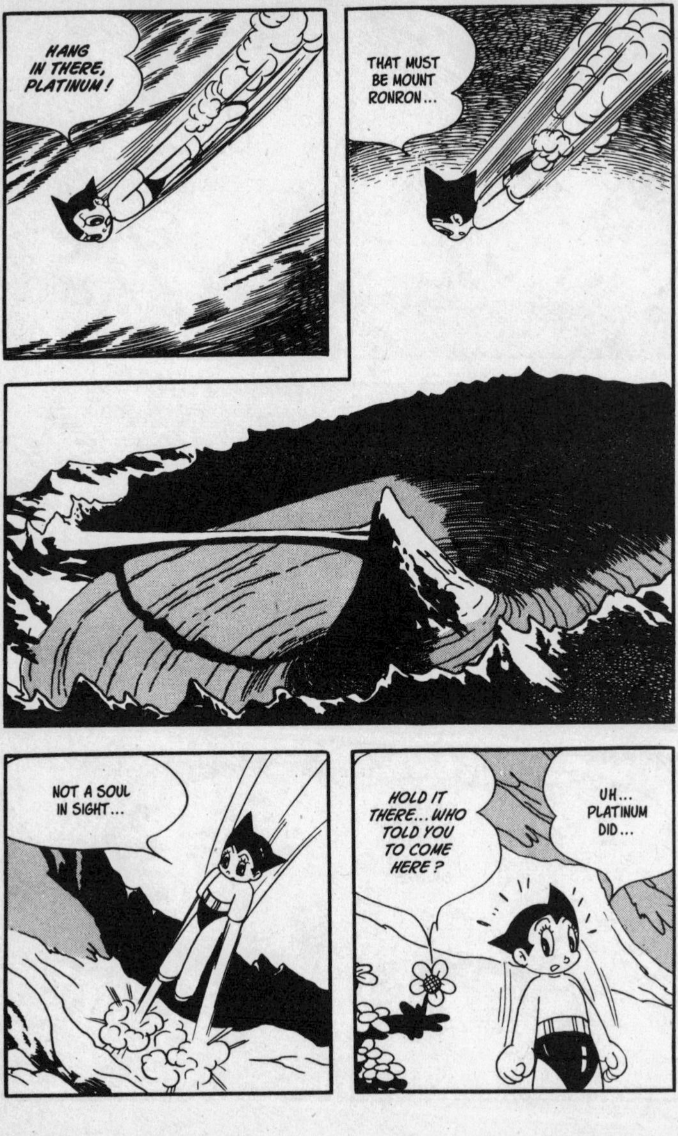
HANG IN THERE, PLATINUM!
THAT MUST BE MOUNT RONRON...
NOT A SOUL IN SIGHT...
HOLD IT THERE... WHO TOLD YOU TO COME HERE?
UH... PLATINUM DID...

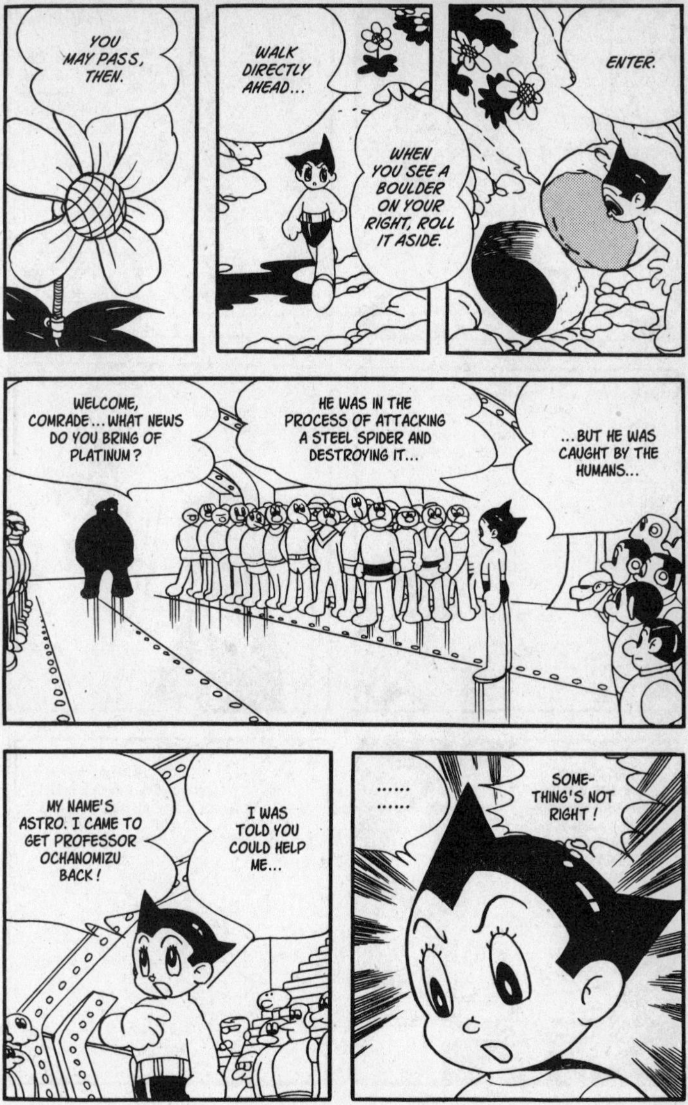
YOU MAY PASS, THEN.
WALK DIRECTLY AHEAD...
WHEN YOU SEE A BOULDER ON YOUR RIGHT, ROLL IT ASIDE.
ENTER.
WELCOME, COMRADE... WHAT NEWS DO YOU BRING OF PLATINUM?
HE WAS IN THE PROCESS OF ATTACKING A STEEL SPIDER AND DESTROYING IT...
...BUT HE WAS CAUGHT BY THE HUMANS...
MY NAME'S ASTRO. I CAME TO GET PROFESSOR OCHANOMIZU BACK!
I WAS TOLD YOU COULD HELP ME...
......
......
SOME-THING'S NOT RIGHT!

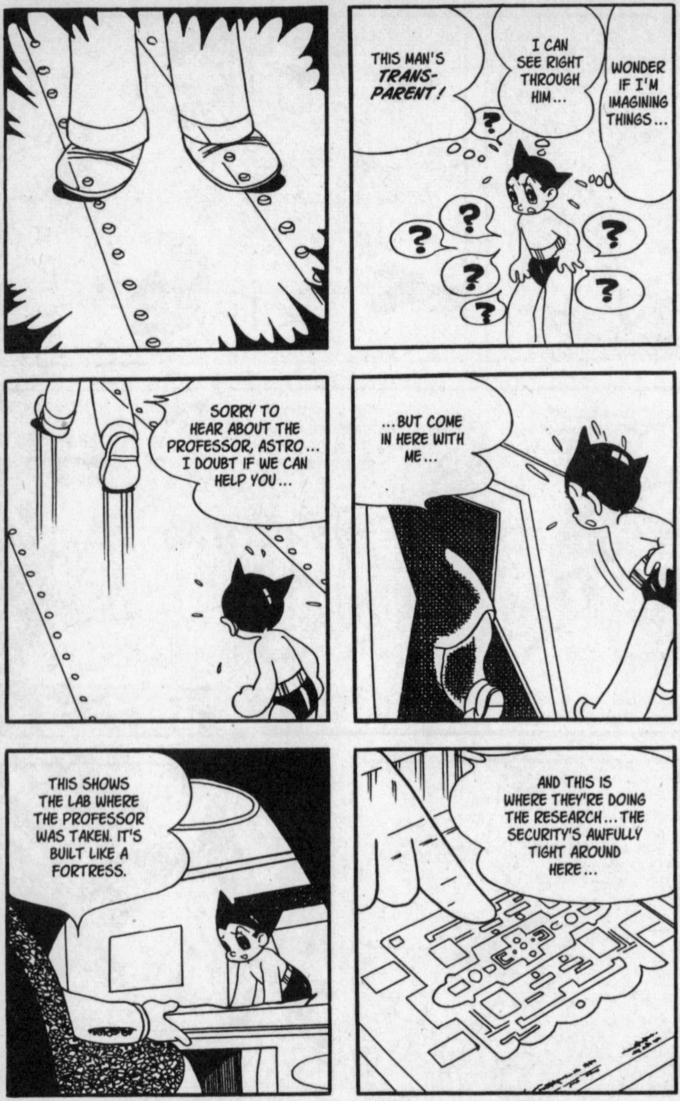
THIS MAN'S TRANS-PARENT!
I CAN SEE RIGHT THROUGH HIM...
WONDER IF I'M IMAGINING THINGS...
?
?
?
?
?
?
?
SORRY TO HEAR ABOUT THE PROFESSOR, ASTRO... I DOUBT IF WE CAN HELP YOU...
...BUT COME IN HERE WITH ME...
THIS SHOWS THE LAB WHERE THE PROFESSOR WAS TAKEN. IT'S BUILT LIKE A FORTRESS.
AND THIS IS WHERE THEY'RE DOING THE RESEARCH... THE SECURITY'S AWFULLY TIGHT AROUND HERE...

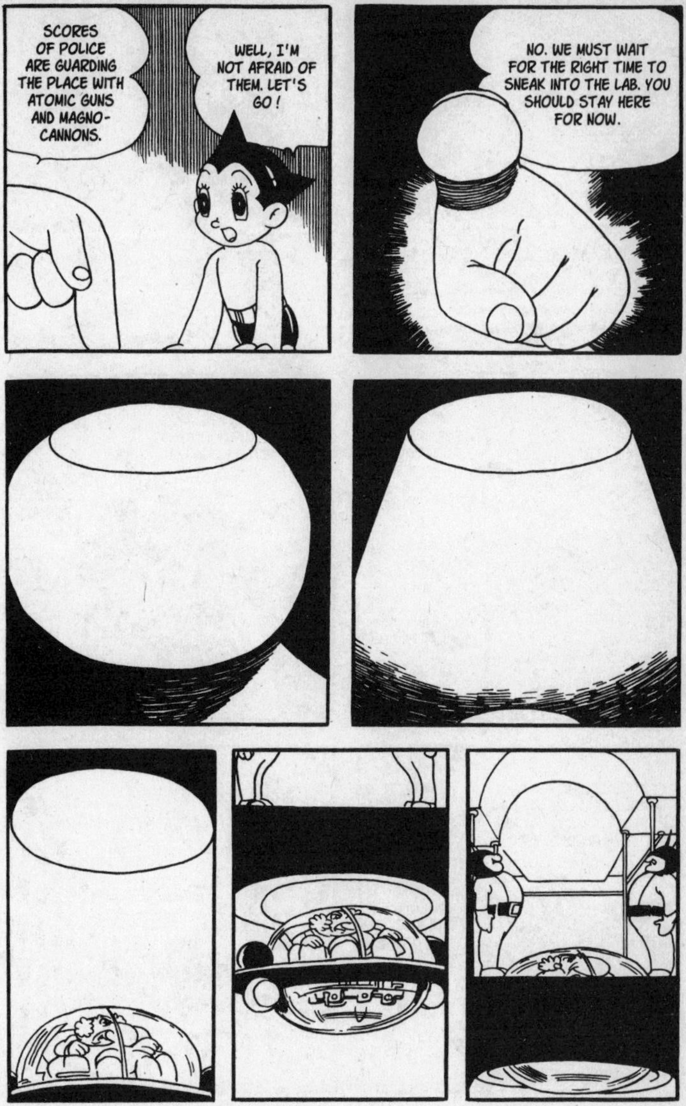
SCORES OF POLICE ARE GUARDING THE PLACE WITH ATOMIC GUNS AND MAGNO-CANNONS.
WELL, I'M NOT AFRAID OF THEM. LET'S GO!
NO. WE MUST WAIT FOR THE RIGHT TIME TO SNEAK INTO THE LAB. YOU SHOULD STAY HERE FOR NOW.

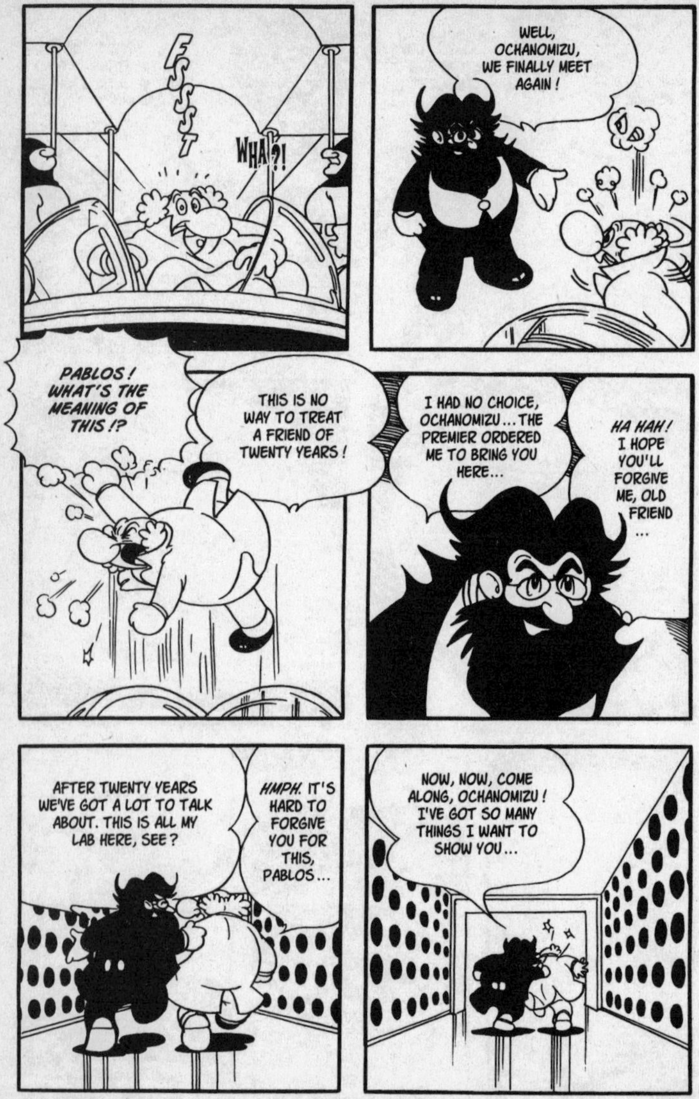
FSSST
WHA?!
WELL, OCHANOMIZU, WE FINALLY MEET AGAIN!
PABLOS! WHAT'S THE MEANING OF THIS!?
THIS IS NO WAY TO TREAT A FRIEND OF TWENTY YEARS!
I HAD NO CHOICE, OCHANOMIZU... THE PREMIER ORDERED ME TO BRING YOU HERE...
HA HAH! I HOPE YOU'LL FORGIVE ME, OLD FRIEND...
AFTER TWENTY YEARS WE'VE GOT A LOT TO TALK ABOUT. THIS IS ALL MY LAB HERE, SEE?
HMPH. IT'S HARD TO FORGIVE YOU FOR THIS, PABLOS...
NOW, NOW, COME ALONG, OCHANOMIZU! I'VE GOT SO MANY THINGS I WANT TO SHOW YOU...

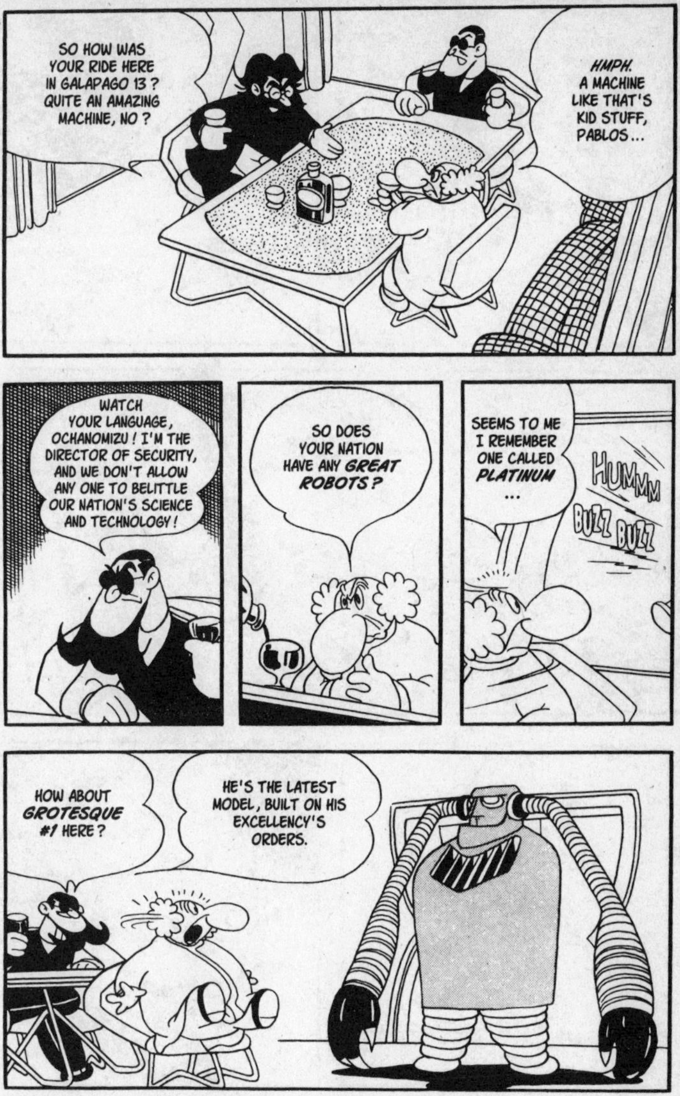
SO HOW WAS YOUR RIDE HERE IN GALAPAGO 13 ? QUITE AN AMAZING MACHINE, NO ?
HMPH. A MACHINE LIKE THAT'S KID STUFF, PABLOS...
WATCH YOUR LANGUAGE, OCHANOMIZU ! I'M THE DIRECTOR OF SECURITY, AND WE DON'T ALLOW ANY ONE TO BELITTLE OUR NATION'S SCIENCE AND TECHNOLOGY !
SO DOES YOUR NATION HAVE ANY GREAT ROBOTS ?
SEEMS TO ME I REMEMBER ONE CALLED PLATINUM ...
HUMMM
BUZZ BUZZ
HOW ABOUT GROTESQUE #1 HERE ?
HE'S THE LATEST MODEL, BUILT ON HIS EXCELLENCY'S ORDERS.

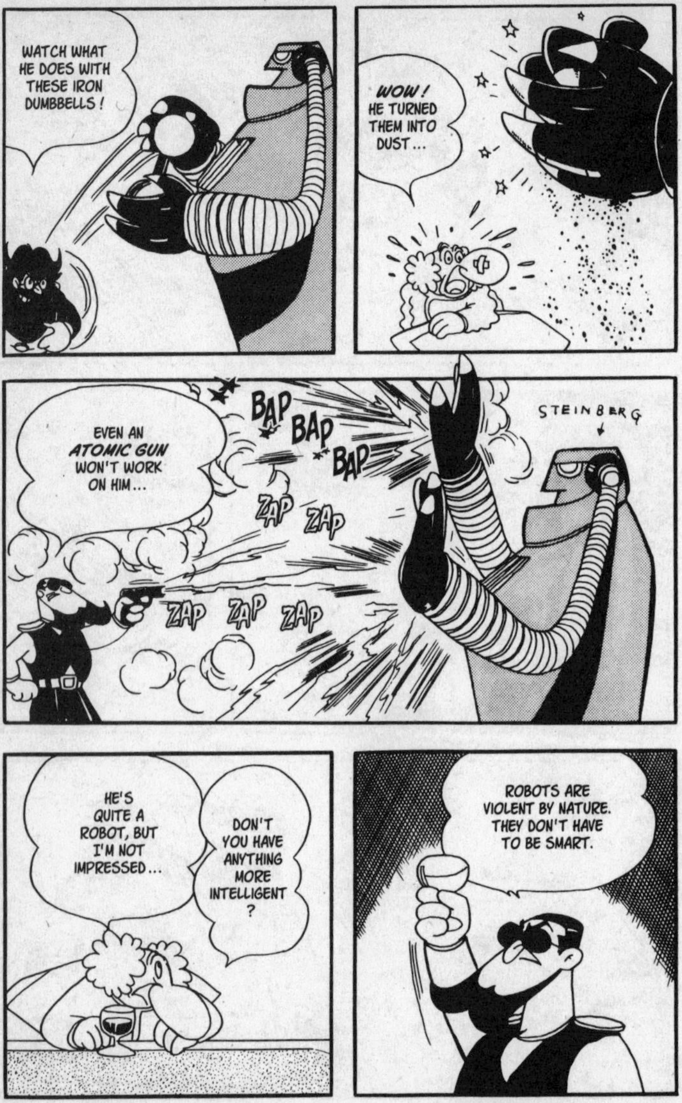
WATCH WHAT HE DOES WITH THESE IRON DUMBBELLS !
WOW ! HE TURNED THEM INTO DUST ...
EVEN AN ATOMIC GUN WON'T WORK ON HIM ...
BAP BAP BAP
STEINBERG
ZAP ZAP
ZAP ZAP ZAP
HE'S QUITE A ROBOT, BUT I'M NOT IMPRESSED ...
DON'T YOU HAVE ANYTHING MORE INTELLIGENT ?
ROBOTS ARE VIOLENT BY NATURE. THEY DON'T HAVE TO BE SMART.

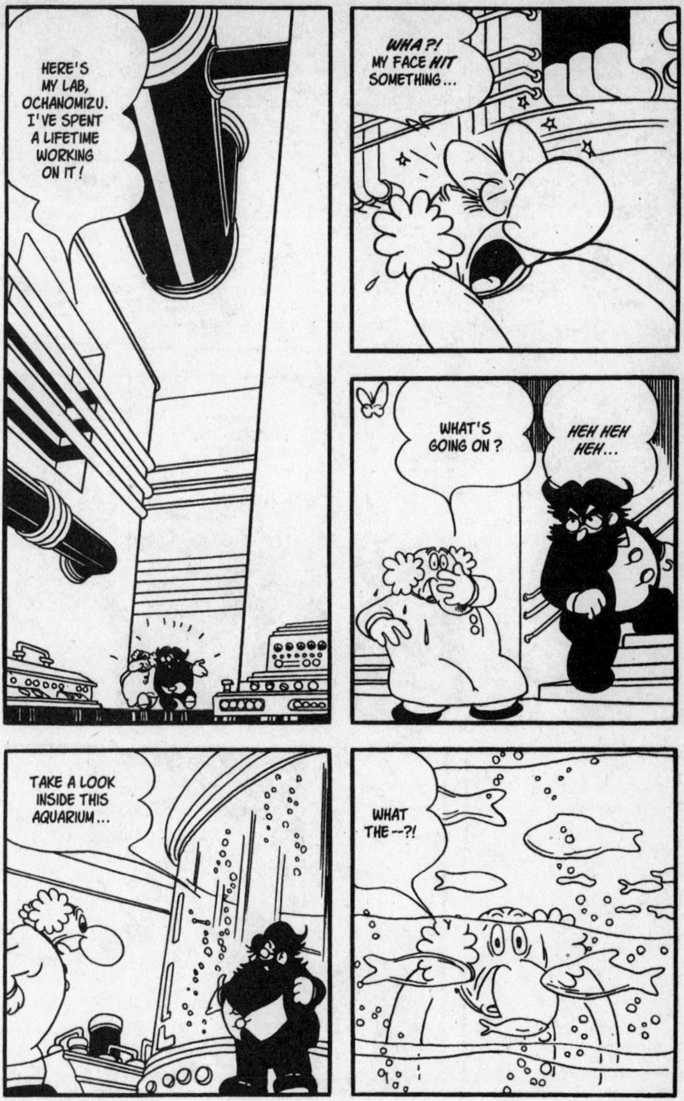
HERE'S MY LAB, OCHANOMIZU. I'VE SPENT A LIFETIME WORKING ON IT!
WHA?! MY FACE HIT SOMETHING...
WHAT'S GOING ON?
HEH HEH HEH...
TAKE A LOOK INSIDE THIS AQUARIUM...
WHAT THE--?!

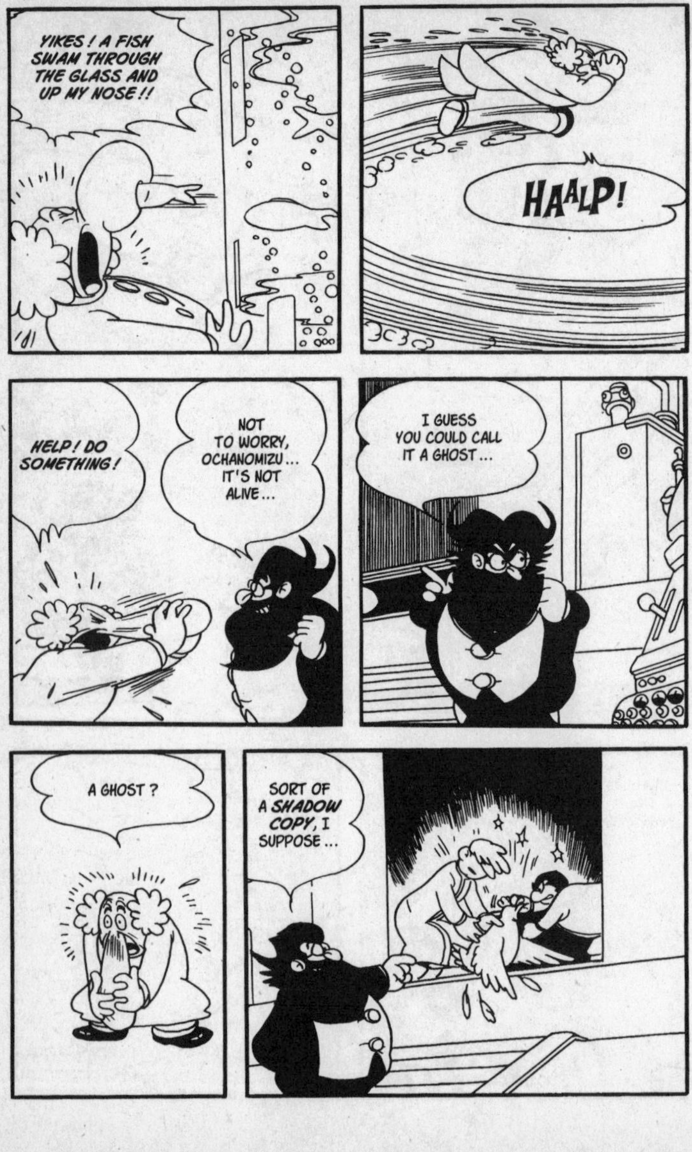
YIKES! A FISH SWAM THROUGH THE GLASS AND UP MY NOSE!!
HAALP!
HELP! DO SOMETHING!
NOT TO WORRY, OCHANOMIZU... IT'S NOT ALIVE...
I GUESS YOU COULD CALL IT A GHOST...
A GHOST?
SORT OF A SHADOW COPY, I SUPPOSE...

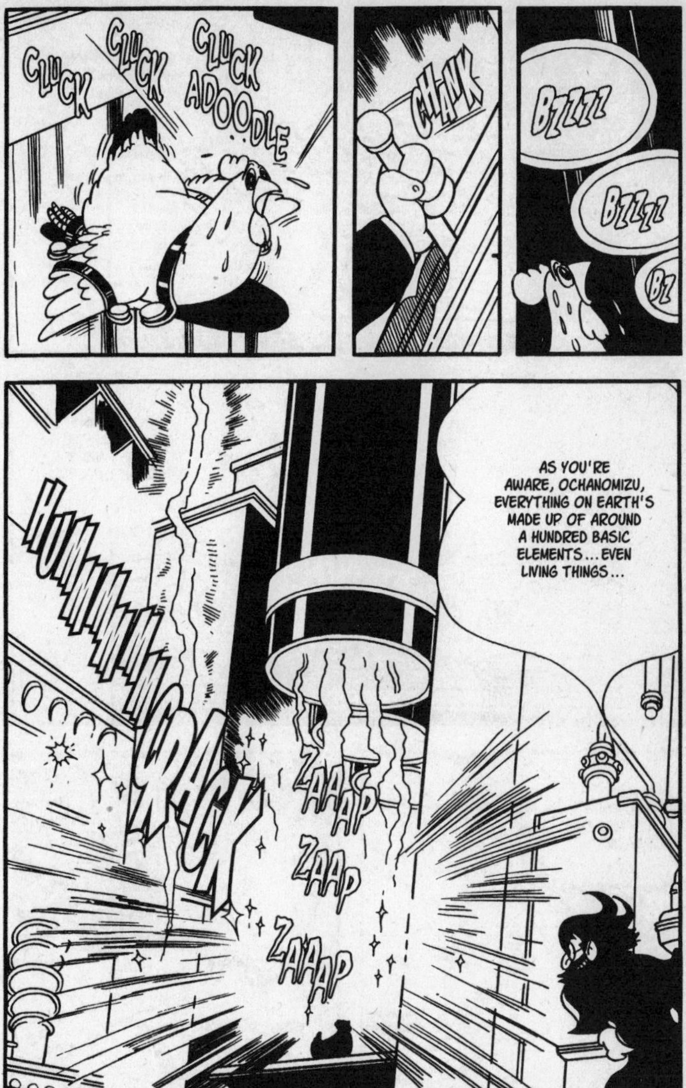
CLUCK
CLUCK
CLUCK ADOOODLE
CHANK
BZZZZ
BZZZZ
BZ
HUMMMMMCRACK
AS YOU'RE AWARE, OCHANOMIZU, EVERYTHING ON EARTH'S MADE UP OF AROUND A HUNDRED BASIC ELEMENTS... EVEN LIVING THINGS...
ZAAAP
ZAAP
ZAAAP

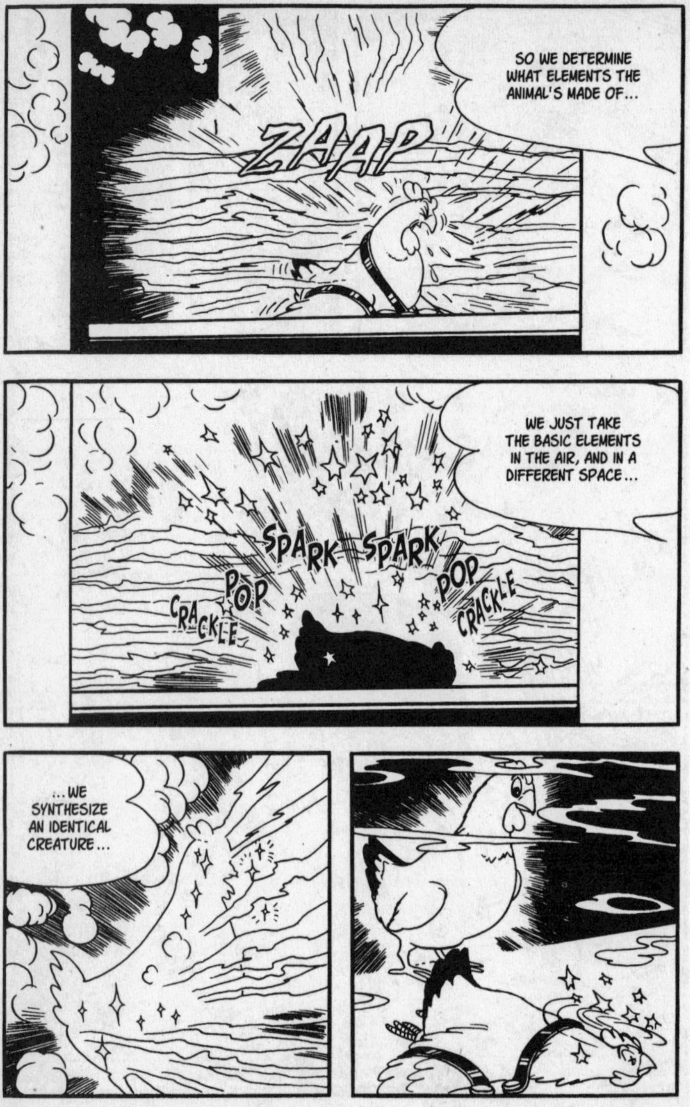
SO WE DETERMINE WHAT ELEMENTS THE ANIMAL'S MADE OF...
ZAAP
WE JUST TAKE THE BASIC ELEMENTS IN THE AIR, AND IN A DIFFERENT SPACE...
SPARK SPARK
POP
CRACKLE
POP
CRACKLE
...WE SYNTHESIZE AN IDENTICAL CREATURE...

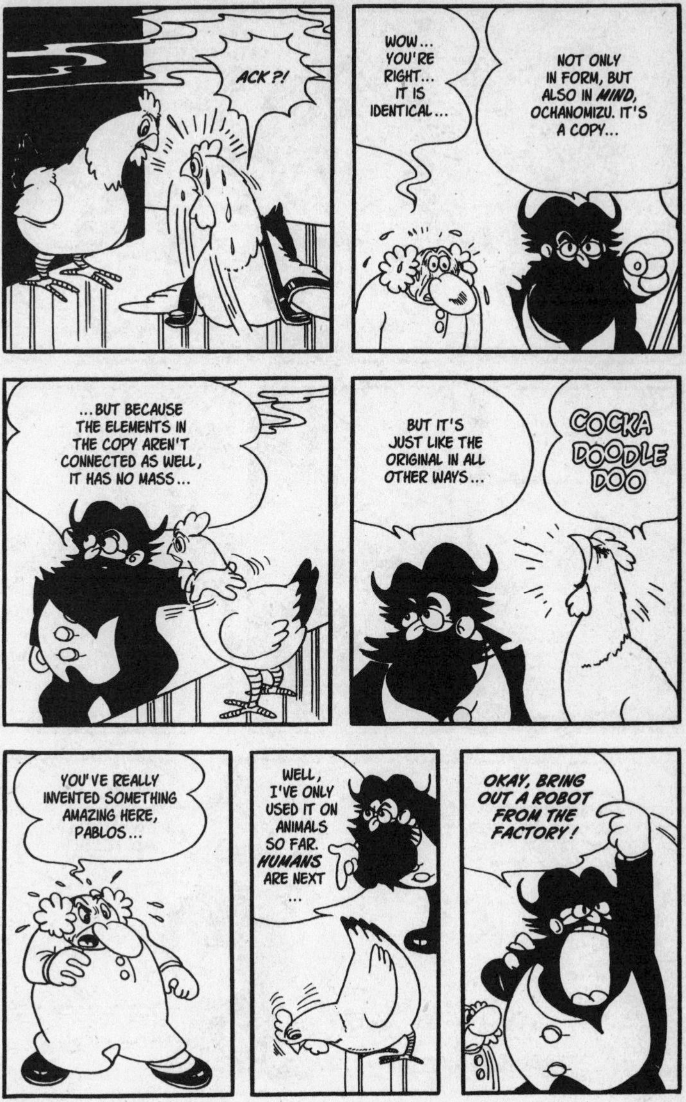
ACK?!
WOW... YOU'RE RIGHT... IT IS IDENTICAL...
NOT ONLY IN FORM, BUT ALSO IN *MIND*, OCHANOMIZU. IT'S A COPY...
...BUT BECAUSE THE ELEMENTS IN THE COPY AREN'T CONNECTED AS WELL, IT HAS NO MASS...
BUT IT'S JUST LIKE THE ORIGINAL IN ALL OTHER WAYS...
COCKA DOODLE DOO
YOU'VE REALLY INVENTED SOMETHING AMAZING HERE, PABLOS...
WELL, I'VE ONLY USED IT ON ANIMALS SO FAR. *HUMANS* ARE NEXT...
OKAY, BRING OUT A ROBOT FROM THE FACTORY!

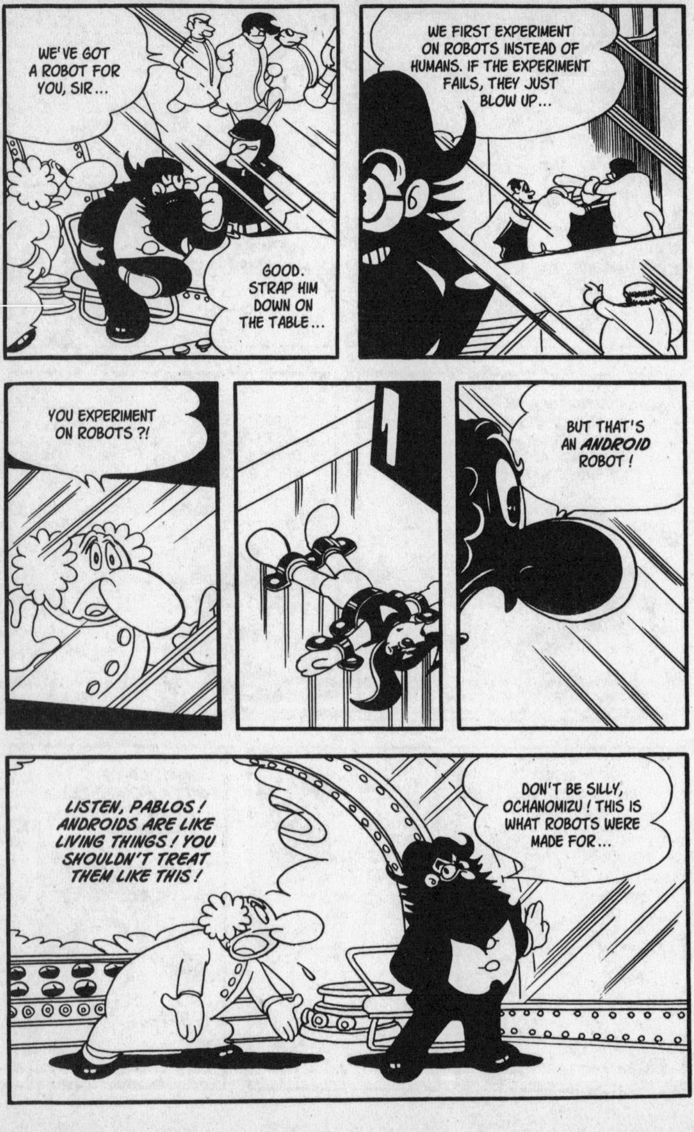
WE'VE GOT A ROBOT FOR YOU, SIR...
GOOD. STRAP HIM DOWN ON THE TABLE...
WE FIRST EXPERIMENT ON ROBOTS INSTEAD OF HUMANS. IF THE EXPERIMENT FAILS, THEY JUST BLOW UP...
YOU EXPERIMENT ON ROBOTS ?!
BUT THAT'S AN *ANDROID* ROBOT !
LISTEN, PABLOS ! ANDROIDS ARE LIKE LIVING THINGS ! YOU SHOULDN'T TREAT THEM LIKE THIS !
DON'T BE SILLY, OCHANOMIZU ! THIS IS WHAT ROBOTS WERE MADE FOR...

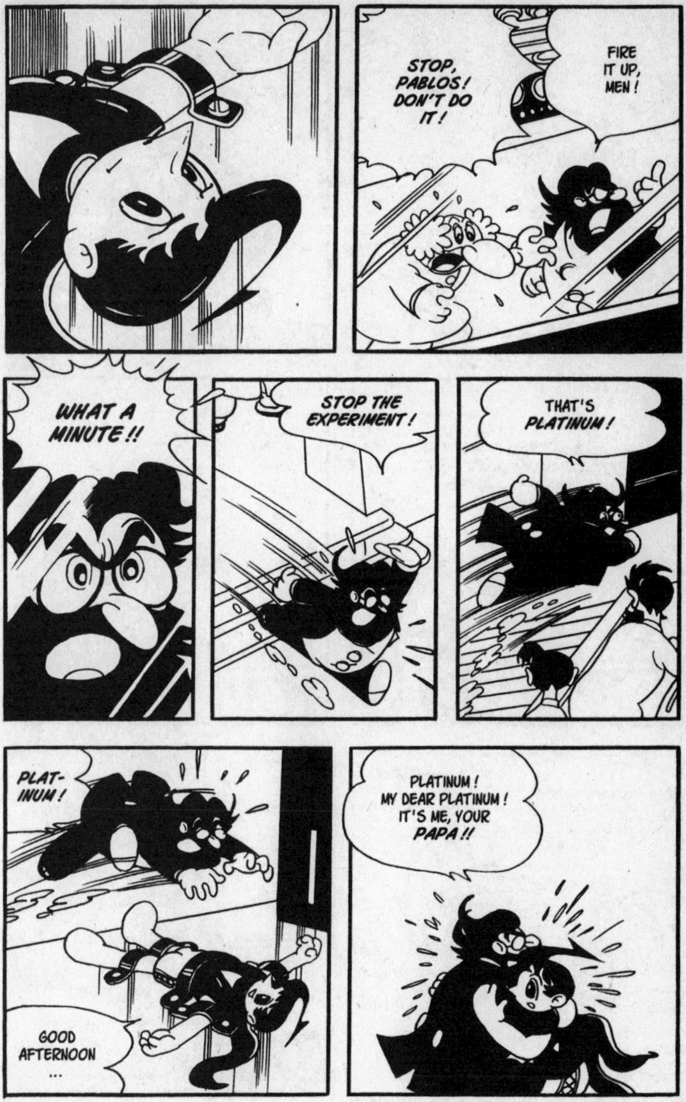
STOP, PABLOS! DON'T DO IT!
FIRE IT UP, MEN!
WHAT A MINUTE!!
STOP THE EXPERIMENT!
THAT'S PLATINUM!
PLAT-INUM!
GOOD AFTERNOON ...
PLATINUM! MY DEAR PLATINUM! IT'S ME, YOUR PAPA!!

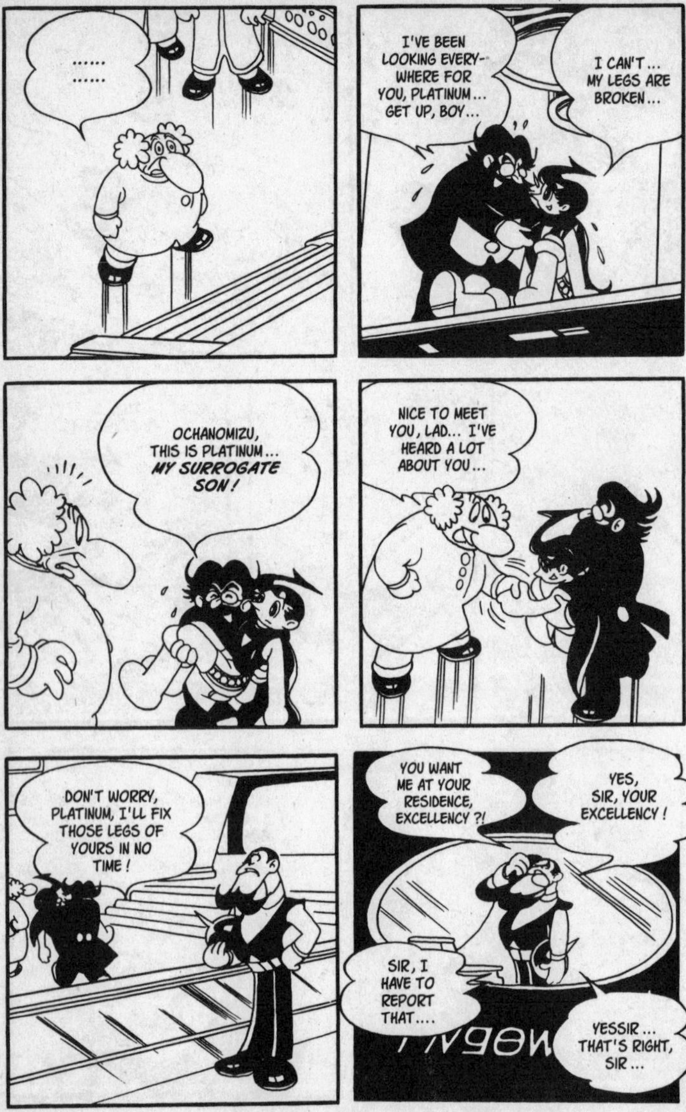
......
......
I'VE BEEN LOOKING EVERY-WHERE FOR YOU, PLATINUM... GET UP, BOY...
I CAN'T... MY LEGS ARE BROKEN...
OCHANOMIZU, THIS IS PLATINUM... *MY SURROGATE SON!*
NICE TO MEET YOU, LAD... I'VE HEARD A LOT ABOUT YOU...
DON'T WORRY, PLATINUM, I'LL FIX THOSE LEGS OF YOURS IN NO TIME!
YOU WANT ME AT YOUR RESIDENCE, EXCELLENCY?!
YES, SIR, YOUR EXCELLENCY!
SIR, I HAVE TO REPORT THAT....
YESSIR... THAT'S RIGHT, SIR...

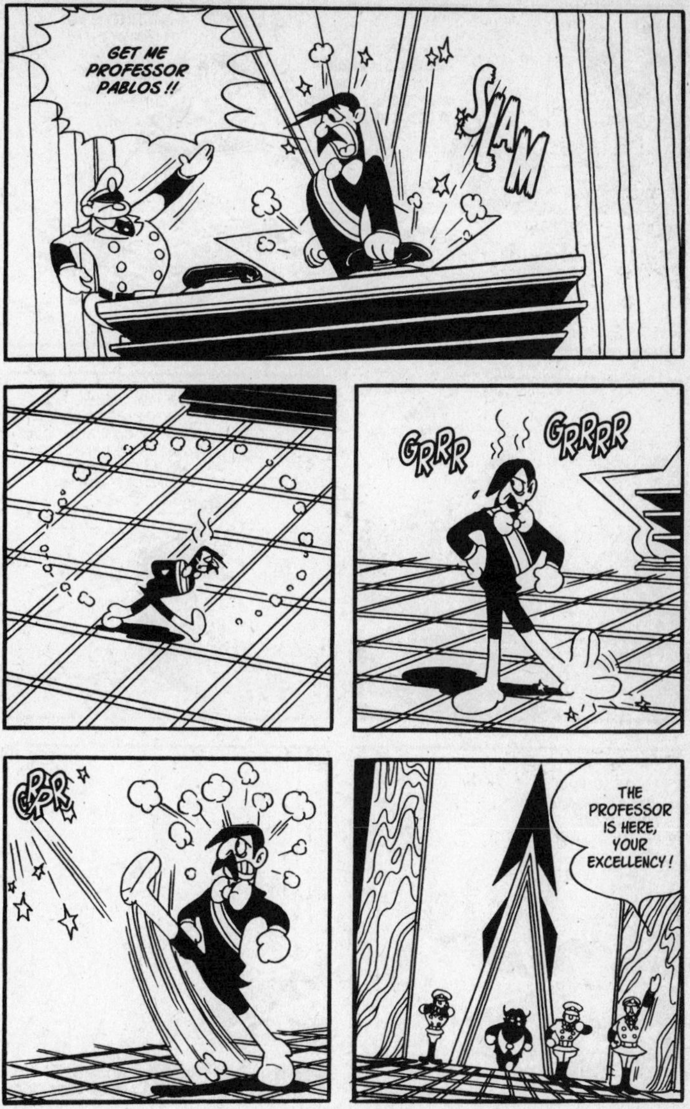
GET ME PROFESSOR PABLOS !!
SLAM
GRRR
GRRRR
GRRR
THE PROFESSOR IS HERE, YOUR EXCELLENCY !

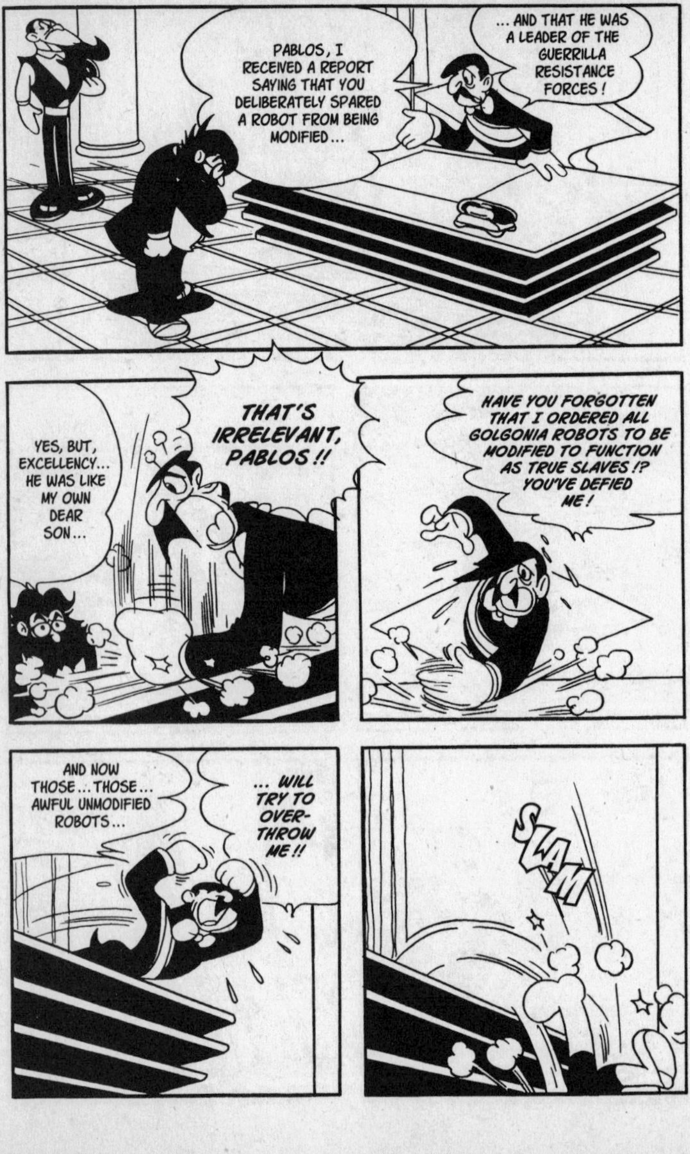

PABLOS, I RECEIVED A REPORT SAYING THAT YOU DELIBERATELY SPARED A ROBOT FROM BEING MODIFIED...
... AND THAT HE WAS A LEADER OF THE GUERRILLA RESISTANCE FORCES!
YES, BUT, EXCELLENCY... HE WAS LIKE MY OWN DEAR SON...
THAT'S IRRELEVANT, PABLOS!!
HAVE YOU FORGOTTEN THAT I ORDERED ALL GOLGONIA ROBOTS TO BE MODIFIED TO FUNCTION AS TRUE SLAVES!? YOU'VE DEFIED ME!
AND NOW THOSE... THOSE... AWFUL UNMODIFIED ROBOTS...
... WILL TRY TO OVER-THROW ME!!
SLAM

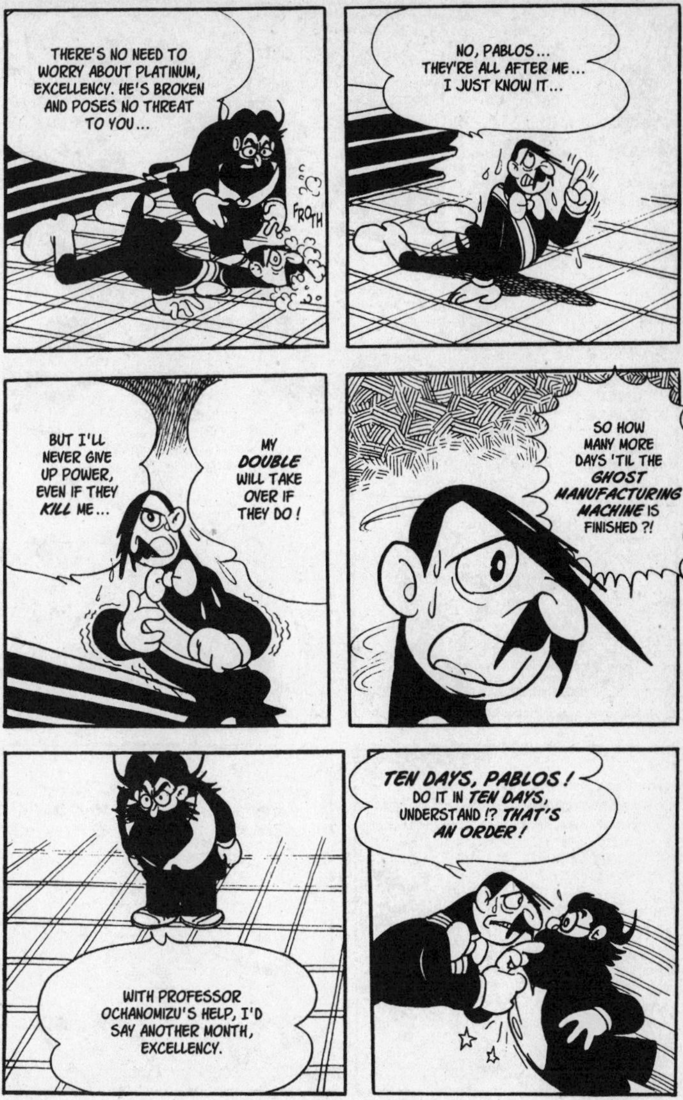

THERE'S NO NEED TO WORRY ABOUT PLATINUM, EXCELLENCY. HE'S BROKEN AND POSES NO THREAT TO YOU...
FROTH
NO, PABLOS... THEY'RE ALL AFTER ME... I JUST KNOW IT...
BUT I'LL NEVER GIVE UP POWER, EVEN IF THEY KILL ME...
MY DOUBLE WILL TAKE OVER IF THEY DO!
SO HOW MANY MORE DAYS 'TIL THE GHOST MANUFACTURING MACHINE IS FINISHED ?!
WITH PROFESSOR OCHANOMIZU'S HELP, I'D SAY ANOTHER MONTH, EXCELLENCY.
TEN DAYS, PABLOS! DO IT IN TEN DAYS, UNDERSTAND !? THAT'S AN ORDER!

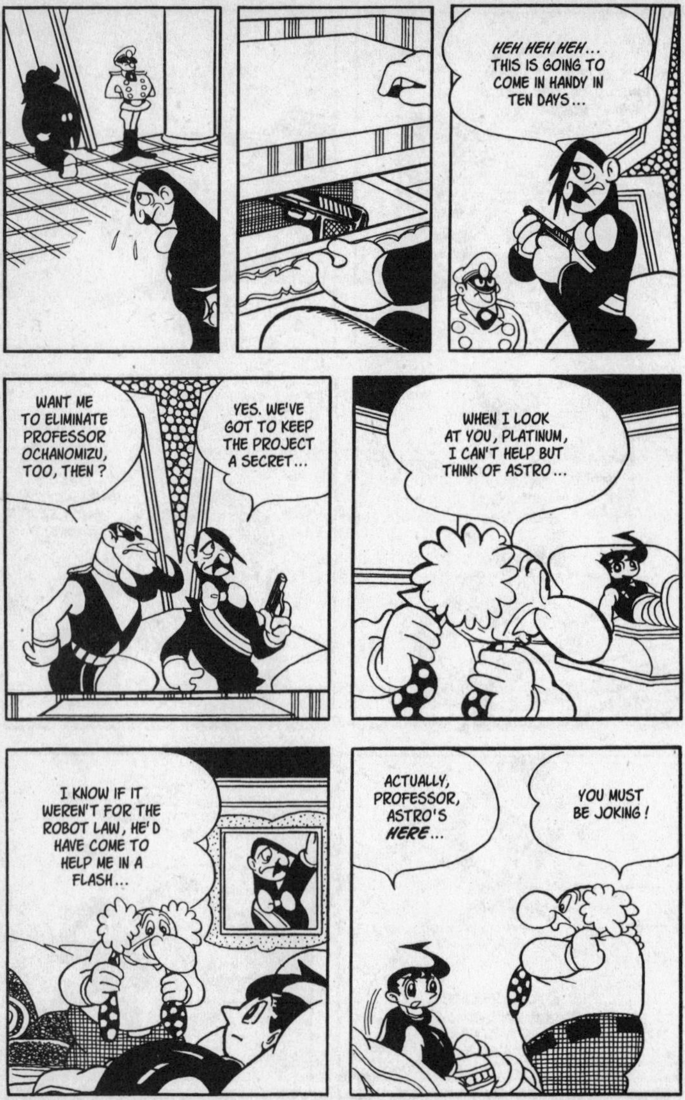
HEH HEH HEH... THIS IS GOING TO COME IN HANDY IN TEN DAYS...
WANT ME TO ELIMINATE PROFESSOR OCHANOMIZU, TOO, THEN?
YES. WE'VE GOT TO KEEP THE PROJECT A SECRET...
WHEN I LOOK AT YOU, PLATINUM, I CAN'T HELP BUT THINK OF ASTRO...
I KNOW IF IT WEREN'T FOR THE ROBOT LAW, HE'D HAVE COME TO HELP ME IN A FLASH...
ACTUALLY, PROFESSOR, ASTRO'S HERE...
YOU MUST BE JOKING!

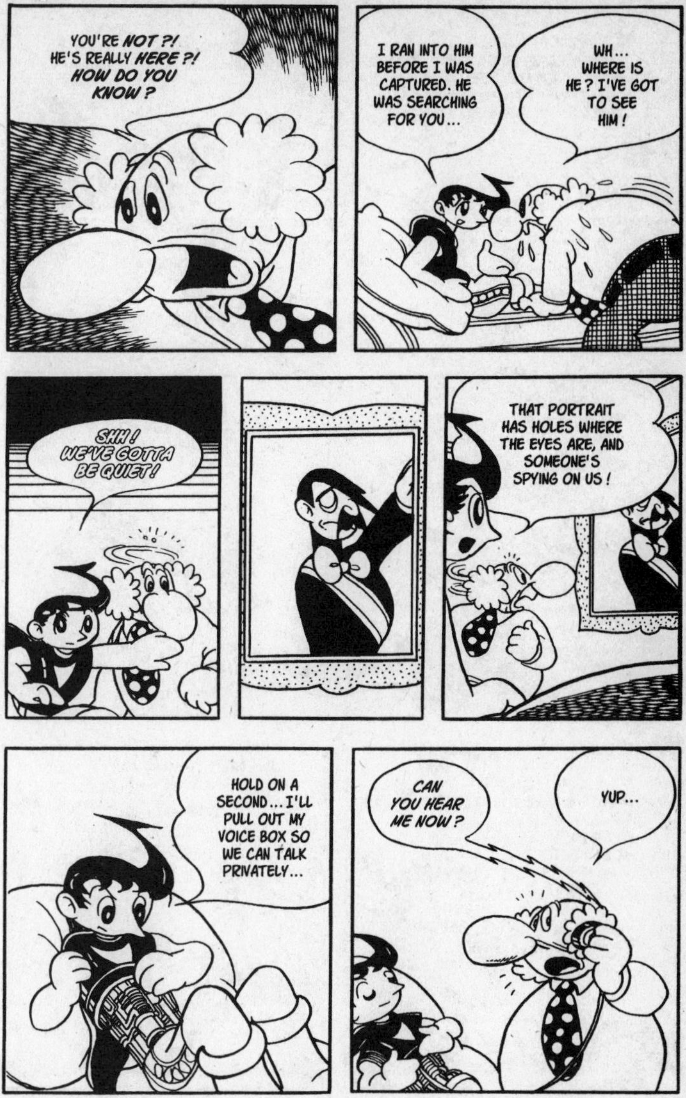
YOU'RE NOT ?! HE'S REALLY HERE ?! HOW DO YOU KNOW ?
I RAN INTO HIM BEFORE I WAS CAPTURED. HE WAS SEARCHING FOR YOU...
WH... WHERE IS HE ? I'VE GOT TO SEE HIM !
SHH ! WE'VE GOTTA BE QUIET !
THAT PORTRAIT HAS HOLES WHERE THE EYES ARE, AND SOMEONE'S SPYING ON US !
HOLD ON A SECOND... I'LL PULL OUT MY VOICE BOX SO WE CAN TALK PRIVATELY...
CAN YOU HEAR ME NOW ?
YUP...

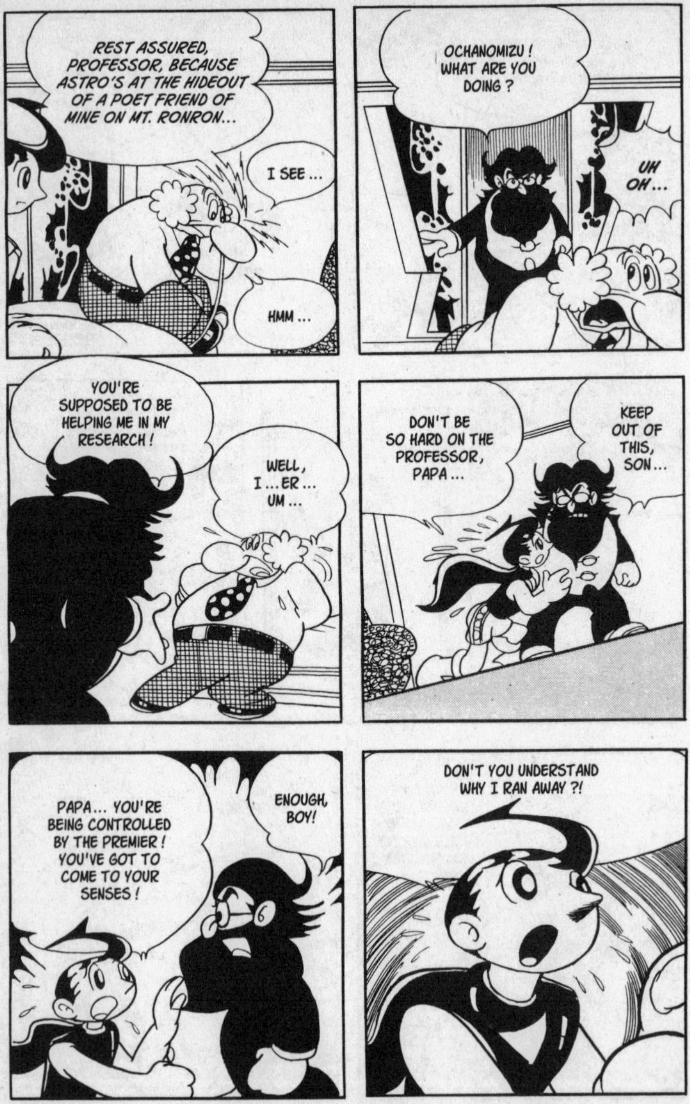
REST ASSURED, PROFESSOR, BECAUSE ASTRO'S AT THE HIDEOUT OF A POET FRIEND OF MINE ON MT. RONRON...
I SEE...
HMM...
OCHANOMIZU! WHAT ARE YOU DOING?
UH OH...
YOU'RE SUPPOSED TO BE HELPING ME IN MY RESEARCH!
WELL, I...ER... UM...
DON'T BE SO HARD ON THE PROFESSOR, PAPA...
KEEP OUT OF THIS, SON...
PAPA... YOU'RE BEING CONTROLLED BY THE PREMIER! YOU'VE GOT TO COME TO YOUR SENSES!
ENOUGH, BOY!
DON'T YOU UNDERSTAND WHY I RAN AWAY?!

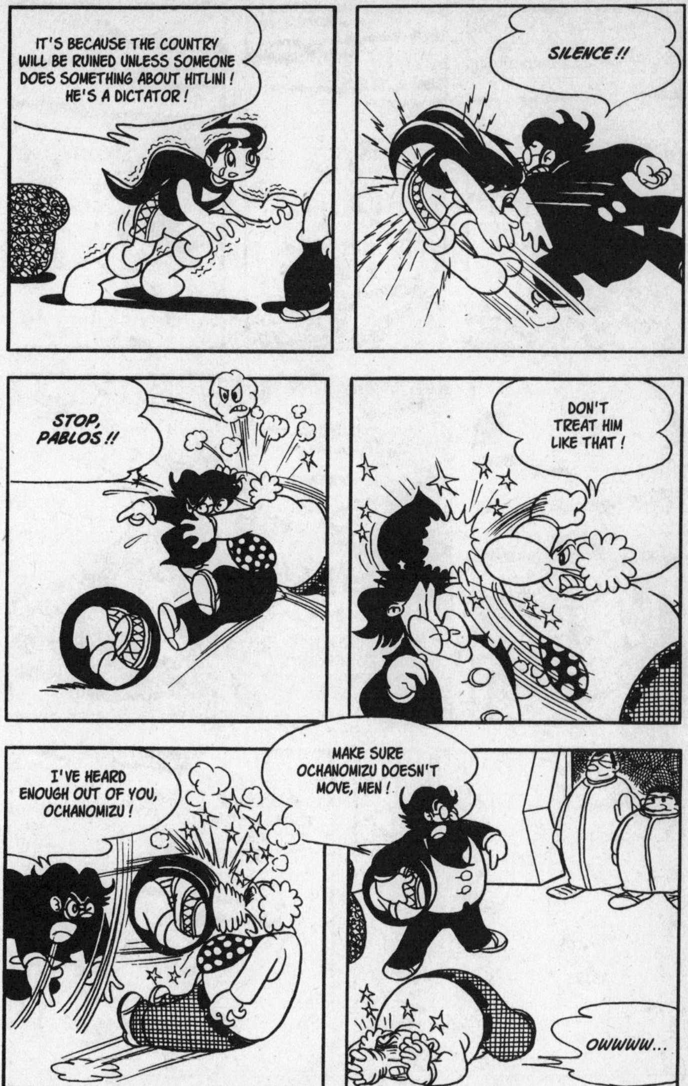

IT'S BECAUSE THE COUNTRY WILL BE RUINED UNLESS SOMEONE DOES SOMETHING ABOUT HITLINI! HE'S A DICTATOR!
SILENCE!!
STOP, PABLOS!!
DON'T TREAT HIM LIKE THAT!
I'VE HEARD ENOUGH OUT OF YOU, OCHANOMIZU!
MAKE SURE OCHANOMIZU DOESN'T MOVE, MEN!
OWWWW...

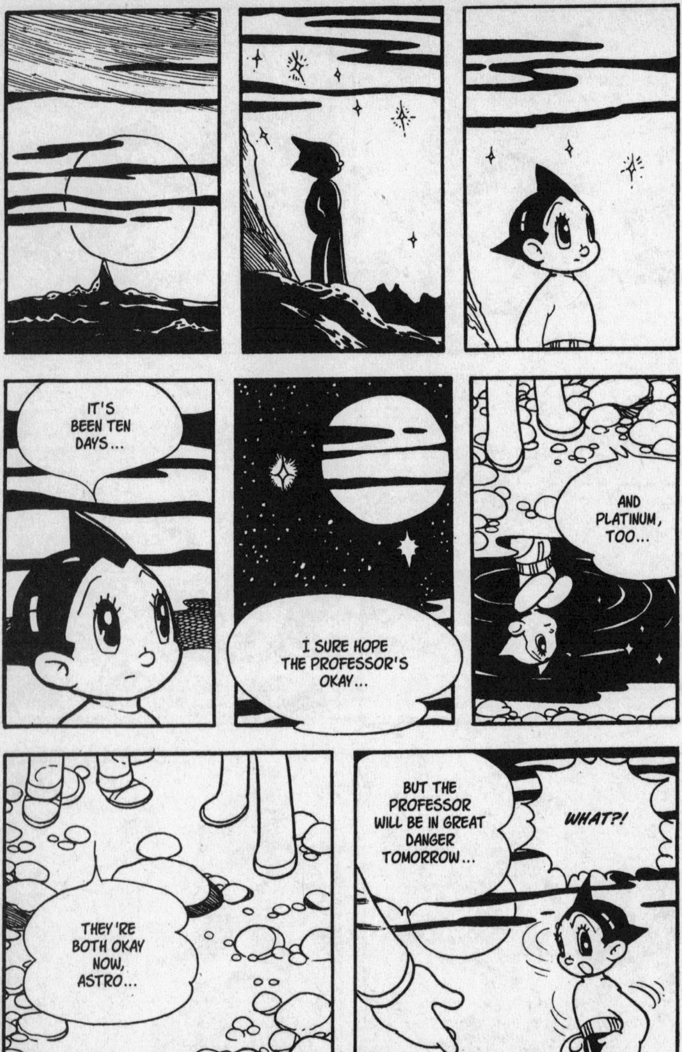
IT'S BEEN TEN DAYS...
I SURE HOPE THE PROFESSOR'S OKAY...
AND PLATINUM, TOO...
THEY'RE BOTH OKAY NOW, ASTRO...
BUT THE PROFESSOR WILL BE IN GREAT DANGER TOMORROW...
WHAT?!

WHY'VE YOU BEEN TELLING ME NOT TO GO HELP THEM IF THAT'S THE CASE!?

BECAUSE THE TIME WASN'T RIGHT... BUT NOW IT IS...

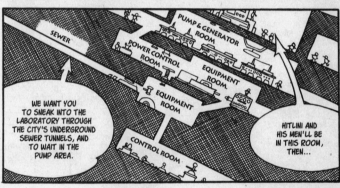

SEWER

PUMP & GENERATOR ROOM

POWER CONTROL ROOM

EQUIPMENT ROOM.

EQUIPMENT ROOM

CONTROL ROOM

WE WANT YOU TO SNEAK INTO THE LABORATORY THROUGH THE CITY'S UNDERGROUND SEWER TUNNELS, AND TO WAIT IN THE PUMP AREA.

HITLINI AND HIS MEN'LL BE IN THIS ROOM, THEN...

... RENDEZVOUS WITH YOU, AND ESCAPE...

GOSH... I HOPE IT WORKS...

WE'VE GOT TO TRY, ASTRO... WE MIGHT NOT HAVE ANOTHER CHANCE...

UNDER- STOOD...

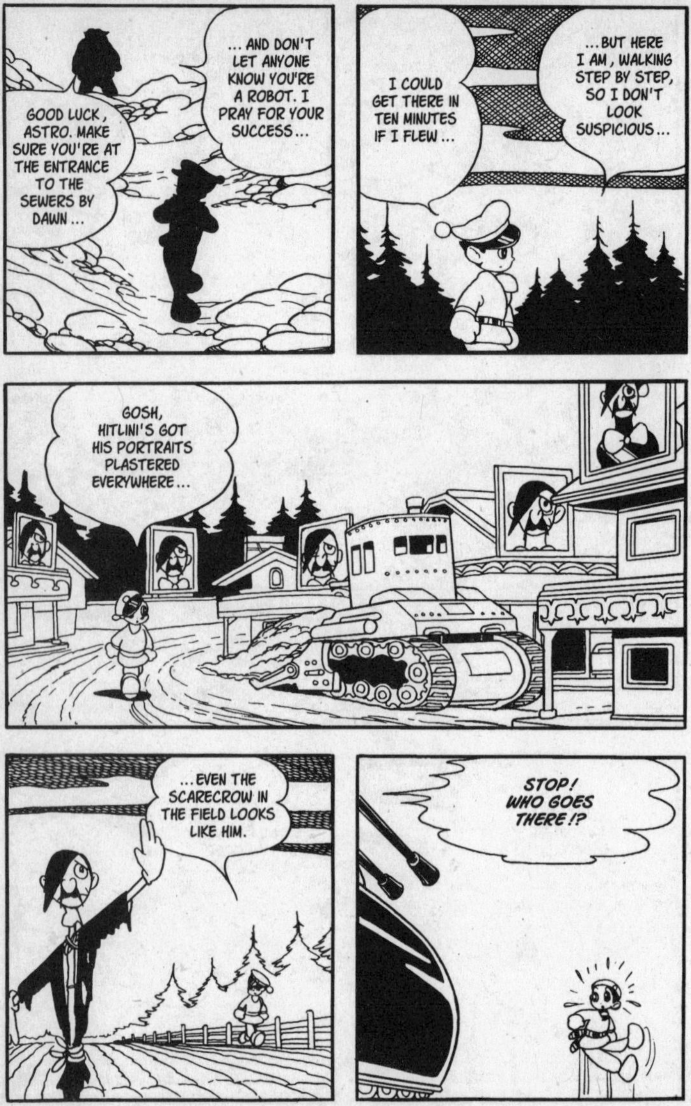
GOOD LUCK, ASTRO. MAKE SURE YOU'RE AT THE ENTRANCE TO THE SEWERS BY DAWN...
... AND DON'T LET ANYONE KNOW YOU'RE A ROBOT. I PRAY FOR YOUR SUCCESS...
I COULD GET THERE IN TEN MINUTES IF I FLEW...
...BUT HERE I AM, WALKING STEP BY STEP, SO I DON'T LOOK SUSPICIOUS...
GOSH, HITLINI'S GOT HIS PORTRAITS PLASTERED EVERYWHERE...
...EVEN THE SCARECROW IN THE FIELD LOOKS LIKE HIM.
STOP! WHO GOES THERE!?

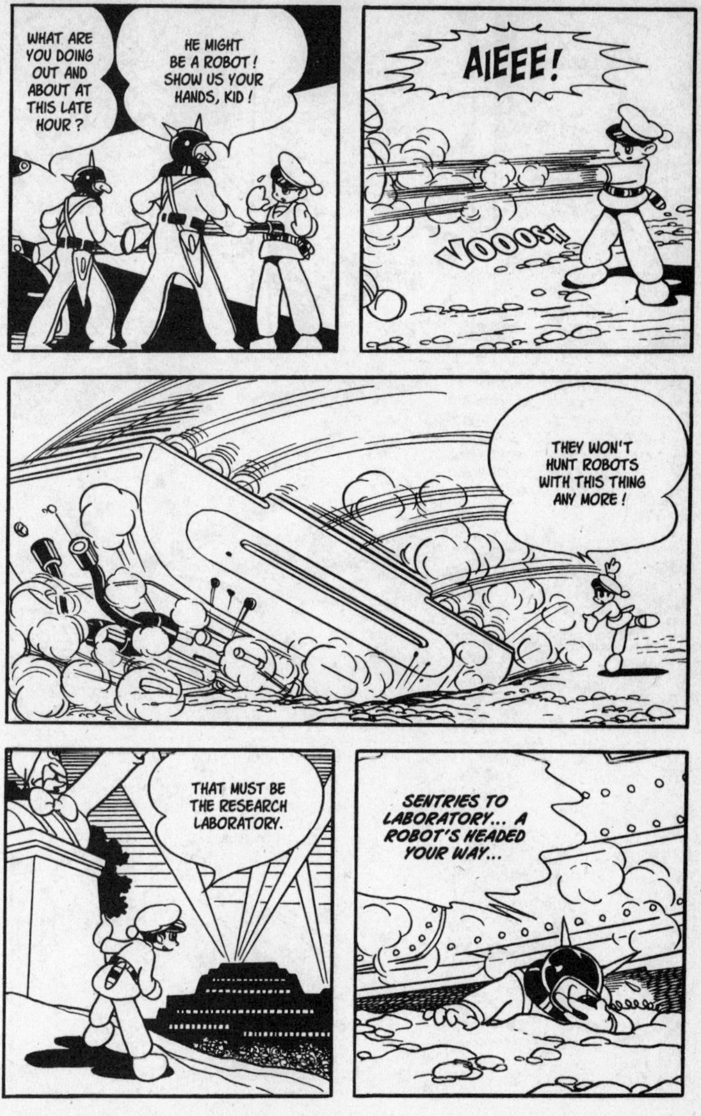
WHAT ARE YOU DOING OUT AND ABOUT AT THIS LATE HOUR ?
HE MIGHT BE A ROBOT ! SHOW US YOUR HANDS, KID !
AIEEE !
VOOOSH
THEY WON'T HUNT ROBOTS WITH THIS THING ANY MORE !
THAT MUST BE THE RESEARCH LABORATORY.
SENTRIES TO LABORATORY... A ROBOT'S HEADED YOUR WAY...

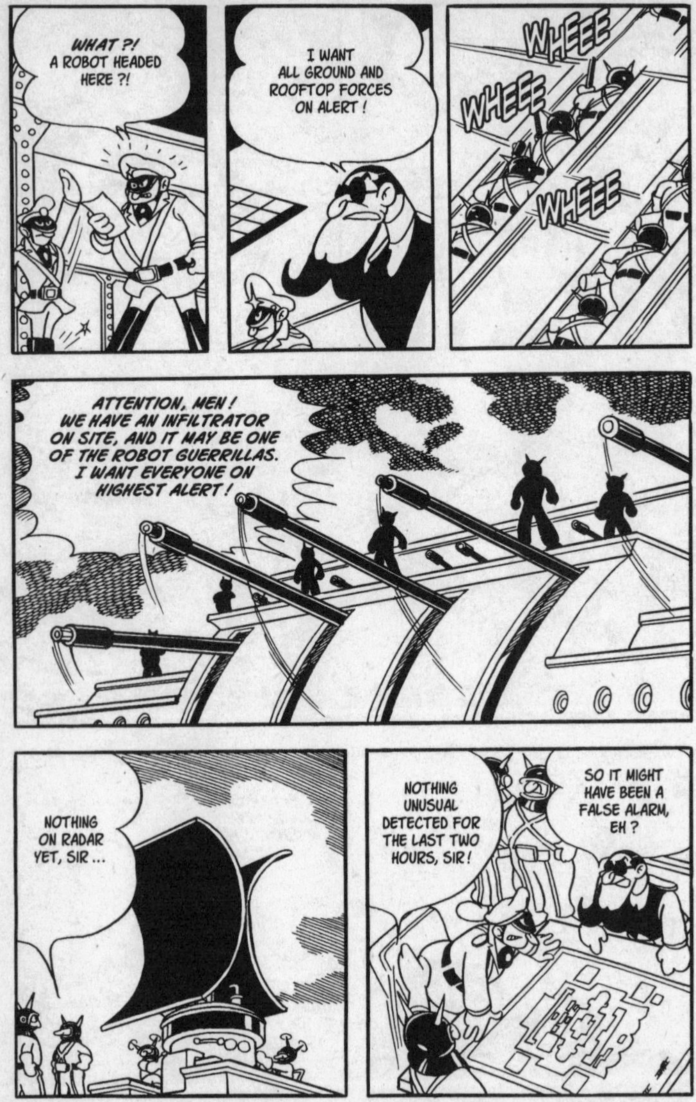
WHAT ?! A ROBOT HEADED HERE ?!
I WANT ALL GROUND AND ROOFTOP FORCES ON ALERT !
WHEEE
WHEEE
WHEEE
ATTENTION, MEN ! WE HAVE AN INFILTRATOR ON SITE, AND IT MAY BE ONE OF THE ROBOT GUERRILLAS. I WANT EVERYONE ON HIGHEST ALERT !
NOTHING ON RADAR YET, SIR ...
NOTHING UNUSUAL DETECTED FOR THE LAST TWO HOURS, SIR !
SO IT MIGHT HAVE BEEN A FALSE ALARM, EH ?

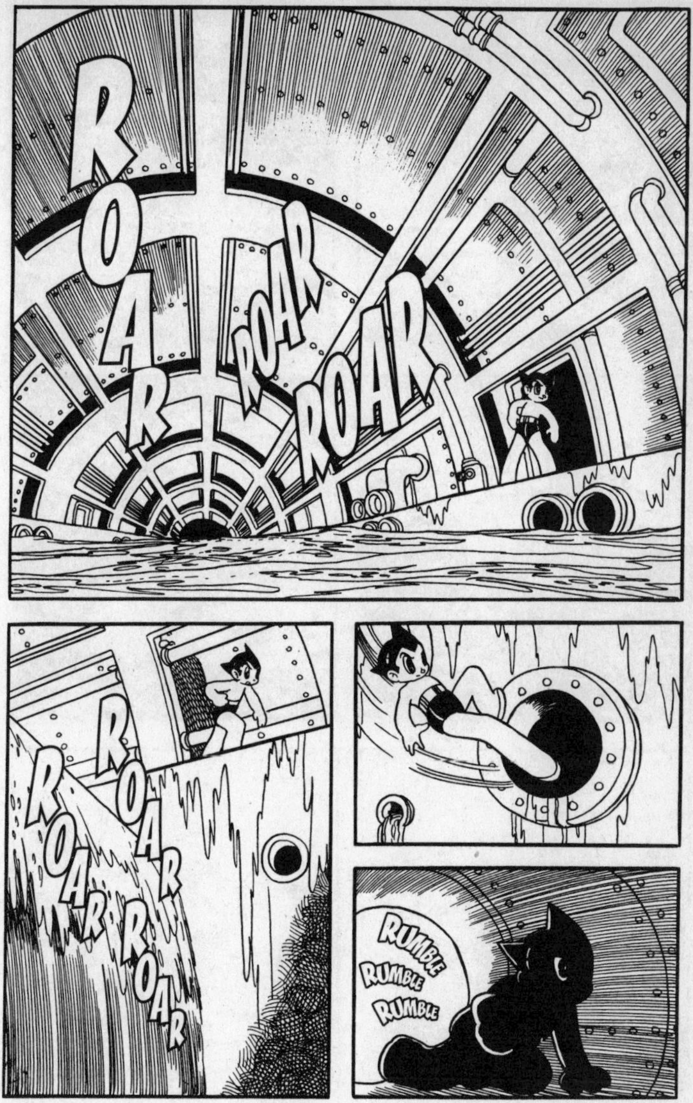
ROAR
ROAR
ROAR
ROAR
ROAR
ROAR
RUMBLE
RUMBLE
RUMBLE

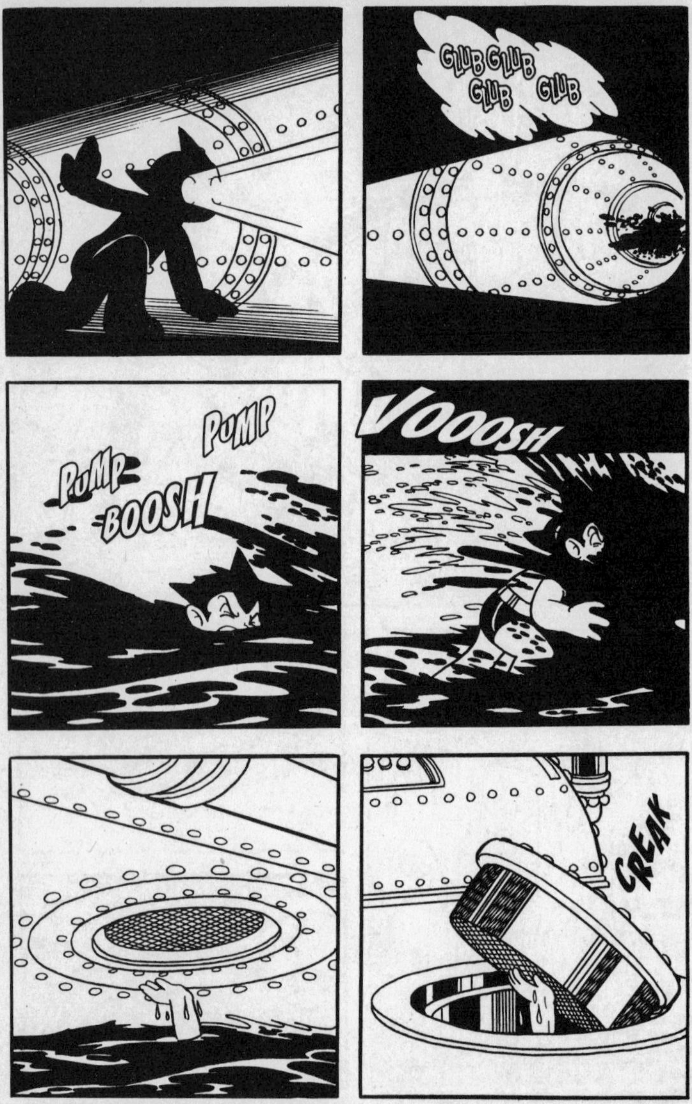
GLUB GLUB
GLUB GLUB
PUMP
PUMP
BOOSH
VOOOSH
CREAK

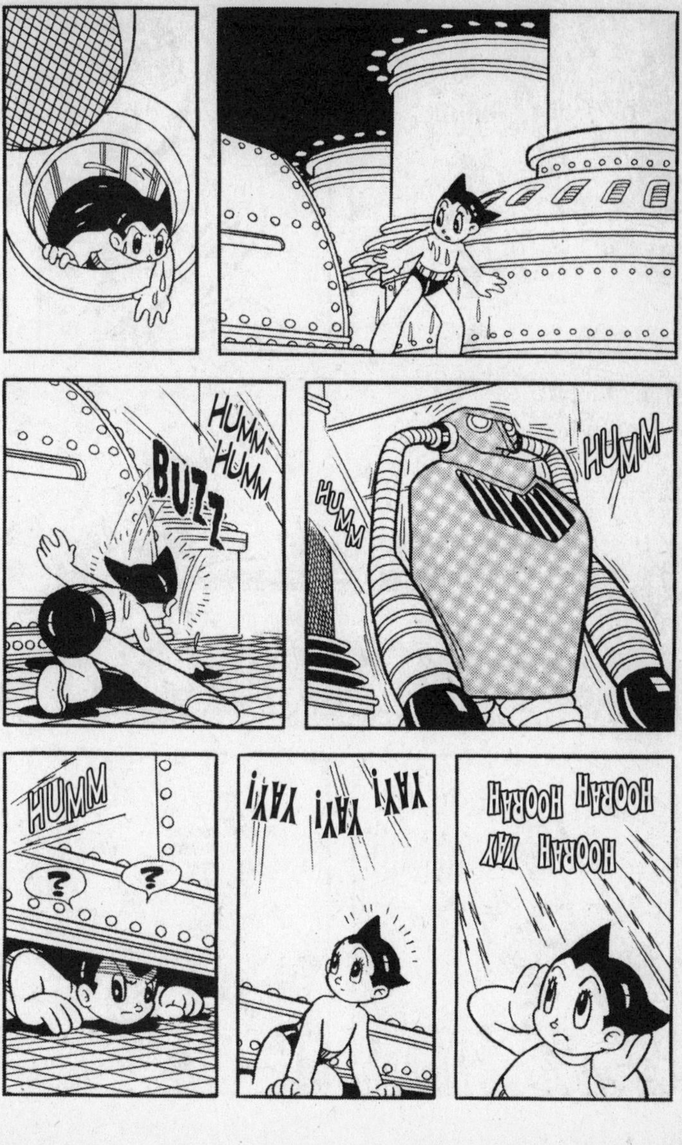
HUMM HUMM
BUZZ
HUMM
HUMM
HUMM
?
?
YAY! YAY! YAY!
HOORAH HOORAH
HOORAH YAY

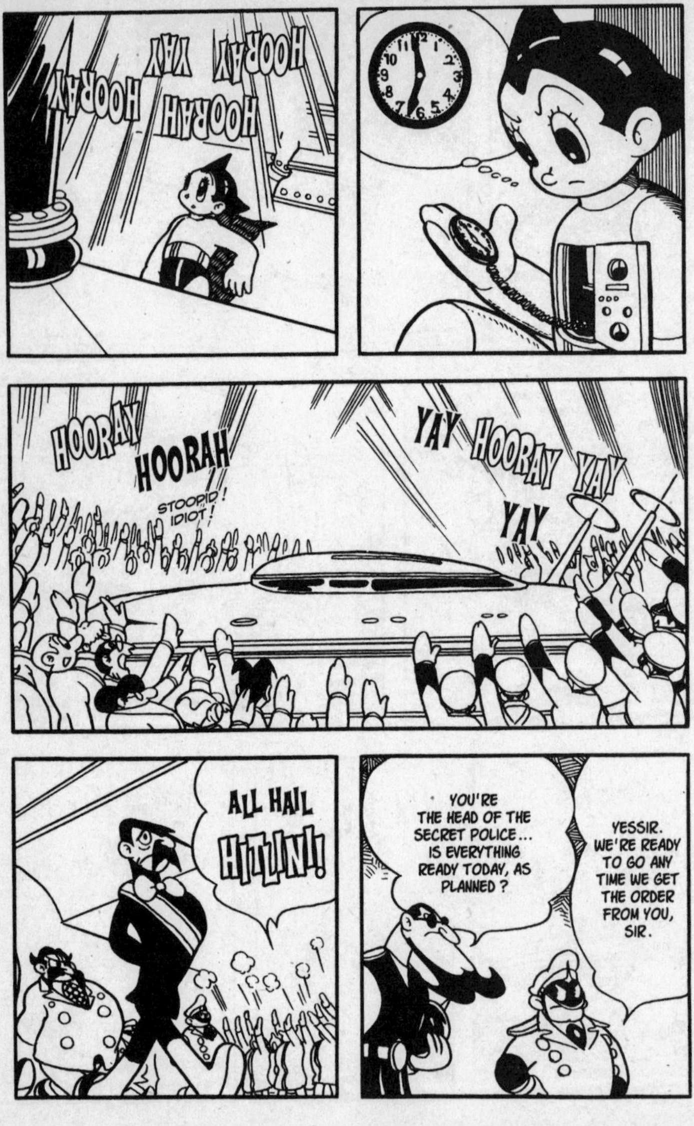
HOORAY
HOORAH
HOORAY YAY
HOORAY
HOORAH
STOOPID! IDIOT!
YAY HOORAY YAY
YAY
ALL HAIL HITLINI!
YOU'RE THE HEAD OF THE SECRET POLICE... IS EVERYTHING READY TODAY, AS PLANNED?
YESSIR. WE'RE READY TO GO ANY TIME WE GET THE ORDER FROM YOU, SIR.

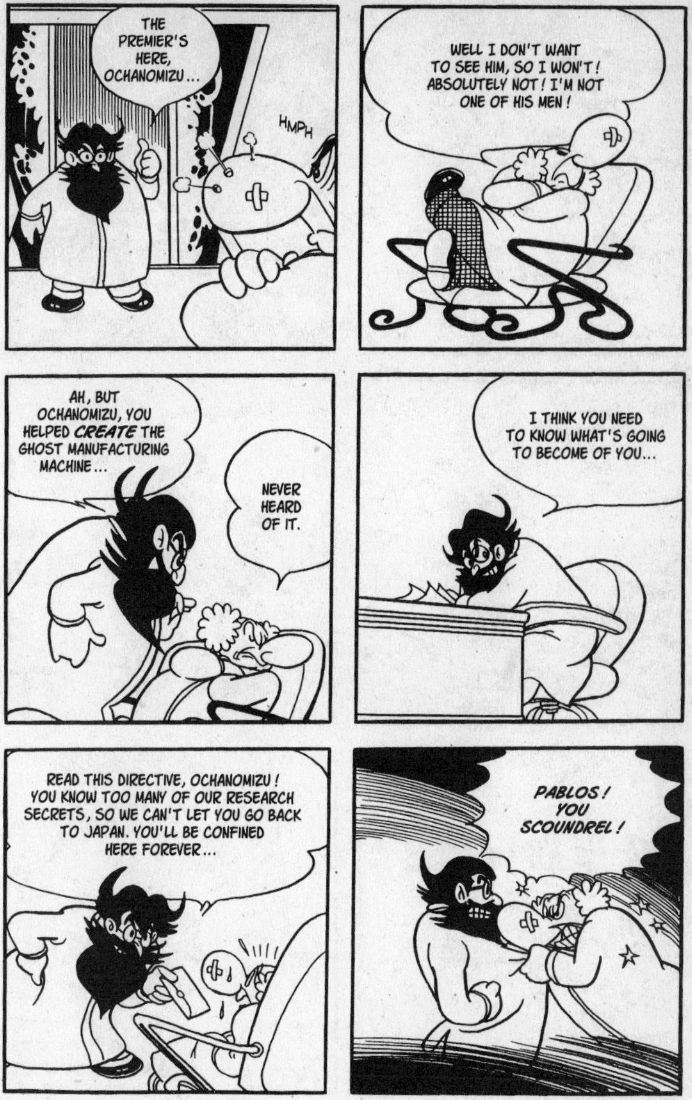
THE PREMIER'S HERE, OCHANOMIZU...
HMPH
WELL I DON'T WANT TO SEE HIM, SO I WON'T! ABSOLUTELY NOT! I'M NOT ONE OF HIS MEN!
AH, BUT OCHANOMIZU, YOU HELPED *CREATE* THE GHOST MANUFACTURING MACHINE...
NEVER HEARD OF IT.
I THINK YOU NEED TO KNOW WHAT'S GOING TO BECOME OF YOU...
READ THIS DIRECTIVE, OCHANOMIZU! YOU KNOW TOO MANY OF OUR RESEARCH SECRETS, SO WE CAN'T LET YOU GO BACK TO JAPAN. YOU'LL BE CONFINED HERE FOREVER...
PABLOS! YOU SCOUNDREL!

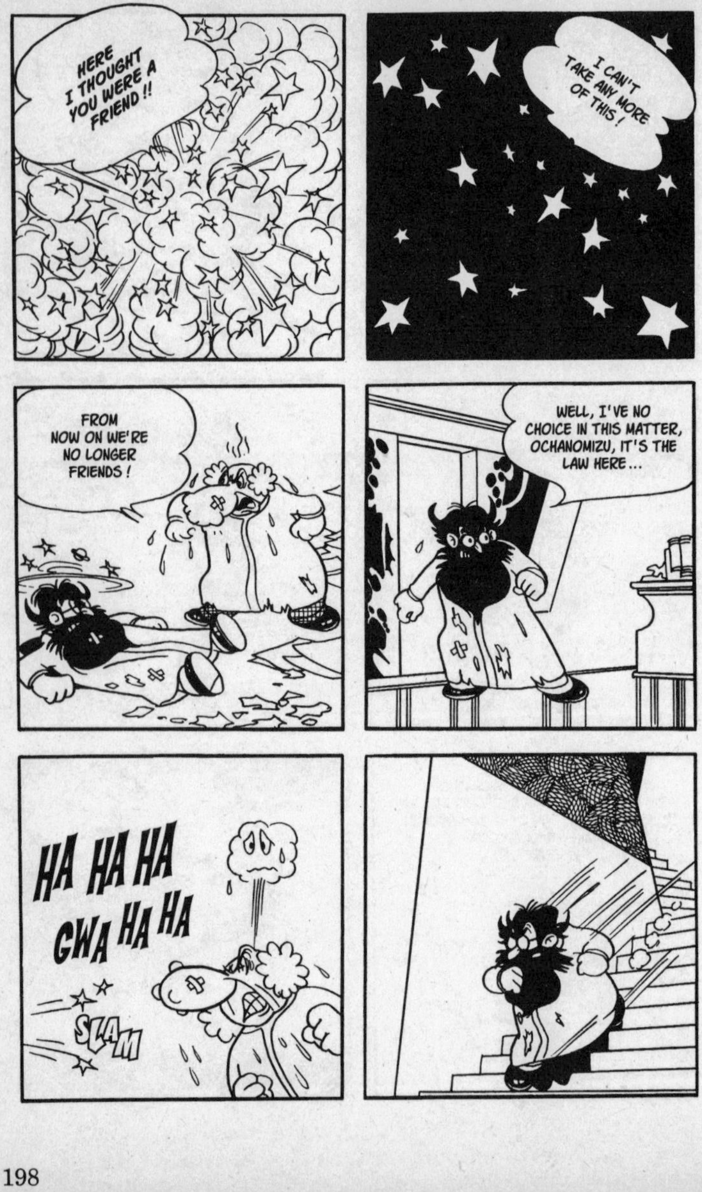

HERE I THOUGHT YOU WERE A FRIEND !!
I CAN'T TAKE ANY MORE OF THIS !
FROM NOW ON WE'RE NO LONGER FRIENDS !
WELL, I'VE NO CHOICE IN THIS MATTER, OCHANOMIZU, IT'S THE LAW HERE...
HA HA HA
GWA HA HA
SLAM

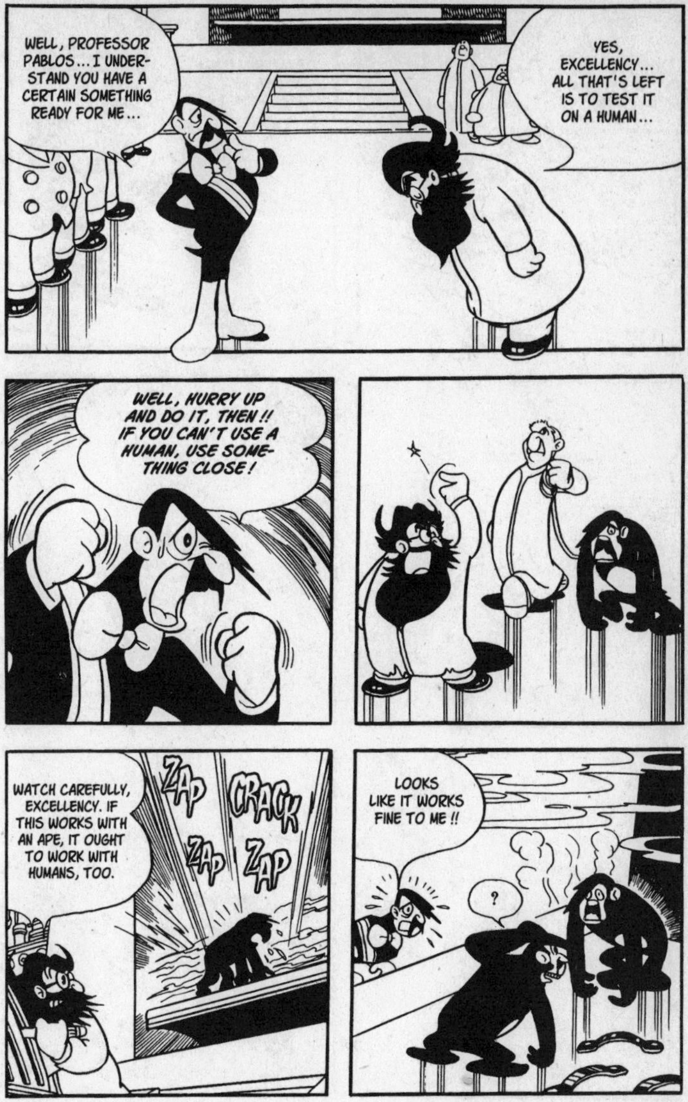
WELL, PROFESSOR PABLOS... I UNDERSTAND YOU HAVE A CERTAIN SOMETHING READY FOR ME...
YES, EXCELLENCY... ALL THAT'S LEFT IS TO TEST IT ON A HUMAN...
WELL, HURRY UP AND DO IT, THEN!! IF YOU CAN'T USE A HUMAN, USE SOMETHING CLOSE!
WATCH CAREFULLY, EXCELLENCY. IF THIS WORKS WITH AN APE, IT OUGHT TO WORK WITH HUMANS, TOO.
ZAP
CRACK
ZAP
ZAP
LOOKS LIKE IT WORKS FINE TO ME!!
?

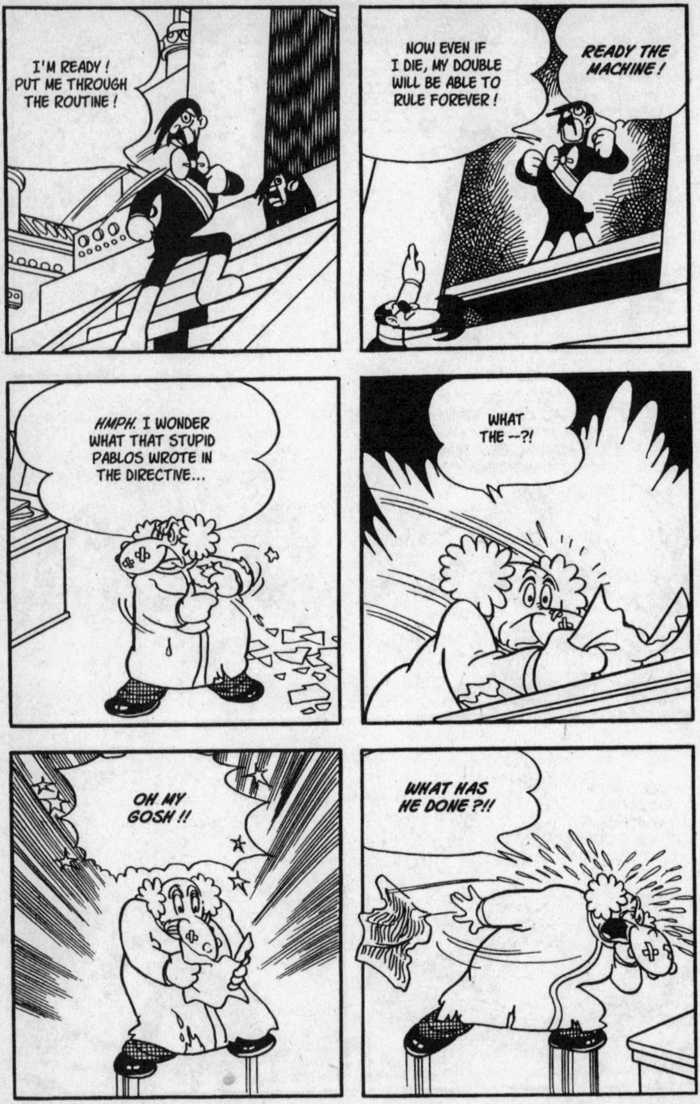
I'M READY ! PUT ME THROUGH THE ROUTINE !
NOW EVEN IF I DIE, MY DOUBLE WILL BE ABLE TO RULE FOREVER !
READY THE MACHINE !
HMPH. I WONDER WHAT THAT STUPID PABLOS WROTE IN THE DIRECTIVE...
WHAT THE --?!
OH MY GOSH !!
WHAT HAS HE DONE ?!!

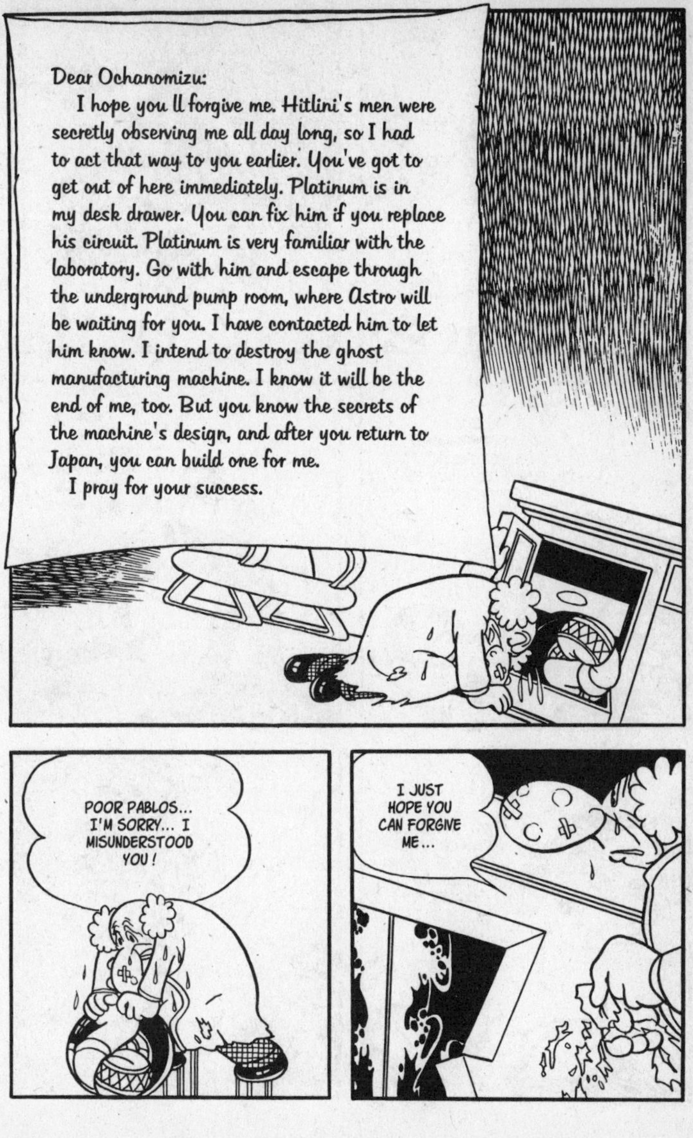
Dear Ochanomizu:
I hope you ll forgive me. Hitlini's men were secretly observing me all day long, so I had to act that way to you earlier. You've got to get out of here immediately. Platinum is in my desk drawer. You can fix him if you replace his circuit. Platinum is very familiar with the laboratory. Go with him and escape through the underground pump room, where Astro will be waiting for you. I have contacted him to let him know. I intend to destroy the ghost manufacturing machine. I know it will be the end of me, too. But you know the secrets of the machine's design, and after you return to Japan, you can build one for me.
I pray for your success.
POOR PABLOS... I'M SORRY... I MISUNDERSTOOD YOU!
I JUST HOPE YOU CAN FORGIVE ME...

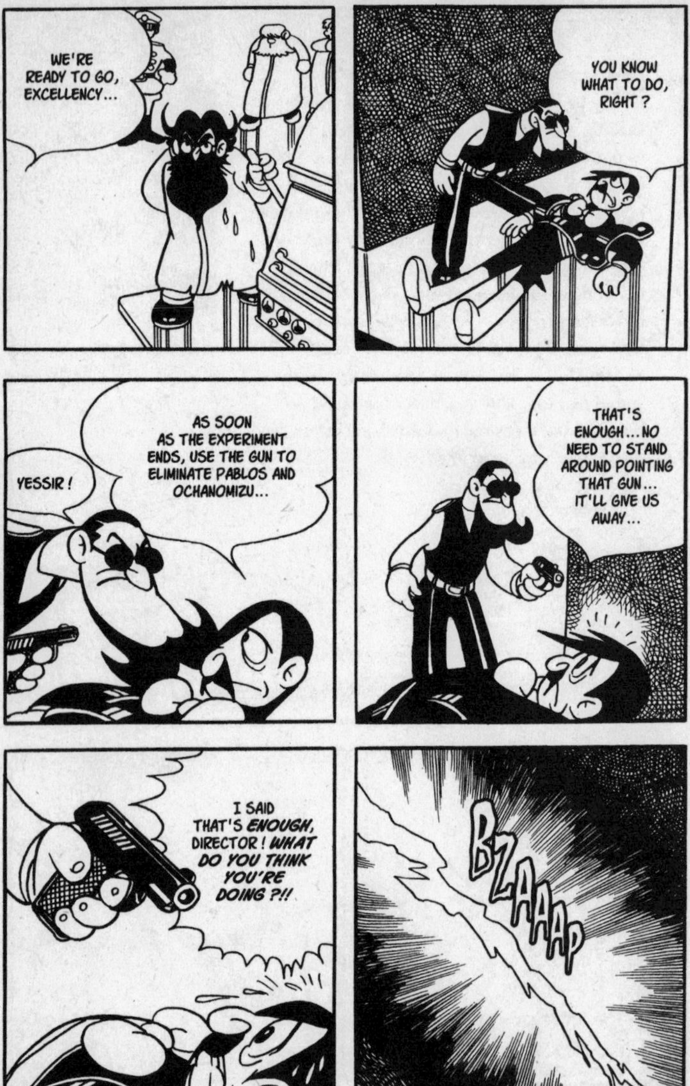
WE'RE READY TO GO, EXCELLENCY...
YOU KNOW WHAT TO DO, RIGHT ?
YESSIR !
AS SOON AS THE EXPERIMENT ENDS, USE THE GUN TO ELIMINATE PABLOS AND OCHANOMIZU...
THAT'S ENOUGH... NO NEED TO STAND AROUND POINTING THAT GUN... IT'LL GIVE US AWAY...
I SAID THAT'S *ENOUGH*, DIRECTOR ! *WHAT DO YOU THINK YOU'RE DOING ?!!*
BZAAAP

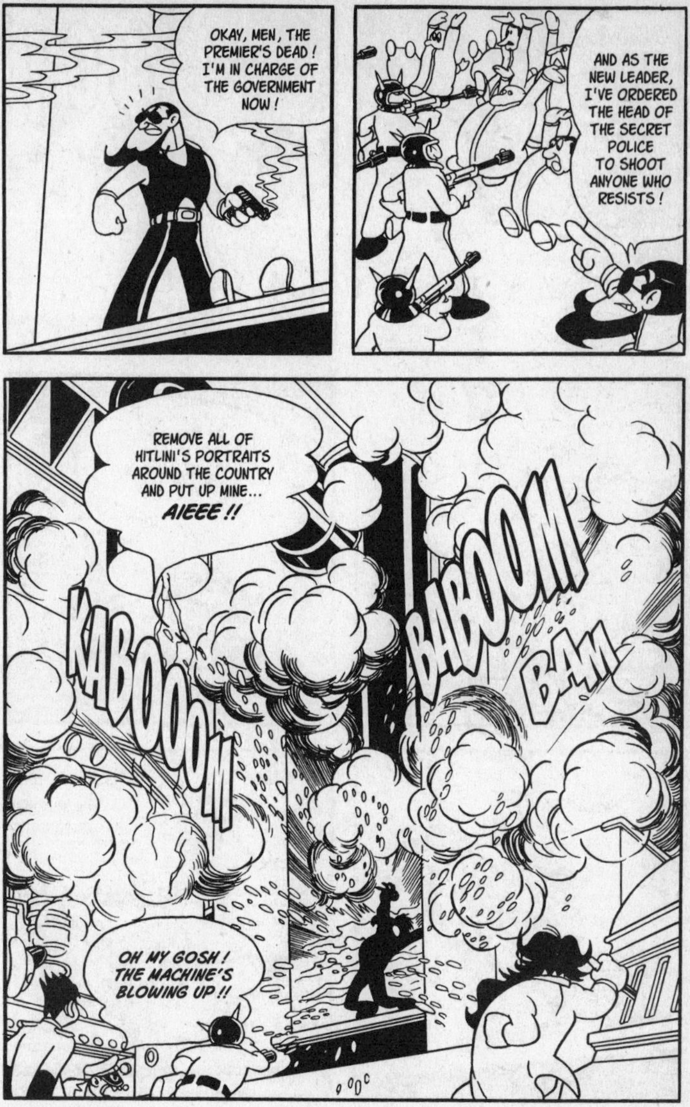
OKAY, MEN, THE PREMIER'S DEAD! I'M IN CHARGE OF THE GOVERNMENT NOW!
AND AS THE NEW LEADER, I'VE ORDERED THE HEAD OF THE SECRET POLICE TO SHOOT ANYONE WHO RESISTS!
REMOVE ALL OF HITLINI'S PORTRAITS AROUND THE COUNTRY AND PUT UP MINE... AIEEE!!
KABOOOOM
BABOOM
BAM
OH MY GOSH! THE MACHINE'S BLOWING UP!!

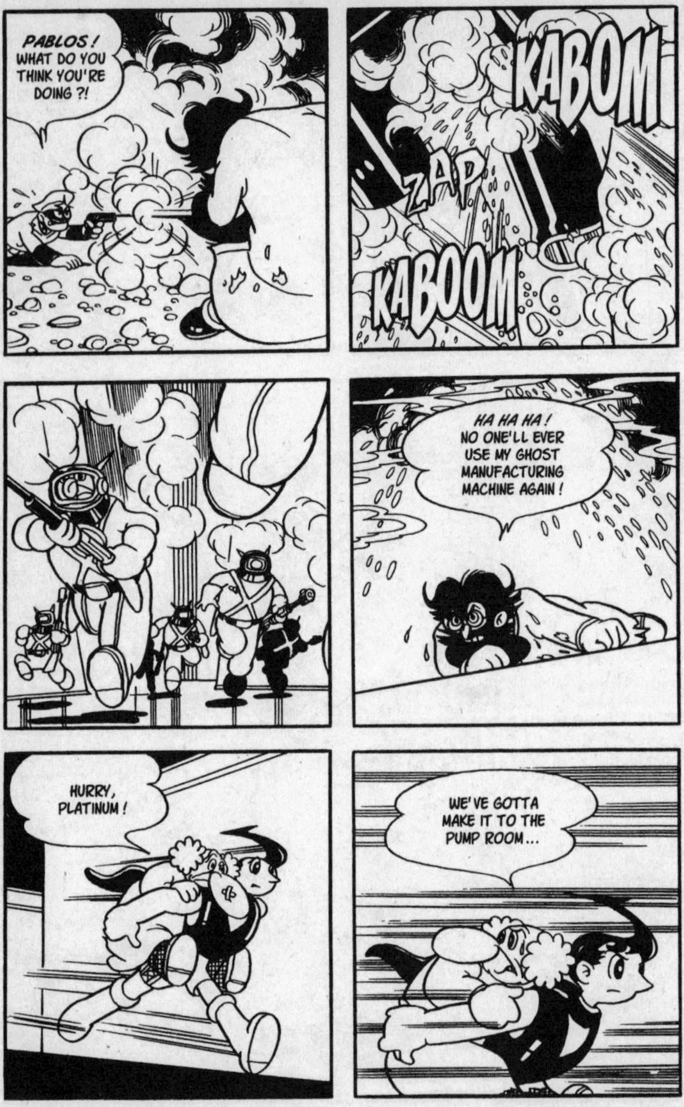
PABLOS! WHAT DO YOU THINK YOU'RE DOING ?!
KABOM
ZAP
KABOOM
HA HA HA! NO ONE'LL EVER USE MY GHOST MANUFACTURING MACHINE AGAIN!
HURRY, PLATINUM!
WE'VE GOTTA MAKE IT TO THE PUMP ROOM...

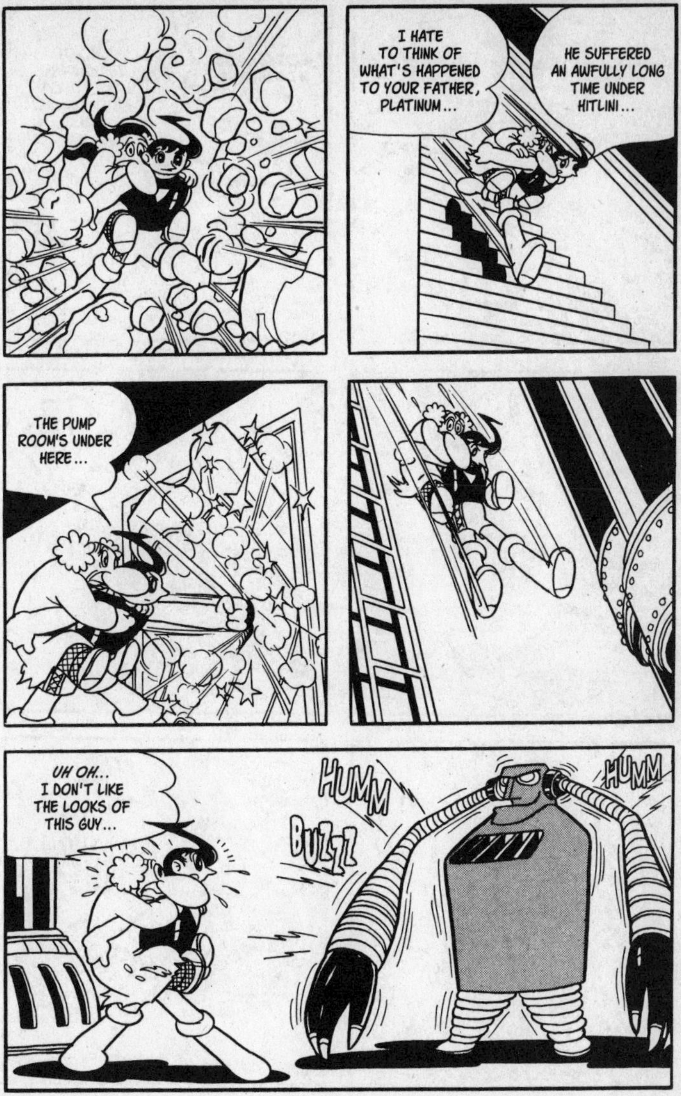
I HATE TO THINK OF WHAT'S HAPPENED TO YOUR FATHER, PLATINUM...
HE SUFFERED AN AWFULLY LONG TIME UNDER HITLINI...
THE PUMP ROOM'S UNDER HERE...
UH OH... I DON'T LIKE THE LOOKS OF THIS GUY...
HUMM
BUZZZ
HUMM

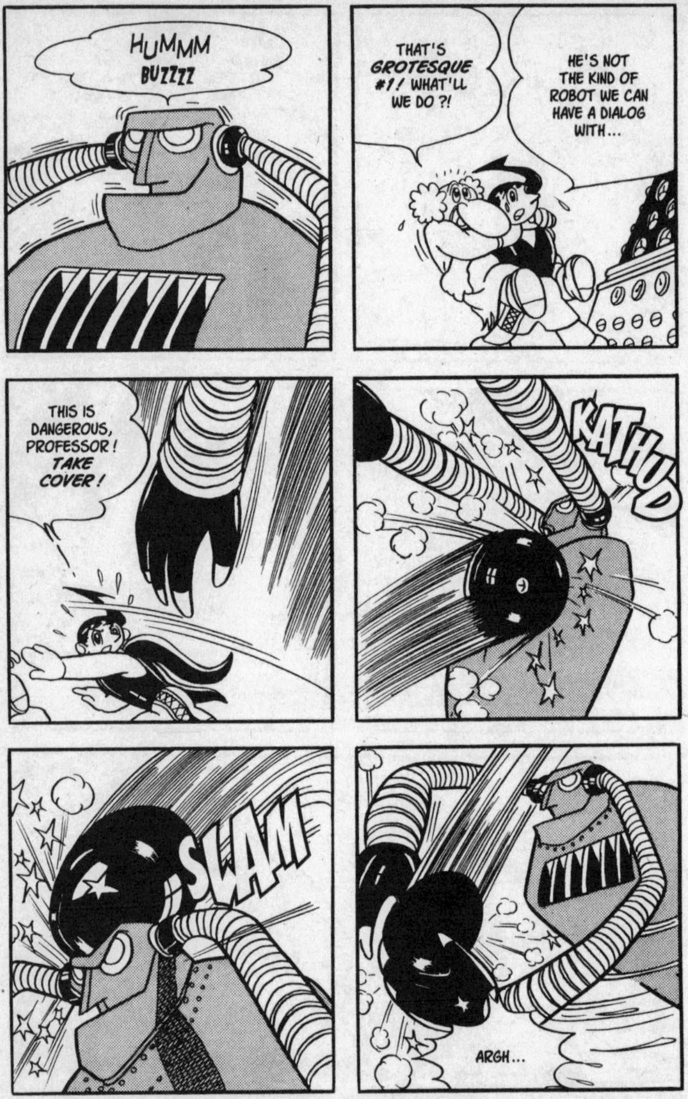
HUMMM
BUZZZZ
THAT'S GROTESQUE #1! WHAT'LL WE DO ?!
HE'S NOT THE KIND OF ROBOT WE CAN HAVE A DIALOG WITH...
THIS IS DANGEROUS, PROFESSOR! TAKE COVER!
KATHUD
SLAM
ARGH...

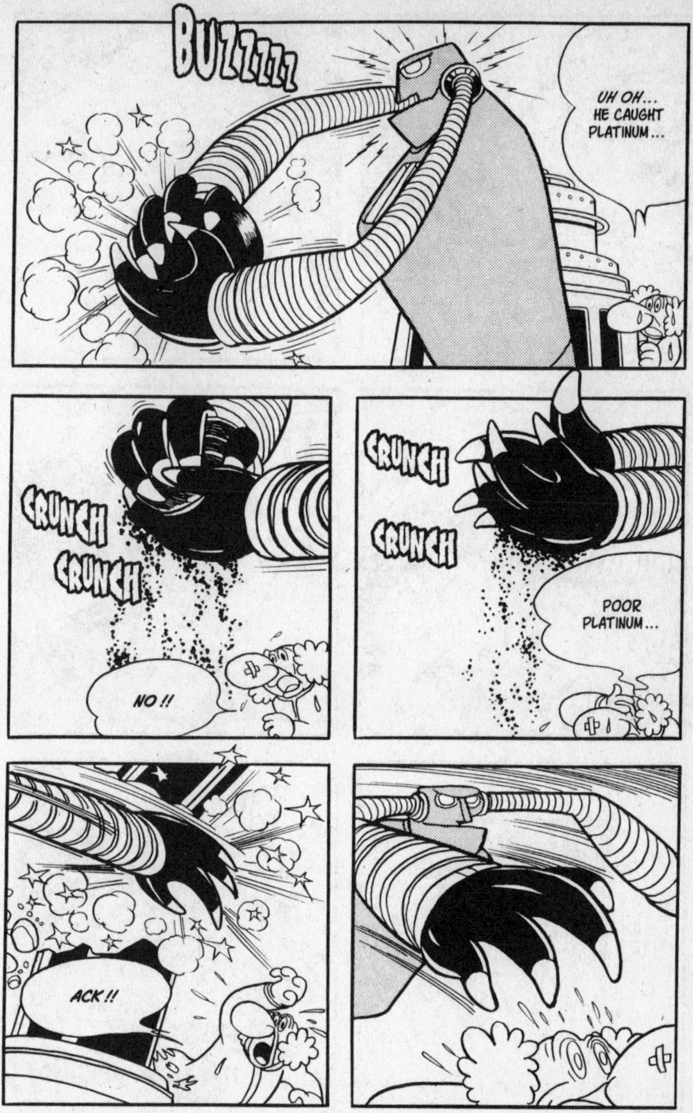
BUZZZZZ
UH OH... HE CAUGHT PLATINUM...
CRUNCH
CRUNCH
NO !!
CRUNCH
CRUNCH
POOR PLATINUM...
ACK !!

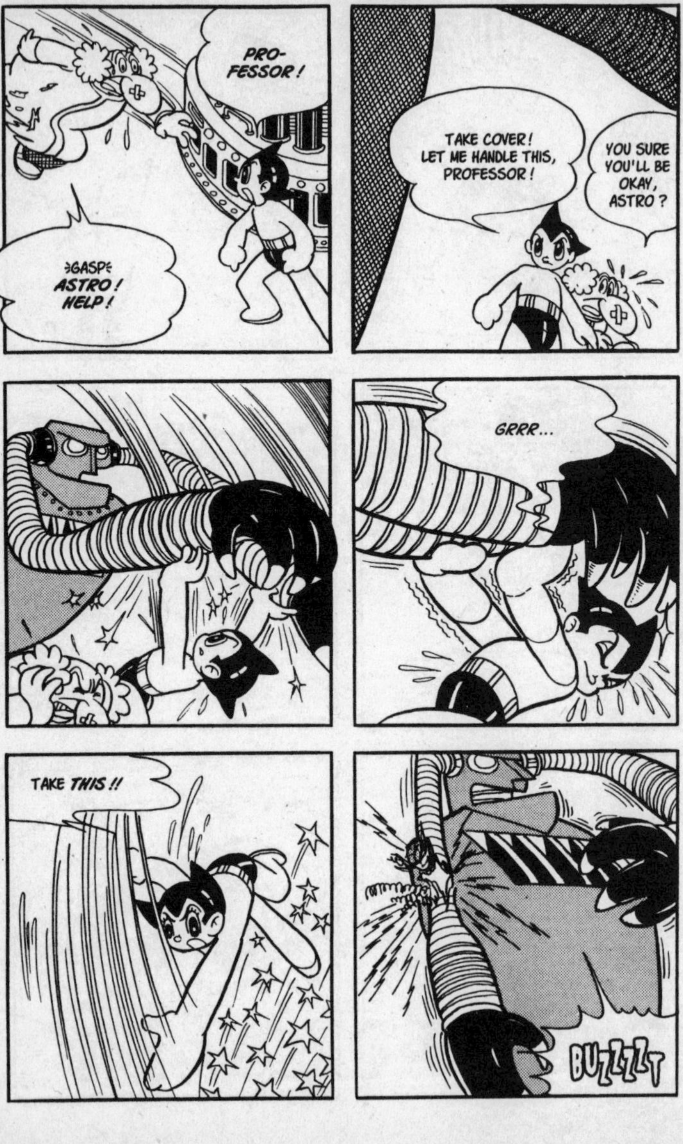
PRO-
FESSOR!
GASP
ASTRO!
HELP!
TAKE COVER!
LET ME HANDLE THIS,
PROFESSOR!
YOU SURE
YOU'LL BE
OKAY,
ASTRO?
GRRR...
TAKE THIS!!
BUZZZZT

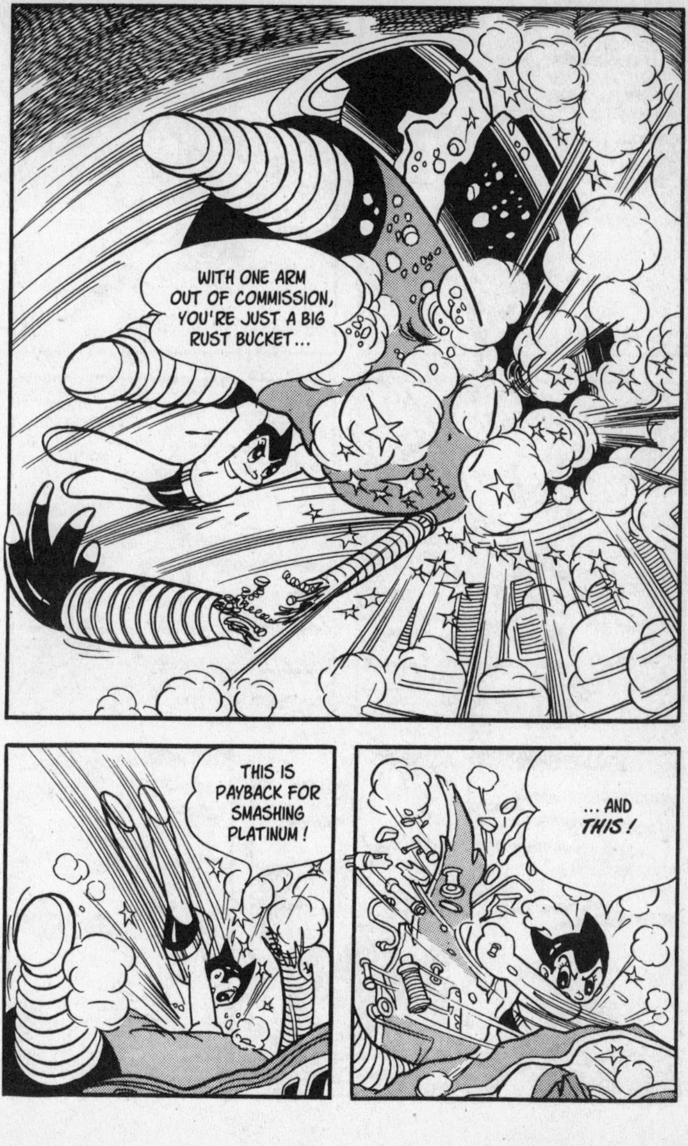
WITH ONE ARM OUT OF COMMISSION, YOU'RE JUST A BIG RUST BUCKET...
THIS IS PAYBACK FOR SMASHING PLATINUM!
...AND *THIS*!

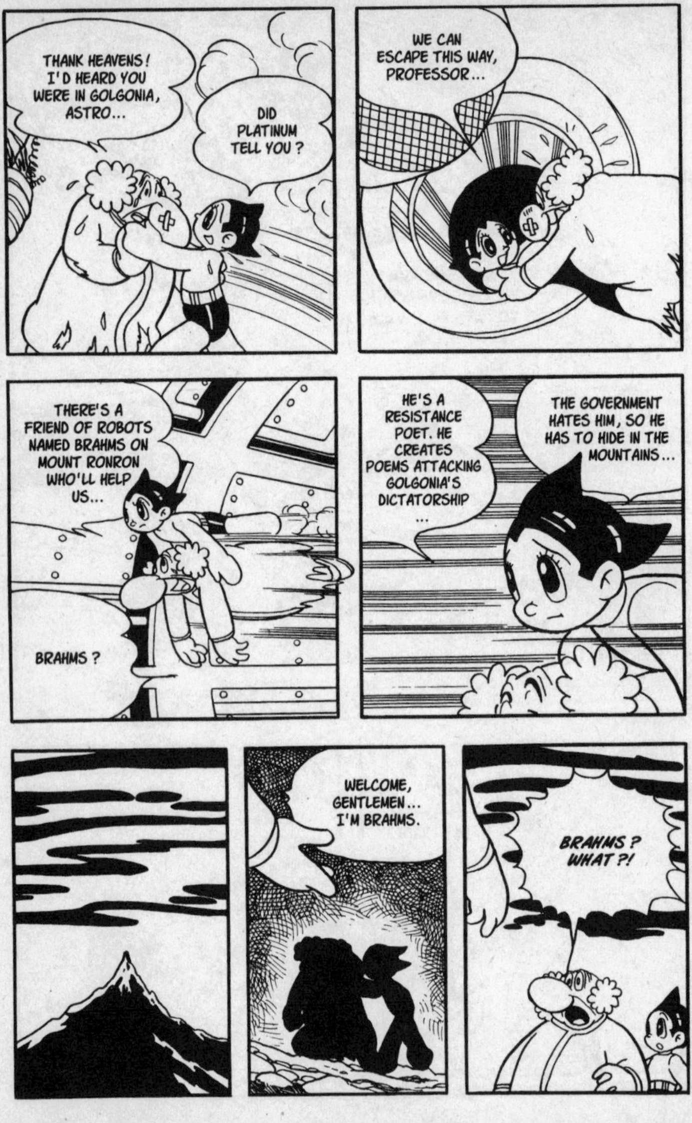
THANK HEAVENS! I'D HEARD YOU WERE IN GOLGONIA, ASTRO...
DID PLATINUM TELL YOU ?
WE CAN ESCAPE THIS WAY, PROFESSOR...
THERE'S A FRIEND OF ROBOTS NAMED BRAHMS ON MOUNT RONRON WHO'LL HELP US...
BRAHMS ?
HE'S A RESISTANCE POET. HE CREATES POEMS ATTACKING GOLGONIA'S DICTATORSHIP ...
THE GOVERNMENT HATES HIM, SO HE HAS TO HIDE IN THE MOUNTAINS...
WELCOME, GENTLEMEN... I'M BRAHMS.
BRAHMS ? WHAT ?!

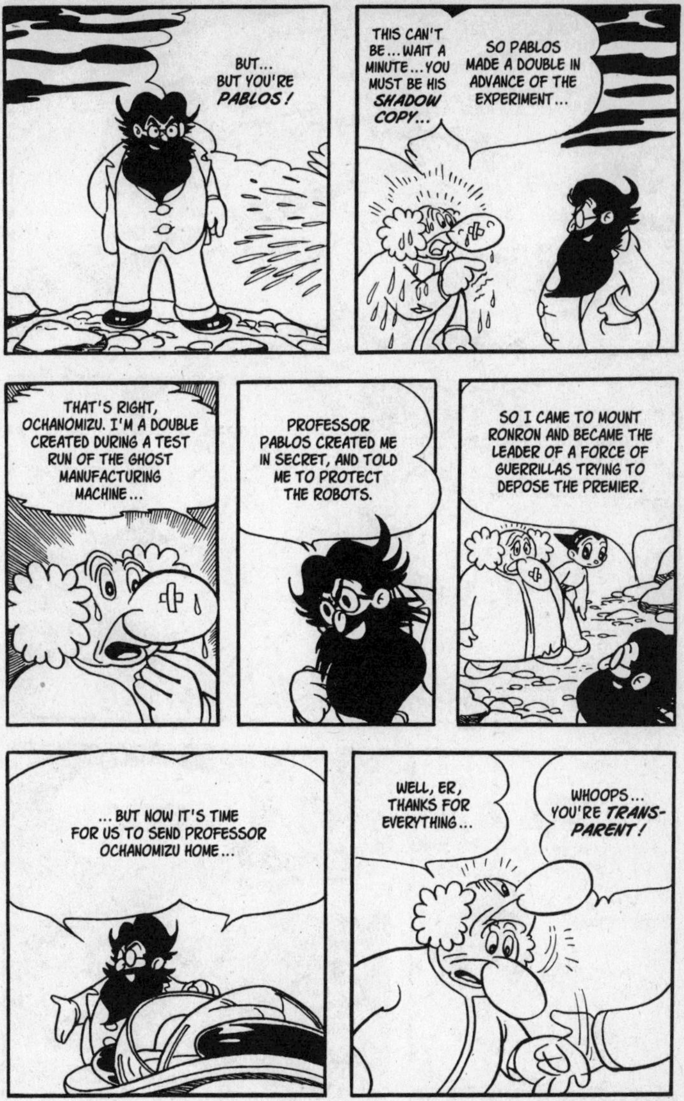
BUT... BUT YOU'RE PABLOS!
THIS CAN'T BE... WAIT A MINUTE... YOU MUST BE HIS SHADOW COPY...
SO PABLOS MADE A DOUBLE IN ADVANCE OF THE EXPERIMENT...
THAT'S RIGHT, OCHANOMIZU. I'M A DOUBLE CREATED DURING A TEST RUN OF THE GHOST MANUFACTURING MACHINE...
PROFESSOR PABLOS CREATED ME IN SECRET, AND TOLD ME TO PROTECT THE ROBOTS.
SO I CAME TO MOUNT RONRON AND BECAME THE LEADER OF A FORCE OF GUERRILLAS TRYING TO DEPOSE THE PREMIER.
... BUT NOW IT'S TIME FOR US TO SEND PROFESSOR OCHANOMIZU HOME...
WELL, ER, THANKS FOR EVERYTHING...
WHOOPS... YOU'RE TRANS-PARENT!

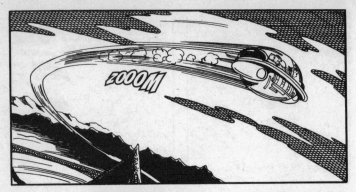

ZOOOM

GOSH, I NEVER EXPECTED THAT... PABLOS' DOUBLE...

DON'T FEEL SO BAD, ASTRO! WE GET TO GO HOME TO JAPAN!

BUT I BROKE THE ROBOT LAW, PROFESSOR...

DON'T WORRY, ASTRO! I'LL DEFEND YOU AGAINST ANY CHARGES. AFTER ALL, THE ROBOT LAW'S GOING TO BE REVISED SOON ANYWAY!

THANKS, PROFESSOR...

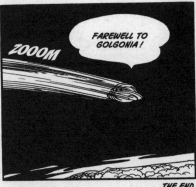

ZOOOM

FAREWELL TO GOLGONIA!

THE END

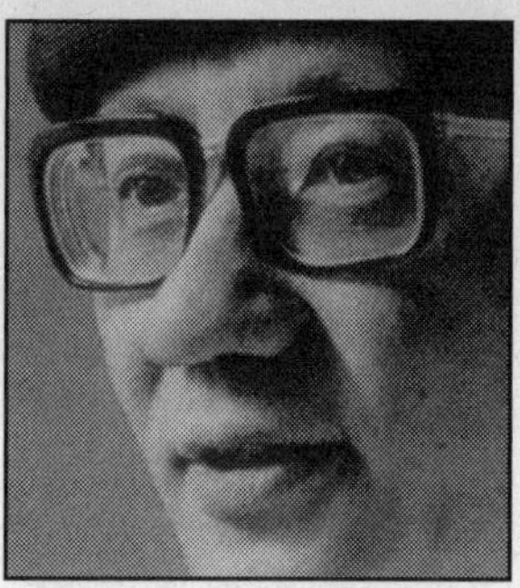

Osamu Tezuka was born in the city of Toyonaka, in Osaka, Japan, on November 3, 1928, and raised in Takarazuka, in Hyogo prefecture. He graduated from the Medical Department of Osaka University and was later awarded a Doctorate of Medicine.

In 1946 Tezuka made his debut as a manga artist with the work *Amachan's Diary*, and in 1947 he had his first big hit with *New Treasure Island*. Over his forty-year career as a cartoonist, Tezuka produced in excess of an astounding 150,000 pages of manga, including the creation of *Metropolis*, *Mighty Atom* (a.k.a. *Astro Boy*), *Jungle Emperor* (a.k.a. *Kimba the White Lion*), *Black Jack*, *Phoenix*, *Buddha*, and many more.

Tezuka's fascination with Disney cartoons led him to begin his own animation studio, creating the first serialized Japanese cartoon series, which was later exported to America as *Astro Boy* in 1963. Tezuka Productions went on to create animated versions of *Kimba the White Lion* (*Jungle Emperor*) and *Phoenix*, among others.

He received numerous awards during his life, including the Bungei Shunju Manga Award, the Kodansha Manga Award, the Shogakukan Manga Award, and the Japan Cartoonists' Association Special Award for Excellence. He also served a variety of organizations. He was a director of the Japan Cartoonists' Association, the chairman of the Japan Animation Association, and a member of the Manga Group, Japan Pen Club, and the Japan SF Authors' Club, among others. Tezuka became Japan's "comics ambassador," taking Japan's comics culture to the world. In 1980, he toured and lectured in America, including a speech at the United Nations.

Regarded as a national treasure, Osamu Tezuka died on February 2, 1989 at the age of 60. In 1994, the Osamu Tezuka Manga Museum opened in the city of Takarazuka, where he was raised. His creations remains hugely popular in Japan and are printed in many languages throughout the world, where he is acclaimed as one of the true giants of comics and animation, his work as vital and influential today as it was half a century ago.

"Comics are an international language," Tezuka said. "They can cross boundaries and generations. Comics are a bridge between all cultures."

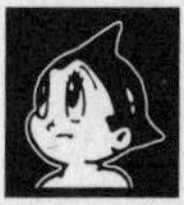